Diversity, Inclusion, Equity and the Threat to Academic Freedom

Edited by
Martín López-Corredoira,
Tom Todd & Erik J. Olsson

Authors (alphabetical order): D. Abbot, T. Agoh, G. Amendt, I. Arpi, D. Benatar, P. Boghossian, Civitas Research Team, D. Díaz Pardo de Vera, P. Domingos, J. Fiamengo, E. Forest, J. Gibert Galassi, N. Goldstuck, J.L. González Quirós, L.M. Krauss, P. Labelle, M. López-Corredoira, H. Mac Donald, M. Malmgren, J. Peterson, C. Polychronakos, E.J. Olsson, P.C. Salzman, A. Strumia, T. Todd, A. Yafaev

SOCIETAS
essays in political
& cultural criticism

imprint-academic.com

Published in the UK by
Imprint Academic, PO Box 200, Exeter EX5 5YX, UK

Distributed in the USA by
Ingram Book Company,
One Ingram Blvd., La Vergne, TN 37086, USA

ISBN 9781788360845 Paperback

A CIP catalogue record for this book is available from the
British Library and US Library of Congress

Contents

Part II.
Race, Ethnicity

Part III.
Diversity, Inclusion and Equity Programmes

Preface by the Editors

The last 30 years have witnessed radical changes in academia. The politics and ideology of diversity, inclusion and equity (DIE) have gradually come to influence or even dominate what can be talked about, researched and taught at institutions of higher education. The size of the problem has manifested itself recently in the formation of large networks of scientists committed to upholding the principles of free speech and independent research: the *Academic Freedom Alliance* (AFA, USA), *Academics for Academic Freedom* (AFAF, UK), *Academic Rights Watch* (ARW, Sweden) and *Netzwerk Wissenschaftsfreiheit* (Germany) — to name just a few.

There can be no doubt that discrimination based on sex, race, ethnicity, religion or political beliefs should not be tolerated. This is true, in particular, for academic research and education where individuals applying for an educational programme or an academic position should be assessed purely on the basis of their academic merits and achievements. One would therefore expect policies emphasizing DIE not only to embrace scientific standards in academia, but to promote adherence to them. Surprisingly, however, this is far from always the case. In recent years, such policies have increasingly led to quite the opposite result, namely a situation in which, for example, allegiance to a "group identity" is increasingly considered relevant when evaluating an individual's suitability for academic study or research — quite in contrast to the famous dictum of civil rights leader Martin Luther King that we all deserve to be judged not by skin colour, but by content of character.

This unfortunate development, which contradicts the very spirit of research and higher education, has been accompanied by an unprecedented attack on freedom of speech — another cornerstone of professional scholarly activity without which universities as we know them will slowly but surely suffocate. Whereas the principles of DIE suggest *prima facie* fundamental tolerance towards all viewpoints, DIE has increasingly placed science in general under suspicion of being an instrument of the allegedly ubiquitous power struggle between the (multiple) sexes and various races. The criteria by which the allegedly prevailing discrimination by gender or race is deemed tangible (or even systemic) are often founded more on subjective sensibilities than on any sound, empirically evidence-based arguments. Inevitably, any proponent of DIE politics must at least in part resort to biased research or censorship as their arguments are, through their renouncement of empiricism, in consequence less and less accessible to rational thought.

The DIE principles have now been incorporated in universities' policies and fundamental values all over the world, practically forcing researchers and teachers to avoid subjects and suppress results that could be seen to violate these policies. Any criticism risks being seen as compelling evidence of non-compliance with those very policies. The effect is a culture of silence in which academics are increasingly reluctant to speak out against DIE policies for fear of possible consequences.

To accomplish their educational missions, universities and research institutes need to be politically neutral and adhere strictly to established scientific standards. The current undermining of these fundamental precepts is not a problem that will eventually fix itself. Rather, we strongly believe that coordinated action is now urgently needed to counter the excesses of identity politics in academia and that such action needs to involve people across the political spectrum.

Many have spoken out recently about these problems. Our purpose here is to pull together some of the most remarkable cases in a single book, with original or republished materials, so that the reader can see we are dealing with a ubiquitous trend and not just isolated complaints. The essays contained here show personal experiences and observations, illustrating the abuse of power, censorship and witch-hunts at many universities and research centres around the world.

This book contains 26 chapters by 25 co-authors and one research team from 11 different countries. The great majority of the authors describe their personal experiences working in academia, while a few others touch on the sociological problems of science and academia in general. The contributions are written in a journalistic style accessible to a wide public, rather than as technical papers for specialists. They are not *scientific* demonstrations of a given hypothesis, since ideologies or their refutations cannot be *demonstrated*; they present, rather, a panorama of the absurdities and human suffering to which these developments in our western society have given rise.

This book is divided into five thematic blocks or sections, although this division is not strict and many of the chapters also touch on topics handled in other blocks. In order to help the reader with the classification of the different chapters, we have labelled each of them with a list of topics covered. Please note that our mission as editors was to collect articles related to the topic and that we do not endorse all of the points of view reflected in the various chapters. The authors were, of course, totally free to express their opinions and we have avoided any interference in their messages.

The first section discusses "feminism and gender mainstreaming". Salzman tells us that feminists are allowed to negate academic freedom, to deny publication of scientific evidence and to bully scientists and suppress scientific conclusions that they do not like. Arpi depicts how Swedish universities are willingly turning themselves into a commissariat for a one-sided and simplistic vision of social justice rather than adhering to the search for truth. In his review on music academia and orchestras, Malmgren thinks that lobbying groups and activists try to achieve gender equity utopia by replacing historical discrimination in one direction with contemporary discrimination in the other. Goldstuck and Polychronakos illustrate in separate chapters their years of experience as researchers and professors in health areas. Goldstuck remarks that wokism, especially feminism and transsexual identity but also race identity, are gaslighting western societies and pushing against reason and logic. Polychronakos is amazed that genital organs not clearly identifiable as male or female cannot be called "disorders" anymore, but "differentiation". He also points out, for example, that raising a child as a boy or as a girl is considered to represent "outdated and stereotyped conceptions of gender and childrearing". Our editor, Todd, describes how transgender activists have turned on "gender-critical" feminists, chasing them out of office because they adhere to the principal of dimorphous/binary sex. We could ignore or criticize these ideas, but the problem, Yafaev notes, is that the freedom to ignore or criticize them is highly restricted. Woke has progressively and insidiously taken hold in academia over the last decade and has now become a dominant doctrine; it genuinely holds sway in academia and is accepted as an article of faith, says Yafaev in his chapter about #*metametoo,* who compares the situation with the old regime in his country when it was part of the USSR. Only a few countries in western civilization have been spared this ideologization of academia: Hungary, for instance, took the drastic decision to remove gender studies from a list of approved masters programmes, arguing that it serves no purpose and is based in ideology rather than science. In a thought-provoking contribution, Fiamengo considers the case for other western countries to follow suit.

A second section is dedicated to the topics of race and ethnicity, another issue on which many intellectuals have feared to speak in the face of politically correct prejudice. But there are authors who say enough is enough in the conformity to a lie, such as Mac Donald, who describes a pessimistic panorama in which universities admit, hire and promote as many black students as it possibly can without regard to their merits or qualification, an effect of the fierce bidding war among colleges for under-represented minorities. As Krauss observes, not only are people without merits hired simply because they belong to a minority group, but there are highly productive scientists whose grants have been rejected not on the basis of science, but because their diversity proposals were insufficiently detailed. Researchers are also removed from their positions when they decide to study issues that include how human genetics might be linked to cognitive ability. Nonetheless, not every place on our planet is dominated by these ideological movements. Forest and Agoh point out some interesting notes of optimism in Japanese society, where wokism, radical feminism and critical race theory do not have much future, possibly due to the very different philosophical and religious background of that society.

The third section describes the DIE programmes in the academic world and the distortions of reality that they inspire. LaBelle reminds us that the DIE ideology does not see people as individuals, but as members of groups compartmentalized according to immutable traits. In the process, they support and implement measures that are themselves the epitome of discrimination. DIE programmes actually promote divisiveness, exclusion and inequity based on immutable traits. Furthermore, Fiamengo in her second contribution discovers in analysing some documents at universities like Berkeley that there is an intent to purge non-left-wing individuals, including women and people of colour, from college campuses. Another example of exclusion in the name of inclusivity comes from one of the editors, López-Corredoira, who explains that the IAU (*International Astronomical Union*; the most important association of astronomers worldwide) has imposed a woke ideology, leaving no leeway for astronomers who do not accept it. All of these political actions lead, writes Saltzman, to the death of meritocracy and to admittance of underperforming, weak students to universities, who are funded, because their sexuality, or race, or gender, is statistically "underrepresented" in relation to their presence in the general population. Is this good for science and academia?

A common response by proponents of DIE to any questioning of their arguments is deplatforming, censorship or even workplace intimidation. This is illustrated in Part IV of our book: Strumia's talk at CERN (*Conseil Européen pour la Recherche Nucléaire*) in 2018 that led to his suspension from research work there (narrated by himself); the rescindment of a visiting fellowship initially offered to Peterson at Cambridge University (UK), in solidarity with the DIE activists (narrated by himself); deplatforming of a speaker, Flemming Rose, invited to give the 2016 academic freedom lecture in South Africa (in the chapter by Benatar); a talk by Abbot cancelled by MIT following social media pressure, which makes him think that woke ideology is essentially totalitarian in nature: it attempts to corral the entirety of human existence into one narrow ideological viewpoint and to silence anyone who disagrees; attempts to censor a conference organized in Germany on family and domestic violence showing how domestic violence is a symmetrical phenomenon, perpetrated equally by both sexes (described in the chapter by the initiator of the event, Amendt, and the organizer, one of the editors, Todd); Boghossian resigned his position at Portland State – as he describes in his autobiographical chapter – after continuous sabotage to his freethinking intellectual activity by the social justice faction at his university. Nonetheless, in the last chapter of this block, Domingos gives cause for some optimism by showing that most cancellation attempts end in failure. The real Achilles' heel of the cancel crowd is its short attention span. Once they have bullied someone into submission, they move on to the next victim.

A final block of chapters discusses more general aspects of the suppression of academic freedom. The Civitas Research Team makes a highly useful analysis of UK universities, showing that most of them experienced some kind of repression of academic freedom in connection with DIE issues – Cambridge, Oxford, London and Imperial College of London being among the most restrictive. We are in grave danger when those who wield political power impose upon society beliefs and rules of conduct grounded in the former, according to González Quirós and Díaz Pardo de Vera. Gibert Galassi tries to understand the reasons why victim-hood culture has been installed in academia, and the confusion of democracy with mediocracy. He writes about academia in Chile, but his thoughts might be well considered globally relevant. Finally, Erik Olsson (also editor) explains his view on of the present decrease of academic freedom in a culture dominated by feminine, soft values. Olsson's paper was presented as an invited lecture at a renowned research institute. Ironically, only two hours after being published, Olsson recalls in a post-script, the video recording was taken off *Youtube* for violating the institute's equity policies, in direct confirmation of his main thesis.

We know there are many more people who have expressed similar ideas, and many others who would like to voice their opinion but for the greater part do not dare to do so, for fear of possible recrimination or jeopardizing their careers. We hope these chapters help all of us to realize that we are not alone in our observations, and to encourage other lecturers and researchers to express their reservations about the machinations of DIE lobbyists within academia. Fear of retaliation is not an option in a world in which silence lends consent to the monster's growth, promoting the potential for totalitarian state systems comparable to Orwellian dystopias. We believe there is a clear and present threat to academic freedom and that we should use the legal instruments still available to us to protect it, or live to regret it and be silenced.

In the end, we will not solve the problem only by documenting the state of affairs, but doing so will serve: 1) to manifest that in our academia there are also people, apart from social justice warriors, who observe and think and will not be coerced by them; 2) to create awareness of and resistance to ill-conceived DIE policies based on radical versions of identity politics which have little, if anything, to do with academic values and scholarly integrity. We believe that university and research institutes must be politically neutral and should adhere strictly to established scientific methods.

We would like to emphasize that our intention is not to promote one ideological stream of thought over another. Although woke ideologies originate primarily in left-wing politics, we are not making a stand for any position on the political spectrum. In fact, we would argue that we need to remedy the politicization of academia and encourage the supremacy of an enlightened, evidence-based and rational discourse that is not afraid to discuss any dimension of thought. A political agenda that prevents this will eventually have the opposite effect it intends; the key to anti-discriminatory society is an open discussion of all the factors that may *or may not* contribute to discrimination. To silence any such debate is to eliminate the path to insight into factors benefiting or detracting from social justice.

As the acronym indicates, the present-day version of "DIE" ideology will not be eternal. We hope that this book will be a useful contribution, together with other similar works, that may inspire a new epoch of changes within the academic world.

Martín López-Corredoira, Tom Todd & Erik J. Olsson
December 2021

Disclaimer

The various chapters of this book contain critical statements that may offend supporters of some ideologies. We have not censored any parts of the original texts presented by the authors because we believe the damage incurred by the suppression of academic freedom is more harmful than any possible offence arising from this freedom.

The editors and publishers do not take any responsibility or accept any liability for the correctness of the contents in each contribution or any possible defamation, libellous accusations or other legal issues. Each chapter is the sole responsibility of its corresponding author. Similarly, although the general opinions of each author of this book have many points in common, the points of views on particular aspects are not necessarily shared by the editors or other co-authors.

Part 1.

Feminism and Gender Mainstreaming

Philip Carl Salzman[1]

Feminists Assault Science[2]

ABSTRACT: Feminism and science are incompatible. Feminism is a political ideology aimed at advancing the interests of females in opposition to males. It provides a set of orthodox answers to all questions. Science is a methodology of investigation and a collection of tentative findings. It is based on inquiry, and judges on the evidence discovered. Because men have been predominant in science, and have traditionally been more interested in science than women, feminists have set the goal of increasing the numbers of females and the feminist control of science, as well as transforming it into "feminist science", an oxymoron.

TOPICS: feminism and gender mainstreaming; general considerations on suppression of academic freedom.
****

Feminism is a closed, partisan ideology designed to lobby for female advantage. Science is an open exploration designed to test and expand knowledge. Feminism and science are entirely incompatible.[3]

Feminism rejects biological knowledge about the differences of males and females. To quote a university student about her feminist courses: "merely mentioning biological differences can be wrongthink. Or worse, as I learned in one of my classes, it can be upsetting to genderqueer or transgender students. Thus, some of the root causes of what makes men

---

[1] Professor Emeritus of Anthropology, McGill University, Canada. Email: philip.carl.salzman@mcgill.ca

[2] Reprinted from *Frontier Center for Public Policy*, 23rd January 2019, https://fcpp.org/wp-content/uploads/EF53FeministsAssaultScienceSalzman.pdf

[3] Berezow, A., 26th October 2016, "Is Modern Feminism Incompatible with Science?", *American Council on Science and Health*, https://www.acsh.org/news/2016/10/26/modern-feminism-incompatible-science-10366

and women differ — hormonal, neurological, and biological differences — is left out of the discussion."[4] Biology is rejected on the grounds that locating gender differences in biology has been used to oppress women.[5]

In place of biology, "social construction" of gender roles explains the differences between males and females, according to feminists. In feminist ideology, "biology doesn't determine fate, but culture. Men are violent not because of hormones, but because of socialization into 'toxic masculinity.' And women, who are more nurturing, do so because of sexist conditioning, says social constructionism."[6]

Feminists deny the most basic facts of biology. A feminist colleague refused to accept that human males are on average physically larger and stronger than human females. She knew perfectly well that female elite athletes could not compete with male elite athletes, but even refused to concede this point. Is "social construction" the reason that there are no female players in the NFL, CFL, NBA, NHL, MLB? Or is there a biological basis to the parallel male and female sports leagues and competitions? The physical advantage of males is behind the controversy over trans-sexual male-to-female athletes competing in events against women.[7]

The biological differences between human males and females are myriad, as they are in the animal kingdom among species with sexual reproduction.[8] Both neurological and hormonal differences can impact emotions and skills.[9] For example, cognitive skills differ, with men being stronger in spatial cognition.

Feminists deny all of this, because genetically-based biological characteristics are not amenable to change for the convenience of benefiting females. And biological characteristics that stand in the way of female equality or superiority cannot be admitted. Therefore, all

---

4   Airaksinen, T., 26th August 2016, "What I Learn in My Women's Studies Classes", *Quillette*, http://quillette.com/2016/08/26/what-i-learned-in-my-womens-studies-classes/

5   "Feminist Philosophy of Biology", *Stanford Encyclopedia of Biology*, https://plato.stanford.edu/entries/feminist-philosophy-biology/

6   Airaksinen, T., 26th August 2016, "What I Learn in My Women's Studies Classes", *Quillette*, http://quillette.com/2016/08/26/what-i-learned-in-my-womens-studies-classes/

7   "Transgender people in Sports", *Wikipedia*, https://en.wikipedia.org/wiki/Transgender_people_in_sports

8   11th June 2013, "New Book Explains Extraordinary Gender Differences in Animal Kingdom", *phys.org*, https://phys.org/news/2013-06-extraordinary-gender-differences-animal-kingdom.html

9   Rhoads, S.E., 2005, *Taking Sex Differences Seriously*, New York: Encounter Books.

differences in gender roles are attributed to "social construction", that is, to culture and socialization. It is thus a basic precept of feminism that genetics and biology are false. This makes feminism an enemy of science.

Feminist animosity to science is seen particularly in the opposition to and suppression of scientific studies that do not conform with feminist ideology. One example is the "Greater Male Variability Hypothesis". Theodore P. Hill, Professor Emeritus of Mathematics at Georgia Tech, and currently a research scholar in residence at the California Polytechnic State University, describes the subject of his recent paper:

> In the highly controversial area of human intelligence, the "Greater Male Variability Hypothesis" (GMVH) asserts that there are more idiots and more geniuses among men than among women. Darwin's research on evolution in the nineteenth century found that, although there are many exceptions for specific traits and species, there is generally more variability in males than in females of the same species throughout the animal kingdom.
>
> Evidence for this hypothesis is fairly robust and has been reported in species ranging from adders and sockeye salmon to wasps and orangutans, as well as humans. Multiple studies have found that boys and men are over-represented at both the high and low ends of the distributions in categories ranging from birth weight and brain structures and 60-meter dash times to reading and mathematics test scores. There are significantly more men than women, for example, among Nobel laureates, music com- posers, and chess champions—and also among homeless people, suicide victims, and federal prison inmates.[10]

This paper was accepted in sequence by two respected journals, and then, after feminist intervention, was rejected by both journals. The feminist group, Women in Mathematics, insisted that the journals reject the article, and feminists lobbied the National Science Foundation to refuse acknowl- edgment as a funder, which it did. Other contributors to the paper were threatened by feminist colleagues with loss of their jobs; Women in Mathematics said, "the paper might be damaging to the aspirations of impressionable young women", and feminist professors at the university of the co-author said, to argue that "women have a lesser chance to succeed in mathematics at the very top end is bias". The chair of the co- author's department said, "sometimes values such as academic freedom and free speech come into conflict with other values to which Penn State was committed."[11] In other words, feminists are allowed to negate

---

[10] Hill, T.P., 7th September 2018, "Academic Activists Send a Published Paper Down the Memory Hole", *Quillette*, https://quillette.com/2018/09/07/ academic-activists-send-a-published-paper-down-the-memory-hole/

[11] *Ibid.*

academic freedom, and to deny publication of scientific evidence. As we see in this case, feminist views not only conflict with scientific evidence, but throughout our governmental and educational institutions feminists are officially allowed to bully scientists and suppress scientific conclusions that they do not like.

Alessandro Strumia, a Senior Scientist at the European Organization for Nuclear Research (CERN) and Professor at Pisa University, on 28th September 2018 presented a talk designed to respond to previous presentations. According to Strumia, "This workshop was continuously telling (saying), 'men are bad, men are sexist, they discriminate against us' — lots of things like this. I did a check to see if this was true... and the result was, that was not true. There is a political group that wants women, and other people, to believe that they are victims."[12]

Strumia presented a series of charts, tables and graphs to demonstrate that, far from being discriminated against, women were favoured, and men were discriminated against. He also said that "Physics [was] invented and built by men." Whatever the historical reasons for it, this is of course true of all sciences. In physics, the subject under discussion, women have won three Nobel Prizes, men 207.[13]

The response was immediate: Strumia was suspended from CERN, and his university has launched an investigation. 1,600 scientists signed a petition against Strumia, saying, among other things, that "Strumia's arguments are morally reprehensible. Belittling the ability and legitimacy of scientists of colour and white women scientists using such flimsy pretexts is disgraceful, and it reveals a deep contempt for more than half of humanity that clearly comes from some source other than scientific logic." There was much high rhetoric in the petition, and most of the counterarguments and allegedly refuting evidence are dubious at best.[14]

It would have been difficult to provide refuting argument about "scientists of colour", because Strumia never mentioned them. The petition also said, "Signatories to the statement agreed that they wanted

---

[12] Embury-Dennis, 2018, "Cern Physicist Suspended Over 'Highly Offensive' Presentation on Sexism in Science", *Independent*.

[13] "Nobel Prize Awards by Gender in Each Category", *areppim*, https://stats.areppim.com/stats/stats_nobel_sexxcat.htm

[14] 31st October 2018, "Gender Controversy Comes to Physics: A Response to the Statement Against Alessandro Strumia", *Areo Magazine*, https://areomagazine.com/2018/10/31/gender-controversy-comes-to-physics-a-response-to-the-statement-against-alessandro-strumia/. As of 4th December 2018, there are 1,962 signatures on a petition "CERN: Return Prof. Strumia to Office!", https://sciencecensored.com/cern-return-prof-strumia-to-office/

to state, in the strongest possible terms, that the humanity of any person, regardless of ascribed identities such as race, ethnicity, gender identity, religion, disability, gender presentation, or sexual identity is not up for debate."[15] Strumia of course said nothing about anybody's "humanity", nor about religion, disability, or sexual identity. What he did say was "The data about citations and hirings show that women are not discriminated (against) in fundamental physics." He said, "We reward merit, irrespective of gender."[16]

The reaction to Strumia was not an impartial scientific challenge based on evidence. Rather, the reaction to Strumia was an indignant rejection of a heretic who violated the religion of progressive feminism's most cherished commandment, that females must make up at least 50% of the people in any enterprise. Strumia received the usual treatment of a heretic: vilification and excommunication. A major part of the vilification was to condemn Strumia for saying things that he never said. The underlying view of his accusers is that if you do not accept feminist ideology and goals, then you are evil.

Where did the idea come from that "justice" is the demographic representation in every activity and enterprise of every category of humanity according to their statistical representation in the general population? And that if equal representation does not exist, it is in every case because of bigotry and discrimination? This precept ignores the differences among different categories of a population, and their different suitability for different activities. For example, members of particular categories who are, on average, short in stature are unlikely to be represented in professional basketball, not due to bigotry, but due to suitability. Why is the illustrious idea of "diversity" in physical type and ability ignored in the equal representation commandment? The equal representation precept also ignores freedom, the ability of people to choose what they prefer. If people of certain categories prefer urban living, must a representative proportion of them be sent to the farms and forests against their wills?

Throughout North American society, in governments, scientific agencies, granting agencies and universities, there is a determined policy, with sanctions attached, to increase the number of females in STEM (science, technology, engineering, mathematics) fields. This has been determined from above, from progressive feminist principles. Below, among students, the enthusiasm of females to commit to STEM has been,

---

[15] Oppenheim, M., 2018, "1,600 Scientists Condemn CERN Physicist's 'Morally Reprehensible' Talk", *Independent*.

[16] *Ibid.*

shall we say, lukewarm. Given the free choice that females have had in universities, they have massively chosen to go into the social sciences and humanities. Females now make up 60% of university graduates across North America, males 40%, so females are already substantially over-represented, but this does not seem to be a violation of "gender equality", at least according to feminists. Nonetheless, feminists are frantic that females do not have a higher representation in STEM. Here are the Canadian figures:

> According to the National Household Survey (NHS), women accounted for 39% of university graduates aged 25 to 34 with a STEM degree in 2011, compared with 66% of university graduates in non-STEM programs.
> Among STEM graduates aged 25 to 34, women accounted for 59% of those in science and technology programs, but accounted for 23% of those who graduated from engineering and 30% of those who graduated from mathematics and computer science programs.
> Women are always less likely to choose a STEM program, regardless of mathematical ability. Among those who went to university, 23% women in the three highest categories of PISA [Programme for International Student Assessment] scores (out of six) chose a STEM program, compared with 39% of men in the three lowest categories of PISA scores.[17]

Furthermore, it appears that gender equality in the society at large is negatively correlated with females in STEM. That is, "In countries that empower women, they are less likely to choose math and science professions." The explanation seems to be that girls, while good at math and science, are better at reading, and prefer reading. And there are more opportunities in economically advanced countries for people with literary backgrounds. "The upshot of this research is neither especially feminist nor especially sad: It's not that gender equality discourages girls from pursuing science. It's that it allows them not to if they're not interested."[18] This evidence does not support the feminist argument that females do not go into STEM because they are discriminated against. Rather, it supports what female students have shown by their free choices, that they prefer non-STEM fields.

Finally, the assault on science continues with a demand that science be transformed into "feminist science". In other words, feminists say that

---

[17] Hango, D., 2013, "Gender Differences in Science, Technology, Engineering, Mathematics and Computer Science (STEM) Programs at University", *Insights on Canadian Society*, https://www150.statcan.gc.ca/n1/pub/75-006-x/20130 01/article/11874-eng.htm

[18] Khazan, O., 18th February 2018, "The More Gender Equality, the Fewer Women in STEM", *The Atlantic*, https://www.theatlantic.com/science/archiv e/2018/02/the-more-gender-equality-the-fewer-women-in-stem/553592/

science as it has been practised during the past 500 years is no good and should be abandoned. After all, say the feminists, "objectivity is male subjectivity."[19]

In its place? Feminist science that "infuses social justice, inclusion and equality into science to advance progressive social change... a socially just science."[20] In other words, feminists do not want to explore reality through the collection and assessment of evidence. Feminists already know the answers that they like, and wish to transform science to fit feminist ideology. That will allegedly "advance progressive social change", although it is likely to end the masculine discovery of the world.[21]

We already know that feminism is toxic to our culture and our educational system,[22] and next it will be toxic to science. Are we smart enough and serious enough to defend science?

[19] Gimborys, K., 15th June 2017, "Creating a More Feminist Science", *National Organization for Women*, https://now.org/blog/creating-a-more-feminist-science/

[20] Nardi, W., 24th January 2018, "'Feminist Science' Event Teaches Researchers How to Do 'Socially Just Science'", *The College Fix*, https://www.thecollegefix.com/feminist-science-event-teaches-researchers-socially-just-science/

[21] *Ibid.*

[22] Salzman, P., 11th July 2018, "Toxic Feminism", *Frontier Center for Public Policy*, https://fcpp.org/2018/07/11/toxic-feminism/

Ivar Arpi[1]

Academic Freedom Under Threat in Sweden[2]

ABSTRACT: The author examines the effects of the Swedish government requirement that gender mainstreaming be implemented at universities. In the political science department at Lund University, for example, the proportion of female authors must never fall below 40 percent of the reading lists. In social sciences, staff are required to ensure that gender and diversity perspectives are represented in the faculty's education and take a course themselves in "Gender and Diversity in Education".

TOPICS: feminism and gender mainstreaming; general considerations on suppression of academic freedom.
****

"You will include Judith Butler in your course." That was announced to Erik Ringmar, senior lecturer in the Department of Political Science at Lund University, after the September meeting of the department's board of directors. Not that there's anything wrong with reading the queer studies feminist Butler. It's just that the course Ringmar teaches is primarily about the reaction to modernity at the turn of the last century, with a focus on fascism.

During earlier semesters it included a part about postmodernism, and within it Butler, but it was removed because it didn't fit in with the rest of the course. "There is not a course committee in the world which can force me to teach Judith Butler unless I want to", Ringmar wrote on his blog.

---

[1] Graduated in political sciences in University Uppsala (Sweden), columnist and writer, editorial columnist at *Svenska Dagbladet* in Sweden. Email: ivar.arpi@gmail.com

[2] Reprinted from *Quillette*, 15th November 2017, https://quillette.com/2017/11/14/academic-freedom-threat-sweden/

This has led to strong protests from student activists, the board, the director of studies and the dean.

Of course, this is no great catastrophe in and of itself. It's just a literature list, after all. But it is part of a much larger process by which academic freedom in Sweden is being circumscribed. What is happening now in the political science department at Lund University is fully sanctioned by the gender mainstreaming that the government has ordered all Swedish universities to implement (more on that later).

A Threat to Academic Freedom

The department's goal, set by the board and approved by the academic board, is that the proportion of female authors must never fall below 40 percent of the reading lists. A course like Erik Ringmar's — "Modern Society and its Critics" — which focuses on original texts from around the turn of the last century, immediately gets into trouble since fascism in the 1930s wasn't exactly a bastion of gender equality. So Ringmar's reading list contained too few female reactionaries for the board to be satisfied. He tried to resolve this by including anarchism as another violent political response to modernity (although it was not really the original idea of the course) and, unlike female fascists, their anarchistic counterparts actually wrote a great deal. But even so, the proportion of female authors on the course's reading list only reached 15 percent.

It wasn't good enough, according to the board. Judith Butler had to be included.

The gender equality plan of the Faculty of Social Sciences makes it clear that teachers must include sufficient literature from gender studies. What's currently happening to Erik Ringmar, a senior lecturer being forced to change his course, has already occurred a number of times according to the political science department's own equality plan. The only difference is that Ringmar protested the decision. The Faculty's Gender Equality Plan further imposes on all subordinate institutions the following: "Make an inspection of whether and how common curriculums and literature lists are being reviewed, ensuring that gender and diversity perspectives are represented in the faculty's education." It doesn't stop there. According to the department's action plan for gender equality, all teaching staff are required to take a mandatory "Gender and Diversity in Education" course, taught in the Faculty of Social Sciences.

All of this is guided by the underlying principle that it is not just about recruiting more women, it is about getting the right kind of gender per-spectives which are influenced by the postmodernist and poststructuralist theories dominant within the humanities. While these perspectives may be interesting in some contexts, they are usually strongly ideological and almost always impossible to falsify.

Gender Mainstreaming

The direction to include Judith Butler on his reading list made the Director of Studies and Erik Ringmar decide to not hold the course again. Students who want to learn about the emergence of fascism at the turn of the twentieth century need to apply to another university, and all this at a time when right-wing reaction is on the rise again in Europe.

This is just one example of academic freedom being traded for a specific vision of social justice, and similar processes are taking place across the country. This process is called gender mainstreaming and it threatens academic freedom at all Swedish universities.

At first glance, this doesn't sound so bad, does it? For who is opposed to gender equality? In Sweden, only a select few. But gender mainstreaming involves much more than that. And in practice, the concept of gender equality in this context masks a much more radical and profound process.

In the appropriation directions for 2016, the government tasked all of Sweden's universities to "develop a plan for how the institution intends to develop gender mainstreaming". The National Secretariat for Gender Research has been given the task of leading the work. It was created by the social democratic government in 1998 to further research in sex and gender and it is led by gender studies researchers. The second in charge, Fredrik Bondestam, wrote in his dissertation about gender inequality that the gender-aware were fighting against a "privileged elite of Swedish-speaking, white, protestant heretics totally uninterested in being informed of their own structural violence". Just the other day, when confronted by this quote, he said he still stood by it and that it had a "very beautiful wording".

People like Bondestam are in charge of mainstreaming their gender ideology – even though their ideology is far from mainstream – if you ask regular Swedes.

For their new task to gender mainstream universities, the secretariat has travelled across the country, holding lectures and workshops for administrators and teaching staff. On 15th May this year, colleges and universities submitted their plans to promote gender equality, which have been strongly influenced by the secretariat's instructions.

While it might sound like it, gender mainstreaming is not just about tackling discrimination. Whereas anti-discrimination efforts aim to create equal opportunity for all, gender mainstreaming is about "reorganising

existing activities" and "changing the power structures that give discriminatory effects".

What power structures is this about? When you read the equality
plans that the universities have written, you get the impression that
Swedish universities are characterized by overt misogyny, racism,
ableism, heteronormativity and other afflictions. In any event, that's how
the universities describe themselves.

At Uppsala University, ranked number 29 on the *Times Higher
Education* (*THE*) list of Europe's best universities (2017), they declare that
their "goal is that as far as possible [they will] work on gender mainstreaming from an intersectional perspective". So what does intersectionality mean? Imagine a pyramid. At the top there are white, able-
bodied, heterosexual men. They are considered to have the greatest power
and are therefore considered the most privileged. From this position
different power structures flow and intersect. Men repress women, whites
oppress non-whites, non-disabled repress disabled, and heterosexuals
oppress LGBTQ people. It might not be a conscious oppression, but
nevertheless the norms created around white, able-bodied, heterosexual
men are oppressive. The oppression is exerted through diffuse power
structures that permeate everything we do and think. That's the theory.

Here's how the psychology professor Jonathan Haidt characterized the
intersectionality ideology when I interviewed him a year ago:

> The first thing you do when you interact with people is that you find out
> which category they belong to. White? That's bad. Male? That's bad.
> Straight? It's bad. It is called intersectionality. You add privilege points
> based primarily on racial background, gender, and sexual orientation.
> Basically, it is a form of racism. It's a form of intellectual cancer because the
> whole idea of universities is that we're supposed to learn to judge each
> other by our ideas and words, not by what categories we happen to belong
> to.

Several universities report in their equality plans that they will work with
"norm critique". Both language and research are mainly, according to
these theories, production and reproduction of power. And the purpose
of research should be to show and break down this power. Therefore,
norm critique is considered central, as norms are by definition power
structures that oppress marginalized groups. Different power structures
cooperate to marginalize and repress different groups in an intersectional
way. In this framework, the purpose of research is to understand these
power structures and deconstruct them in order to build a fairer world
free from oppressive norms. Again, this is not a fringe phenomenon. It's
now entering the core of the universities through gender mainstreaming.

One would think that the universities would have carried out an investigation to determine the extent to which the oppressive power structures they purport to exist permeate their organizations and student bodies. (Generally, when you contend that something exists, you need to prove it.) But the National Secretariat for Gender Research recommends against this.

In their feedback, those who have surveyed the situation at their own universities are mildly reprimanded: "There may be educational and knowledge benefits of making local mappings of identified problems, but generally speaking it's not relevant to present already known structural injustices." No further investigations are needed. The secretariat already knows what society looks like and the reasons for it.

A number of universities established that gender perspectives should be integrated into all education strands. In the department of political science at Stockholm University it's mandatory to include gender studies at all levels of the education and to include an equal number of female authors in the reading lists. At Malmö University, it means, among other things, that parts of the education of a specialist nurse will be earmarked for gender studies.

At the Karolinska Institute — ranked 10th in Europe according to *THE* — they tie themselves into knots in an attempt to make the gender scientists of the secretariat happy without violating the science of medicine at the same time. In explaining why gender perspectives must be included in the education of future physicians, they state quite reasonably that "research that does not take into account differences in biology and pathology between the sexes... may affect the development of medicines and care." Yet on the same page they also state that they aim to "incorporate more gender-conscious and/or norm-critical literature in education". In other words, they will try to use gender studies — where gender is viewed as a social construction — while at the same time investigating biological sex differences and sex effects in medical treatment. Reconciling these two perspectives might prove challenging, to say the least.

Malmö University will review the allocation of research funding so that they don't result in "unequal consequences". The equality here is not about giving equal opportunities. No uneven distribution between gender categories is acceptable, even though prior interests, preferences and aptitudes may differ. The heads of the departments must annually make "gender-aware and norm-critical surveys and analyses of the allocation of assignments, time and economic resources between men and women". Everything must be gender mainstreamed: "Education plans, curricula, learning objectives, local degree goals, course guides, course literature, teaching methods and educational information are reviewed and revised based on national gender equality policy goals."

At the Royal Institute of Technology (KTH) – ranked 83rd in Europe according to *THE* – they have taken it one step further by setting up a special inspection body called the Equality Office, with at least three full-time positions. In addition, new faculty services have been created in the field of gender and organization research. The work is led by the Vice Principal of Equality and Basic Values, Professor Anna Wahl, and will have its own budget. What does a vice principal of basic values even do? It brings to mind some kind of theological activity rather than a scientific activity, performed at a university.

Generally, KTH's plan, to a very small extent, is about gender equality, and to a very large extent it is about sanctioning a theory of power structures according to intersectionality and gender studies. Furthermore, its only stated definition of an equality analysis is "about visualising the problems that arise from the fact that we divide humanity into two categories and ascribe one category more value than the other." The conclusion is thus already done before the analysis is even made. It's unclear how the engineers trained at KTH benefit from this. No such evaluation has been done.

Sometimes one hears that it is exaggerated how far the Swedish state's gender equality work has gone. Or that phenomena such as norm critique and intersectionality are peripheral. This is not the case, which the gender mainstreaming of all of Sweden's universities shows.

Is there even evidence that norm criticism and anti-prejudice training actually improve education? This question is not asked by either the Secretariat for Gender Research or by the institutions themselves. This is not about improving education. Nor is it about conducting better research. Instead of dealing with actual gender equality, in the sense of combating discrimination, a small agency like the National Secretariat of Gender Research has interpreted its mission much more broadly. All college staff must be educated in the right gender perspectives which are now renamed as "competencies". So one is either competent or incompetent in their perspective. If you want to teach or research in a university you either accept the directives or you don't. So what happens next?

I asked Erik Ringmar if all this was really such a bad thing. Why should university teachers not also take responsibility to try to create a socially just society? He answered that there are a lot of problems in society that the universities can help to analyse. The best and only way to do this is to maintain the integrity of the intellectual activities that are undertaken within these institutions. I am right-wing, Erik is left-wing.

But our politics should not matter. The important thing is the integrity of the academic process. If destroyed, then the core of the university is destroyed.

Control processes, budgets, allocation of research funds, reading lists, curriculums — all aspects of university life are being mainstreamed by the National Secretariat's gender studies ideology. Meanwhile nothing has been written about it in our Swedish newspapers. The few times it's been mentioned in the parliament, it has only been in positive terms by Social Democrats boasting about their own policies.

Why is everyone so quiet? Is it because they agree with what's happening? Or is this deafening silence driven by fear?

The universities' mission is to seek the truth. That is not possible without academic freedom. Right now, Swedish universities are willingly turning themselves into a commissariat for a one-sided and simplistic vision of social justice. And when the search for truth and the ideology of social justice collide, which do you think is likely to win?

Martin Malmgren[1]

Self-Censorship in Times of Ideological Conformity

ABSTRACT: For more than two years, a debate has raged in Finland on questions relating to gender parity, the musical canon and representation in the classical music world. Sweden has often been highlighted as a pioneer when it comes to equality — but who actually decides what true equality is? A closer examination of Swedish cultural policies reveals a confusion between equality of opportunity and equality of outcome, where cultural workers and academicians prefer to stay silent rather than bite the hand that feeds them.

TOPICS: feminism and gender mainstreaming; race, ethnicity; diversity, inclusion and equity programmes
****

> We can all agree that the censorship of artists by tyrannous regimes is an abomination, and yet there is something even more dispiriting about an artist who surrenders his or her freedom of expression voluntarily. (Andrew Doyle — from "Free Speech and Why it Matters")

LvB — Ladies versus Beethoven[2]

"Is Beethoven alone more interesting than all of the world's women?" When journalist Maria Pettersson asked this pointed question at a panel

---

[1] Musician (pianist), PhD student at the DocMus Doctoral School of Classical Music, Sibelius Academy (Finland). Email: martin.malmgren@gmail.com
[2] This heading is taken from a festival that was meant to happen in March 2020 at the Stockholm Concert Hall, where each concert included a Beethoven symphony and a work by a female composer: https://www.mynewsdesk.com/se/konserthuset-stockholm-kungliga-filharmonikerna/pressreleases/ladies-versus-beethoven-a-different-kind-of-beethoven-festival-at-konserthuset-stockholm-2020-2850383

discussion[3] in Helsinki, it sounded like an echo from a Swedish media scandal in 2013, highlighting the fact that Beethoven occupied as much space in Swedish orchestras' programmes as all female composers combined.[4] Efforts to highlight inequality in today's classical music world often call attention to such statistics; the organization Donne—Women in Music recently reported that out of 100 orchestras in 27 countries, only 5% of the previous season's programmes was composed by women.[5] It was also deemed to be alarming that only 1.1% of the music was written by black or Asian women, with no more than 2.4% by their male counterparts. In Finland, it was the daily *Hufvudstadsbladet*[6] that initiated the debate in 2019, by presenting concert programme statistics from the capital region's orchestras and categorizing works by "male" and "female", "living" and "dead" composers—also noting a total absence of African composers.

The question arises as to whether such statistics-fixated organizations and journalists are at all familiar with the origins of western art music. A reasonable counter-question to that of Maria Pettersson's would have been to ask why anyone even thinks about using contemporary ideals of racial and gender equality retroactively, with regards to a centuries-old art form with European roots? Serfdom had recently been abolished in the Holy Roman Empire that Beethoven grew up in—is anyone really surprised that the issue of gender equality among composers was not at the forefront of society during those times? It appears self-evident that the "imbalance" seen in today's concert programmes reflects how vastly different expectations of men and women were earlier in music history. We see this in the life of the enormously talented Fanny Mendelssohn,

---

3   27th September 2021, "Female Composers Sidelined by History"—a panel discussion with conductor Susanna Mälkki, researcher Nuppu Koivisto-Kaasik and doctoral researcher and music journalist Markus Virtanen, moderated by journalist Maria Pettersson, *Taidepiste*, https://www.uniarts.fi/en/events/ taidepiste-female-composers-sidelined-by-history/

4   16th September 2013, "Lika mycket Beethoven som kvinnor", *Sveriges Television*, https://www.svt.se/nyheter/lokalt/norrbotten/lika-mycket-beeth oven-som-kvinnor

5   9th September 2021, "Women Compose Only 5 percent of the Pieces Scheduled in Classical Music Concerts Today", *Classic FM*, https://www.classicfm.com/ discover-music/women-in-music/compose-five-percent-pieces-classical-concerts/

6   3rd September 2019, "HBL granskar: Orkestrarna säger att könsbalansen är viktig—men bara 4,3 procent av verken är av kvinnliga tonsättare", *Hufvudstadsbladet*, https://www.hbl.fi/artikel/hbl-granskar-orkestrarna-sager -att-konsbalansen-ar-viktig-men-bara-43-procent-av-verken-ar-av-kv/

who was told by her father that her musical inclinations had to be "only an ornament", while her younger brother Felix was encouraged to develop his musical talents in full. Numerous historical women composers ended up publishing under a pseudonym, and Fanny Mendelssohn had works published under the name of her more famous younger brother. But in the absence of obvious counter-questions, the chief conductor of the Helsinki Philharmonic Orchestra, Susanna Mälkki, declared that classical music lags several decades behind other art forms regarding gender equality. She lamented that the orchestral world is a conservative environment characterized by professional and psychological laziness. How was it at all possible, pressed Maria Pettersson, to have such poor gender representation in the year of 2021? The generic comments from Mälkki avoided any mention of the fact that, during the 21/22 season, she herself was scheduled to conduct 31 works by male composers compared with only 4 works by women—several of these also short in duration.

When journalists and activists demand a certain outcome regarding artistic content and representation, the natural impulse could be to defend artistic freedom; the fact that Mälkki conducts significantly more music of one gender than the other is neither remarkable nor worthy of criticism. But although many in the classical music world are critical of today's identity politics, the vast majority of them have opted for self-censorship over speaking out publicly. Let us investigate the consequences of this path.

Indisputable Gender Perspectives

During the early 2000s, a number of Swedish government investigations focusing on gender equality were published, paving the way for profound changes in areas including academia and culture. The report "Claim the Spotlight" from 2006 was a result of the government asking the then-Minister of Culture, Marita Ulvskog, to convene a committee "with the task of submitting proposals on how gender- and equality perspectives can become an undisputed and influential force in the field of performing arts".[7] Few appear to have been alarmed that the authorities demanded these perspectives to be indisputable. The report argues that "artistic competence, quality and skill are concepts that can be exclusionary", and in a text by Kristina Hultman, the reader is told that art music today is

---

[7] 26th April 2006, "Plats på scen", *Ministry of Culture*, https://www.regeringen. se/49bb98/contentassets/4dab59fc022b4d789f9d7d9f02373a32/plats-pa-scen-del-1-av-2-missiv---kap.-5-sou-200642

permeated by "gender power-related privileges for men and prejudices against women". A source reference is missing. But since Swedish law prohibits discrimination on the basis of gender, the question arises as to how many legal cases have been pursued regarding discriminatory male "gender power-related privileges"? Hultman, who at the time also acted as a parliamentary candidate for the political party Feminist Initiative, did not seem to have much prior experience of the industry she was asked to write about, yet her conclusions were soon being quoted and taken as fact in other state-funded investigations.[8] As the state began earmarking millions of SEK for projects focusing on gender equality, a large number of groups were unsurprisingly willing to take up the cash that was offered. Organizations such as KVAST (Female Gathering of Swedish Composers), KUPP (Women Up On the Podium), Konstmusiksystrar (Art Music Sisters) and Kvinnoorkestern (The Women's Orchestra) have, over the years, received several million SEK from the Swedish Performing Arts Agency, the Swedish Gender Equality Agency, the Swedish Arts Council and others. The Swedish Performing Arts Agency began supporting projects that tried to "create a canon of works written by female composers", and among other things they advocated for a mandatory introductory course on gender for music college teachers—a prerequisite for employment.[9] In the Swedish Arts Council's scholarship applications, a new policy clarified that "a maximum of 60 percent should benefit an overrepresented gender".[10]

It is unsurprising that statistical equality of this sort would soon find itself on a collision course with reality. In areas such as dance and children's literature, women form a significant majority, whereas the balance is the opposite among composers. On closer inspection, it appears to be the case that exceptions to the 40/60 ideal are regularly made in situations where it would otherwise lead to an unfair outcome for women; the Swedish Arts Council has made an exception in scholarships for dance, where the 40/60 principle has been replaced by 30/70 "because female applicants often make up almost 70 percent of received grant

8   27th November 2009, "Komponisternas villkor", see p. 23: https://www. konstnarsnamnden.se/Sve/Nyheter/PDFer/Komponisternas%20villkor.pdf

9   "Statens musikverks jämställdhetsuppdrag—rapport för verksamheten 2011", https://musikverket.se/wp-content/uploads/2014/10/Statens-Musikverks-Jamstalldhetsuppdrag-rapport-for-verksamheten-2011.pdf

10   "Kulturrådets årsredovisning 2017", https://www.kulturradet.se/globalassets /start/om-oss/arsredovisningar/arsredovisningar-dokument/arsredovisning ar/kulturradets-arsredovisning-2017.pdf

applications".[11] No such exception is mentioned in areas where male applicants are in the significant majority. In the Council's annual reports, it is noticeable that the 40/60 principle is frequently ignored in cases where it is women who are overrepresented among the applicants, while overrepresentation for men is almost never passes the 60% mark.[12]

How are such discrepancies possible in a society that claims to promote equality for both men and women? The answer is that we are dealing with an ideology that rejects the idea that we are all equal today: it refers to historical injustices, claims that white, straight men as a whole have been the most privileged group of the past, and thus reaches the conclusion that they still hold "gender power-related privileges" that must be redressed. This way of thinking results in a type of guilt by association that must be examined critically, since it can hardly be said that the average man of today enjoys privileges similar to men of the nobility during the lives of Beethoven and Mozart.

Similarly, it is no coincidence that the supposedly "exclusionary" concepts of "quality", "skill" and "artistic competence" are viewed with suspicion. Once again it is claimed that white men — not, for example, performers or the concert audiences of our times — have decided for the rest of us what "quality" is, and the fact that the outcome is far from 50/50 is seen as proof that the very concept of "artistic quality" is male-coded.

Legal Confusion

In practice, we see a confusion in both Swedish cultural policy and legislation between the concepts of equality of opportunity and equality of outcome. The Swedish constitution informs that law or other regulation "must not mean that someone is disadvantaged because of their gender, unless that regulation is part of an effort to achieve equality between men and women".[13] But who defines what true equality is? The Swedish Gender Equality Agency gives the impression that it is about *"equal*

---

[11] 19th December 2017, "Tystnadskulturen måste brytas", *Konstnärsnämnden*, https://www.konstnarsnamnden.se/default.aspx?id=21223

[12] See p. 38: https://www.kulturradet.se/globalassets/start/om-oss/arsredovis ningar/arsredovisningar-dokument/arsredovisningar/kulturradets-arsredovi sning-2017.pdf, and p. 73: http://www.e-magin.se/paper/tkj3c1nt/paper/ 1#/paper/tkj3c1nt/72

[13] 22nd November 2018, "SFS 2018:1903 Lag om ändring i regeringsformen", *Lagboken*, https://www.lagboken.se/Lagboken/start/forvaltningsratt/kungor else-1974152-om-beslutad-ny-regeringsform/d_3404519-sfs-2018_1903-lag-om-andring-i-regeringsformen

opportunities for women and men to participate... and influence", but already the next sentence states that "an *equal distribution* of power and influence between men and women in all sectors of society... is a crucial precondition for qualitative aspects of the exercise of power to be able to change in an equal direction" (my emphasis).[14] The latter quote would require social engineering on an enormous scale and contradicts the first quote, since implementing such a policy wouldn't truly give men and women equal opportunities, if all sectors of society are expected to have precisely 50/50-equal distribution of power and influence. Men and women make different career and life choices, which inevitably lead to real differences in matters of power and influence.

It gets murkier with the law and how it functions in practice. According to the current discrimination legislation, an employer must "in the case of new employment, make a special effort to get applicants from the under-represented gender". The Royal Academy of Music goes a step further in some announcements about professorships, stating that they— in appropriate cases—will make a special effort to *recruit* the under-represented gender, while clarifying that women are underrepresented among professors.[15] This comes as little surprise, since the Swedish state clearly mandates that academic institutions must hire a greater number of female professors overall.[16] This, of course, raises the question of how an academic institution could possibly recruit objectively, when everybody involved knows the gender required to improve the current imbalance. Another dilemma of the same sort is seen in the report "Claim the Spot-light", where the Värmland Opera notes that a "more even distribution between the genders becomes a problem as auditions always take place behind a screen".

The introduction of "blind auditions", where applicants perform behind a screen, has previously been considered an important step towards equality, ensuring a fair process where no aspect other than the

---

[14]   14th December 2017, "En jämn fördelning av makt och inflytande", *Jämställdhetsmyndigheten*, https://web.archive.org/web/20210226124121/https ://www.jamstalldhetsmyndigheten.se/om-jamstalldhet/sveriges-jamstalldhetspolitik/1-en-jamn-fordelning-av-makt-och-inflytande

[15]   Professor of Cello, job announcement, Royal Academy of Music: https:// webcache.googleusercontent.com/search?q=cache:LhLYd_ZJJAkJ:https://ww w.musicalchairs.info/lib%3Fpsection%3Djo%26pid%3D36247%26file_id%3D4 612+&cd=1&hl=en&ct=clnk&gl=fi&lr=lang_fi | lang_en

[16]   4th January 2021, "Fortsatt satsning på jämställdhet i akademin", https://www.regeringen.se/pressmeddelanden/2021/01/fortsatt-satsning-pa-jamstalldhet-i-akademin/

quality of each applicant's playing is judged. However, according to this new doctrine, not being able to register an applicant's gender or skin colour suddenly turns into an obstacle in the fight for equity.[17] Among recent examples of misguided diversity policies, one that received widespread attention was when the English Touring Opera replaced 13 of its white musicians for the sake of diversifying the ensemble.[18] Meanwhile, we can note that most academies, as well as municipalities and orchestras, do find it difficult to comply with diversity and equality requirements, according to which it apparently is extremely unequal in schools, health care and nursing, and where the relative lack of male applicants is not enough to counteract the overall female dominance.[19]

Clashes with reality have in no way prevented the 50/50 ideal from becoming the norm in many areas. At a recent opera symposium arranged by the Royal Swedish Academy of Music,[20] panellists received a welcoming email where participants were numbered and divided into two equally-sized columns according to gender. Each panel discussion was planned to be 50/50 — a distribution that, in the end, did not fully succeed. Unsurprisingly, there were both female and male participants wondering who had been invited based on merit and who had ended up on the programme more as a pawn in the game of equal outcomes.

Though the concept of equal opportunities continues to be confused with equal outcomes, it is worth noting that the Royal Academy of Music's former principal, Cecilia Rydinger, opposes the idea of 50/50-distribution: "Admission must be in proportion to the number of applicants, quality and ability to assimilate the education. Regardless of

---

[17] 16th July 2020, "To Make Orchestras More Diverse, End Blind Auditions", *New York Times*, https://www.nytimes.com/2020/07/16/arts/music/blind-auditions-orchestras-race.html

[18] 10th September 2021, "MU Appalled to Hear About English Touring Opera's Recent Action", *Musicians' Union*, https://musiciansunion.org.uk/news/mu-appalled-to-hear-about-english-touring-opera-s-recent-action

[19] One example comes from the municipality of Nora: "An increase in the proportion of men should be sought, especially in preschool activities, schools and care and nursing. Unfortunately, there are often no or very few male applicants for advertised jobs and temporary positions in these areas", https://www.nora.se/kommunpolitik/reglerochstyrdokument/jamstallhetsplan.4.70d9418166bea2e7521727.html

[20] "Mötesplats Opera 2021", *Kungliga Musikaliska Akademien*, https://www.musikaliskaaakademien.se/kalendarium/kalendarie/motesplatsopera2021svenskoperakonstnutidframtidhistoria.2845.html

gender. All students must succeed in music life, that is why we have entrance exams."[21]

Gender as an Asset

A striking aspect of the current *zeitgeist* is that many have become fully aware that their gender identity can have a decisive impact on their careers. The conductor Anna-Maria Helsing has noted that "in many ways it is easier to be a woman, because there are not so many of us [female conductors], we tend to get a special place",[22] and similarly, the composer Cecilia Damström observes that she herself has not experienced discrimination—"rather the opposite. People usually remember 'that female composer' because of course you also differ from the masses by your gender."[23] Echoing these thoughts, composer Tytti Arola points out that "right now my gender is directly helpful in getting opportunities".[24] The transsexual pianist Sara Davis Buechner noted during Pride Month 2021 that the new cultural focus on diversity meant that the part of her identity that previously damaged her career had now become an asset, and that her calendar had become "the fullest it has ever been".[25] And in 2020, conductor Ruut Kiiski explained that "right now, my position in the labor market is perhaps even better than some men's, when women are given more opportunities."[26]

These observations of gender privilege stand in stark contrast to the principled stance of the previously-mentioned conductor Susanna Mälkki: "My standpoint has always been that since I do not wish that my gender

---

[21] 17th October 2020, "'När är det lämpligt att skaffa barn?' I enrum har Cecilia Rydinger fått frågorna som kvinnliga dirigentstudenter bara ställer till andra kvinnor", *Hufvudstadsbladet*, https://www.hbl.fi/artikel/nar-ar-det-lampligt-att-skaffa-barn-i-enrum-har-cecilia-rydinger-fatt-fragorna-som-kvinnliga-diri/

[22] 2nd October 2011, "Anna-Maria Helsing. Savonlinna, 2011", *Sonorama Magazine*, https://www.youtube.com/watch?v=cP5GLB0WztU

[23] 1st April 2015, "Cecilia Damström: Kompositris år 2015", *Hufvudstadsbladet*, http://gamla.hbl.fi/opinion/impuls/2015-04-01/744586/impuls-kompositris-ar-2015

[24] 16th August 2021, "Tytti Arola toivoo monenlaisten ihmisten päätyvän säveltäjiksi", *Teosto*, https://www.teosto.fi/teostory/tytti-arola-toivoo-monen laisten-ihmisten-paatyvan-saveltajiksi/

[25] 22nd June 2021, "Pride Month Special: Breaking Barriers", *Yamaha*, https://hub.yamaha.com/brand/b-artists/pride-month-special-breaking-barriers/

[26] 17th November 2020, "Förebilderna är a och o på vägen till dirigentyrket—så svarar fyra kvinnor i HBL-enkät", *Hufvudstadsbladet*, https://www.hbl.fi/artikel/forebilderna-ar-a-och-o-pa-vagen-till-dirigentyrket-sa-svarar-fyra-kvinnor-i-hbl-enkat/

is something that is held against me, I also shall not use it to benefit from it. Music, with the capital M, remains its own independent entity—and that, for me, is the best part."[27]

I have previously noted that the 50/50 policy has resulted in female composers having chances four times higher of getting commissions from Swedish orchestras, since only about 20 percent of Swedish composers are women.[28] Such statistical disparities have prompted composer Kalevi Aho, also chairman of the Finnish Symphony Orchestras Association, to ask whether we could now talk about discrimination against male composers in Sweden.[29] A different perspective was put forth by Nicholas Collon, the Finnish radio orchestra's new chief conductor, who was asked what he would say to contemporary male composers who feel disadvantaged as a result of the targeted focus on female composers. Collon's response was that "women have been disadvantaged for so many centuries that I think we, as men, can take it".[30]

The remedy for an historical injustice is thus to introduce a new discrimination—the son is held accountable for the privileges of his most powerful ancestors. Collon's words are in direct opposition to the mindset of his predecessor as chief conductor, Hannu Lintu, who has argued that it would be unhealthy for the future to push for equality through quotas,[31] and mentions that there are "those who say that it is an escape from the problem to refer to artistic criteria, but surely the same criteria must apply, regardless of whether the author is male or female... If we strive for a 50-50 distribution, we will inevitably make decisions that are to the detriment of all parties."[32]

Hannu Lintu points to something important, because it is not just one gender that is the loser in the current distribution policy. The idea that

[27] 31st December 2021, "A Conductor Considers Her Future", *New York Times*, https://www.nytimes.com/2021/12/31/arts/music/classical-music-susanna-malkki.html

[28] 15th May 2021, "When Gender Equality Rings False", *Kvartal*, https://kvartal.se/artiklar/when-gender-equality-rings-false/

[29] 17th November 2020, "Musiikkia korona-aikaan", *Suomen Sinfoniaorkesterit ry*, https://www.sinfoniaorkesterit.fi/fi/artikkeli/?id=42&ofs=1

[30] 4th September 2021, "Vi måste spegla hela samhället", *Hufvudstadsbladet*, https://www.hbl.fi/artikel/vi-maste-spegla-hela-samhallet/

[31] 25th November 2020, "Moi Lontoosta! Päätös on nyt tehty", *Suomen Kuvalehti*, https://suomenkuvalehti.fi/jutut/kulttuuri/kirjat/torstaina-19-marraskuuta-klo-18-30-hannu-lintu-paatti-kuka-saa-kaunokirjallisuuden-finlandian/

[32] 4th September 2019, "Hannu Lintu: Helt onaturligt att åstadkomma en 50-50-fördelning", *Hufvudstadsbladet*, https://www.hbl.fi/artikel/hannu-lintu-helt-onaturligt-att-astadkomma-en-50-50-fordelning/

women are in need of special support and treatment is perceived as infantilizing, and is something many women themselves oppose.[33]

If the positively-discriminated-against female practitioners occasionally speak openly about the prevailing situation that is favourable to them, the disadvantaged men are all the quieter in public. They entrust me with information strictly under anonymity, as few dare to criticize "indisputable" gender equality policies in public. Both established and younger composers and conductors frequently have proposed commissioned works and performances cancelled, strictly due to their gender. I am told by multiple reliable sources about an opera house manager who had decided in advance what gender the chief conductor's assistant should have — in auditions for candidates of both genders. A rather peculiar event was when a female conductor had to cancel an appearance in Sweden due to illness — which resulted in panic for the management, since the ill female conductor could only be replaced by another female. It is now commonly joked about how it would be easier to hire male conductors or commission works by male composers if only they underwent a gender-reassignment surgery. A source says that he had raised the dilemma of ensuring gender equality in discussions with concert house managers, who are said to be "aware of the problem, but also have political directives to relate to. Although the subject is a bit complex, no one I have spoken to seemed personally happy about the quota zeal. Unfortunately, simplified reasoning and slogans have guided the political debate and the directives have been as one could expect."

"Start with the Chicks"

Being denied commissions due to gender is typically confirmed indirectly and orally — usually through a publisher rather than from the concert houses themselves. Sources from within several Swedish concert houses' programme committees confirm that gender is often the first thing discussed when deciding who is being searched for — whether it be a composer, conductor or soloist. Magdalena Fronczak, producer at the

---

[33] "As we have seen, even in the absence of legislation women are entering the workplace in greater numbers. In this regard, the demand for quotas to ensure a certain number of posts are filled by women appears to be a solution in search of a problem. Worse, quotas, like other forms of positive discrimination, undermine women with the implication that promotion has been granted on the basis of biology rather than merit. Women are quite capable of making it to the top without such special measures being put in place", from *Women vs Feminism* by Joanna Williams, Emerald Publishing Limited 2017.

Gothenburg Concert House, calls the strategy to "start with the chicks"[34] — as a way of avoiding the situation where "sweaty concert house bosses" contact Fronczak just before the programme book is to be printed, when it dawns upon them that they have forgotten the issue of women composers, and request "tips on an opera written by a woman".

Experience has shown that it can be risky for institutions to neglect the "chicks". Organizations such as KVAST have collaborated with the media, in particular public service, to "sharpen the tone towards the orchestras"[35] if they do not deliver good results. The orchestra that does not align itself with these demands thus risks being shamed by the media as an institution that "plays mostly male composers".[36] As a remedy for this, KVAST has offered to "enter into a partnership with the orchestras" to allow the institutions to set their own "quantitative, measurable goals for their own repertoire development".

Threats have also come directly from high-ranking politicians. During meetings, former Minister of Culture Alice Bah Kuhnke informed orchestral administrators that they would either have to improve, or the state would be compelled to earmark money specifically for gender equality.

As a result, it is hardly surprising that some orchestras falsify statistics to appease the media, the politicians and the activists. Stefan Forsberg, director of Stockholm's Concert Hall, proudly declared in an interview that almost 40 percent of the composers in the Concert Hall were women.[37] That season, however, only 11 of 78 orchestral works — 14 percent — were written by women. How could this statistical discrepancy be explained? It turns out that the Concert Hall counted composers only once, no matter how many times they were played, and included not only orchestral concerts but also the smaller chamber music concerts, where many short works by *different* female composers were programmed — seemingly in a strategic way. With such statistics, Beethoven is counted

---

[34] August 2020, "Börja med burden — Metoder för jämställd programläggning", *Den andra operan*, http://denandraoperan.se/wp-content/uploads/2021/08/Bo%CC%88rja-med-bruden_webb.pdf

[35] 16th September 2013, "Kvinnliga tonsättare skärper tonen mot orkestrar", *Sveriges Radio*, https://sverigesradio.se/artikel/5644395

[36] 12th June 2015, "Västerås Sinfonietta spelar mest manliga kompositörer", *Sveriges Radio*, https://sverigesradio.se/artikel/6185003

[37] 17th September 2019, "I Stockholm är knappt 40 procent av tonsättarna kvinnor — men könsbalansen är alltjämt ett spänningsfält", *Hufvudstadsbladet*, https://www.hbl.fi/artikel/i-stockholm-ar-knappt-40-procent-av-tonsattarna-kvinnor-men-konsbalansen-ar-alltjamt-ett-spannings/

once even if all nine symphonies are performed during a season, whereas short chamber musical works by different female composers make the Concert Hall appear more "equal". In such a statistical universe, a hypothetical "Ladies versus Beethoven" match would most definitely result in a knockout of the latter by the former.

How Free are the Arts?

The conflict between artistic freedom and demands on artists to tick boxes on diversity, inclusion and equality in grant applications has been topical in Swedish cultural debate for over a decade. However, it wasn't until recently that a government agency investigated this issue, the result of which can be seen in the report "How is Artistic Freedom Doing Under State-Funded Arts Institutions?".[38] Survey responses showed that 33 percent of artists had previously refrained from applying for a grant, due to assessment criteria that were perceived to be in conflict with their understanding of artistic freedom. More remarkably, nearly half of the respondents admitted that they had amended the content of a planned work of art or cultural activity in their applications, in ways that did not increase the quality of the work or activity, but in a way that they thought would result in higher chances of receiving grants. It appears to be a generational issue: in the group 55–64 years, 36 percent have adapted their artistic content, whereas the corresponding figure for the group 25–44 years is close to 60 percent.

Jury members interviewed for this report have taken note of the tendency among applicants to adjust the content to certain themes, in particular diversity and gender issues, "in a way that feels constructed and strategic, and that places the artistic idea in the background". Perhaps the most crucial piece of information in this context is that the experts "describe a desperation among artists and cultural creators, who are often in a difficult financial situation and willing to do and write anything to get an opportunity to devote themselves to their art".

Being quiet and adaptable appears to be much more favourable than openly criticizing current dogma. The vastness of the problem of self-censorship in the arts transcends national borders and can hardly be understated—a recent "Freedom of Expression" survey by the British organization Arts Professional offers "a disturbing and permanent testimony that shines a light upon coercion, bullying, intimidation and

---

[38] 26th June 2021, "Så fri är konsten", *Myndigheten för kulturanalys*, https://kulturanalys.se/publikation/sa-fri-ar-konsten/

intolerance among a community that thinks of itself as liberal, open minded and equitable".[39]

Talentless Men and Symphonic Cathedrals

As has been noted, lobbying groups and activists believe that a good way to achieve gender equality utopia is by replacing historical discrimination in one direction with contemporary discrimination in the other. We now have courses like Popkollo specifically for girls and transgender people,[40] and in Finland the course "Yhdenvertaisesti säveltäen" ("Composing through Equity") which wants to "alleviate professional segregation by gender in the field and promote equal opportunities for participation" — by offering the course primarily for girls.[41] A gender prerequisite was in place during the years when *Kultur i Väst* arranged a course for young conductors—no prior knowledge in conducting was required, however.[42] The course was awarded the Västra Götaland region's gender equality award[43] and was later visited by Sweden's then-Minister of Culture Alice Bah Kuhnke.[44] Among the course's teachers was Marit Strindlund, who said that it is mainly orchestras and opera houses "that can actively work towards giving 50% of the assignments to female conductors".[45] The course's remaining all-female teaching staff included Kerstin Nerbe, who in a radio interview[46] explained that one must use quotas, even if she herself had been against it before. She said that society has changed to actively start pushing for quotas, "because you see that there are good women who have to stand back for a less good man—because it is a

---

39 20th February 2020, "'Culture of Censorship' as Arts Workers Fear Backlash", *Arts Professional*, https://www.artsprofessional.co.uk/news/exclusive-culture-censorship-arts-workers-fear-backlash

40 https://www.popkollo.se/om-oss/

41 https://www.yhdenvertaisestisaveltaen.fi/hankkeesta/

42 "Dirigent—för kvinnor som vill fördjupa sig i dirigentyrket", https://web.archive.org/web/20170224045326/http://www.kulturivast.se/musik/dirigen t-for-kvinnor-som-vill-fordjupa-sig-i-dirigentyrket

43 2nd February 2016, "Kultur i Väst får regionens jämställdhetspris", https://www.mynewsdesk.com/se/kulturivast/pressreleases/kultur-i-vaest-faar-regionens-jaemstaelldhetspris-1307102

44 22nd January 2018, "Kulturministern besöker Kultur i Västs dirigentkurs", https://www.pressmachine.se/pressrelease/view/kulturministern-besoker-kultur-i-vasts-dirigentkurs-27489

45 10th March 2015, "Vill få fler kvinnor att bli dirigenter", *Sveriges Radio*, https://sverigesradio.se/artikel/6113276

46 22nd November 2015, "Kvinnor som dirigerar—Orkestern är mitt instrument", *Sveriges Radio*, https://sverigesradio.se/avsnitt/638039?programid=4112

man". Furthermore, she argued that the term "quality" is "a total non-sense word, because it means nothing, it is something you hit someone on the head with. No, we must have quotas, you have to... have 20% Swedish women [who conduct] with the orchestras." Nerbe thus deemed herself able to ascertain that "talented women" are excluded in favour of "less talented" men, while simultaneously rejecting the concept of "quality".

Are gender-segregated educational programmes truly in line with today's ideas about gender equality? I would argue that segregation of this kind is not beneficial to the participants—it deprives them of opportunities for free competition by protecting them from the complexities of life. Above all, the participants are brought up to believe that the gender they were born into is what defines them as human beings; that these immutable characteristics are what makes them interesting and worthy of special treatment.

Someone who reasons completely differently from Nerbe regarding quotas for Swedish female conductors is Helena Wessman, former director of Berwaldhallen and now principal of the Royal Academy of Music: "We work with conductors at a high level, we are compared with orchestras such as the Berlin Philharmonic Orchestra, the Vienna Philharmonic Orchestra, the London Symphony Orchestra, and we are also looking for conductors at that level. And at present, no Swedish woman is clearly at that level." She goes on to compare the symphonies with the architectural complexity of a cathedral building, where building an arch requires precise adjustment to the millimetre, so that it does not fall down. Arguing that there is a similar level of complexity in symphonic music, Wessman says that "if the composer is the architect, the conductor is the builder"—which in itself is a big assignment, requiring the highest level of technical mastery and skill. "The knowledge of an orchestra is endless. There are a hundred people [in the orchestra] who have dedicated their lives to this, their knowledge is infinite. And if you want to gain their trust, you must know much more than them."

***

It sounds like a legitimate and valuable idea to give space and opportunities to historically disadvantaged groups. Much music has unfairly fallen into oblivion, which is sometimes explained by various forms of injustice that afflicted the composers, whether they were women, from ethnic minorities or living under dictatorships. Having said that, I do not think that we are doing these composers much more than a disservice if we highlight them on the basis of their identity. As a performing musician, I see qualitative differences in approaching a composer's work because of a deep connection with the music, versus doing so because of the composer's identity. We have ended up in a situation where composers are no longer just composers, but rather representatives of different groups based on skin colour and gender. Sinfonia Lahti's first guest conductor, Anja Bihlmaier, confirms that there indeed are quotas for female conductors in Scandinavia, and sees it as a complex issue because "nobody wants to be a quota woman".[47]

An unusual idea regarding questions about representation and concerts with only music by women came recently from the music critic Sofia Nyblom, who was against the idea of all-female programmes with music from times when women did not have the same opportunities as men:

> They did not get the same resources, and… to collect the works of women who have not really been allowed to blossom fully, it can be a bit like, well, that wasn't particularly exciting. But if you instead integrate some of these works that are good—maybe not fantastic—in a program of good and bad works by male composers or some other gender, then you instead get a span and a picture of a time and a picture of a context where you do not have to think "is it good, is it bad, yes, it is by women, yes, then it will not be good"—then it confirms the stereotype… so I don't think we should continue with it.[48]

The one who confirmed the stereotype in this case, however, was the one who spoke. I wonder who would feel thrilled about going to a concert with "good and bad" works by male composers and "maybe not fantastic" works by historical female composers.

A Humiliation for the Music

Among the names that are rarely mentioned when discussing representation of female composers is Galina Ustvolskaya. When faced with questions on this subject, she responded: "Can one really distinguish between music written by men and music written by women?… I am of the opinion that such a division should not be allowed to continue. We should only play music that is genuine and strong. If we are honest about

[47] 23rd August 2021, "Haagse chef-dirigent Anja Bihlmaier: 'Ik ben zo'n type dat vindt dat je alles moet doen, en ook nog goed'", *NRC Handelsblad*, https://www.nrc.nl/nieuws/2021/08/23/haagse-chef-dirigent-anja-bihlmaier-ik-ben-zon-type-dat-vindt-dat-je-alles-moet-doen-en-ook-nog-goed-2-a4055729

[48] 12th November 2021, "En kväll för Allmän rösträtt", *Sveriges Radio*, https://sverigesradio.se/avsnitt/direkt-en-kvall-for-allman-rostratt?fbclid=iwar29g2sm3b2d21r_fn36hiljnfl9cid6ybsv40u3f1fhgxsiwppukgaly4m

it, a performance in a concert by women composers is a humiliation for the music."[49]

Ustvolskaya's words may sound harsh, but should be understood as a suggestion to let the music stand alone on its own merit, regardless of the composer's identity. It would be perfectly possible to abandon the zeal for representation and return to common perceptions of quality and the canon. Gender equality activists may argue that the music is not enough, and that if representation is skewed, it tarnishes the artistic experience. However, there is no indication that a majority of concert visitors feel this way.

The absolute lack of a robust debate on these subjects in the classical music world in Sweden, as well as in Finland, can only be explained by a culture of self-censorship. The arguments put forth in this text have been discussed with a wide range of composers, concert hall managers, conductors, soloists, artistic directors, writers, singers, orchestral musicians and beyond — yet in spite of a wide agreement on the content, few speak out publicly on these matters. The path towards a healthier society, with a greater plurality of viewpoints expressed in the public discourse, would require a more fearless and courageous approach from people in the cultural field. Having said this, there are nevertheless many positive developments worth noting: members of orchestral programming committees in both Finland and Sweden inform me that their committees have successfully rejected proposals of implementing stricter racial and gender quotas. Though the public debate has been one-sided, a wider spectrum of opinions has been shared behind closed doors.

On the surface, this essay deals with a specific issue of representation in a relatively narrow sector of the cultural sphere. In fact, it is about what kind of society we want to live in. At present, we accept that a small group of people are given great influence on issues that make our cultural life swirl ever deeper in an endless identity-political spiral. It is entirely possible to reject these ideas and stop being subordinated by activist dogma — after all, somebody out there will always be provoked by independently-made artistic choices. May I humbly propose tuning out from the demands of the activists and tuning in to the music instead?

---

[49]   Spring 2007, "Masculinity versus Femininity: An Overriding Dichotomy in the Music of Soviet Composer Galina Ustvolskaya", *eSharp*, https://www.gla.ac.uk/media/Media_41213_smxx.pdf

Norman Goldstuck[1]

Fifty Years of Experience of Academia

Is Academic Freedom an Illusion?

ABSTRACT: My student and postgraduate years suggest to me that true academic freedom is largely an illusion. This observation can be verified by looking back at history. The current threat which is due to the diversity, inclusion and equity idea is not a plot of the illuminati, globalists and "new world order" brigade. It is a direct result of the feminist movement, as I shall demonstrate. It is also not new. The form may be different from the experiences of previous millennia but the process and the outcome will be the same.

TOPICS: feminism and gender mainstreaming; race, ethnicity; general considerations on suppression of academic freedom
****

The notion of academic freedom is an illusion, like all utopias. It may have existed for small periods of time in some places but has never been universally sustained. Perhaps it's not really sustainable. Threats to academic freedom have come from politics, religion and general culture. In the Middle Ages it was religion that was the threat. Obviously, it was politics in Nazi Germany and the communist Soviet Union. Now it appears to be culture which is driving the threat to academic freedom and this cultural change is becoming entwined with politics.

I first entered university in 1966 in Johannesburg, South Africa. The apartheid government was the threat to academic freedom as it would not

---

[1] Honorary Consultant in Family Planning, University of Stellenbosch and Tygerberg Hospital, Bellville, Western Cape, South Africa. Email: nahumzh@gmail.com

permit the university to accept students or lecturers of colour. We protested the lack of "academic freedom". I have never held a university appointment but my research as a clinical pharmacologist in the pharmaceutical industry has meant working with academics at universities in the United Kingdom, Canada and South Africa. I have also taught students in all these countries and seen how academia has evolved over nearly 60 years.

As early as the 1970s at least, academia in the UK was subject at least in part to government policy. However, where there are no external factors which exist to challenge academic freedom and a vacuum is created, it needs to be filled. Nature abhors a vacuum and so academia rushes in to fill it. For the most part this is what we are witnessing now. Academics in South Africa, especially those few who were in academic positions in the apartheid years and who stood up to the government, are uncomfortable not being dictated to by the government. They solved this problem by imagining how they would like to be dictated to and going along with it.

South African universities discriminate especially against white male lecturers and students, for example because they think this is what the government wants, or would please government policy, based on its rhetoric. While the government has imposed racial quotas in sports teams this is not true of academia, at least not yet, so South African academia, like the rest of the world, is attempting to go along the road of "woke". Woke is therefore the current threat to academic freedom. Woke is two things; firstly, it is a caste system where white heterosexual old men are at the bottom and everyone else rises up from there, and secondly it has features of Schroedinger's cat, which may be unfamiliar to those who don't know anything about quantum physics.

Schroedinger's metaphorical cat was in a box both alive and dead simultaneously. You only know which when you look into the box. In 'woke', men and woman are identical and gender is a social construct in some situations or very different in others. Like the cat, you only know when you open the box which it is. This is why, for example, the United States can appoint a woman as a four star "combat" general even if the biggest fight she has ever had was with her husband or boyfriend or female partner, and deny a more talented man a job as a physics or maths professor. Interestingly in woke, you cannot be bi-racial simultaneously. Richard Dawkins, who appears to be reasonably woke, thought this. Apparently that is going too far.

"Wokism" is not new. It has arisen at the terminal phase of great empires such as the Greek, Babylonian and Roman empires. Obviously, it was not identical to today's wokism but there were many similarities.

Women had great privilege in certain social strata. They were known to breed with the gladiators (the alpha males of the time) seemingly with the consent of their emasculated patrician husbands who probably had low testosterone and sperm counts, like many of today's males. Currently we blame low testosterone levels on plastic. Who knows what their excuse was? This is obviously not true since it only affects western men and testosterone levels are rising, not falling, in women and the oestrogenic environment is not making women more feminine, quite the contrary. Women, then as today, resorted to total removal of all bodily hair as an expression of neotany, lack of responsibility and the declaration that the whole body was public and no area was private. Many of these actions have returned now under the term of "feminism". What effect the feminism of the Roman era had on its institutions of learning is unclear but it's most likely it threatened the academic freedom of the time.

Wokism is an offshoot of feminism and the gravest threat to academic freedom as it comes from within and is not an external force.

How Feminism Gaslights the World

The biological purpose of all living organisms is to reproduce. Lower organisms reproduce asexually, some use both sexual and asexual means and in some sexuality is not fixed and can vary. Some of these species fight to become the father rather than the mother since it is easier. Mammals reproduce sexually and there are only two sexes despite rare genetic anomalies. With the exception of the duck billed platypus, female mammals carry their offspring. Female mating strategy is to get the male with the best genes and to get the same or another male to provide resources. Males do not understand the concept of "fatherhood" and therefore attempt to mate with as many females as possible so that, in case they don't fertilize a given female or if she or the baby dies, he will be able to somewhere along the line pass on his genes.

Naturally these behaviours have evolved in humans but the development of the human mind has enabled us to understand fatherhood, to the extent we have developed paternity tests. Our minds have developed to be able to attempt to and succeed in overriding our own bodies and biology. The human imagination is very powerful, so men can think they are women and vice versa. It's also possible to think you are God, Napoleon or, like the Roman Emperor Caligula, think you are a horse but that does not mean its necessarily true.

It is also useful to realize that for males the ejaculation that leads to fertilization does not differ from any other in terms of bodily physiological changes. In females the ovulation that is fertilized begins to produce physiological changes within a week or so. In fact, the differences between men and women are so profound that most children appreciate them. I am belabouring the obvious so that the reader will be able to appreciate the profound delusions supposedly "normal" people can harbour and to illustrate how these delusions are perceived as normal and are used to infect objective and rational learning and research.

The top general medical journals, especially the American ones, have all become infected with this delusion. I will not name them because most people with medical interest know which they are. It is very difficult to publish a paper in one of these journals, especially if it was not a large expensive multicentre study. Articles and editorials are consumed with racism and sexism which is apparently everywhere. If you were to submit a paper entitled "The incidence of Covid-19 in copper miners with emphysema in central Chile", it would be less likely to be published than if it was titled "The racial and gender disparity of Covid-19 in copper miners with emphysema in Chile."

Gender does have an effect on clinical conditions like diabetes and heart disease and even to some extent broken bones, like a fractured radius, but it undeniably plays a role in reproductive medicine for obvious reasons. I work in the area of reproductive pharmacology. One would think wokism and "gender neutrality" would be difficult for journals of gynaecology and andrology. You would be wrong. Of course, while it is no problem to find articles showing that endometriosis and fibroids are racist, because of the demographic they affect, we learn that there are "people" who are suffering from heavy menstrual bleeding, and "people" who use emergency contraception. In fact, these diseases I am sure will be labelled sexist because they do not affect men. Naturally the diseases that men suffer is simply their own fault. I attended a webinar and one of the talks was entitled "The use of IUDs in transgender people." The presenter appeared to be female with very short hair and the individuals wanting these IUDs were women who thought they were men or who wanted to become men or something like that. She gave the talk with a straight face. Had I been in the audience I would have been unable to control my mirth. This is nothing new. Years ago I attended a meeting which was petitioning the World Health Organization to spend a lot of money on what I thought was a relatively minor concern in contraception. The main proponent of the study maintained that if this was a male problem the money would rapidly be found. The audience nodded wisely, except for me. I asked, if so much money is spent on research for male problems, then as males live a shorter life than females one must conclude that i) yet more money needs to be spent or ii) the money that is being spent is not being spent wisely.

A woke captain of a sinking ship today would say, "People and children to the lifeboats first." I think that is where Schroedinger's cat would simultaneously determine that some "people" are "women" at the same time. Wokism is all very well but can be overridden of course if drowning is an imminent prospect.

While these delusions in adults are one thing, it is quite another to take them seriously in children. Children who identify as members of the opposite gender are given puberty blockers until further treatment can be given, even over parental objections. Doctors like me who refuse to be drawn into this nonsense are being threatened with losing their medical licences in some places. I wonder, when CRISPAR gene therapy is more advanced, will children who identify with their pets as dogs or cats be allowed to have genetic alteration so they can have a tail? This is the kind of wokism affecting academic medical practice but it is my understanding that it is affecting all branches of science including the physical sciences.

Wokism is an offshoot of feminism because it is feminism that assumes that there is no difference between men and women. This is leading to population collapse and the collapse of marriage rates. Women who believe that having multiple sexual partners is the same for women and men when clearly it has been demonstrated to have different biological and psychological problems, such as the inability of women with multiple sexual partners to truly pair bond, among other things. Women are by nature hypergamous and solipsistic. Men are driven by aggression and dominance. Civilization must hold all these forces which are part of our prehistoric past in check, or else western civilization as we know it will break down. The problem is that feminism wants to hold back basic male drives, and keep them in check as a civilizing force while releasing basic female drives because it is "repressive". Without controlling both male and female basic drives society is destabilized.

So how does this affect scientific publication and consequently academic freedom? In the Middle Ages very few people could read. Even if you could the Church held access to knowledge. Even after the development of the printing press, universities held most books. Likewise in the more modern area libraries have controlled access to scientific information and even what was published was defended and promoted by an elite mafia. Access became more universal with the photocopy machine but was controlled by subscription. The internet has allowed "open access" publication and so knowledge is spreading. The more "prestigious" journals still have a "peer review" mafia which I do not like, especially as I am somewhat part of it. Although I am against the woke part of it.

I predict scientific journals as we know them will die, and control of the internet by big technology and its opinions will also end and scientists will freely publish sense or nonsense. The argument that many people then read and believe nonsense is spurious. Academic orthodoxy and peer review has not prevented belief in first "global warming" and now "climate change", whatever that may mean without any really good evidence despite what is published in reviewed journals. Peer review does not really protect against scientific fraud and nonsense, only the diligent deployment of the scientific method which has got us where we are today does. Universities, especially in the USA, are a leftist money-making scam. Even the so called "ivy league" ones have not been left untouched. Oxford University in the United Kingdom already gives female students more time for mathematics examination papers, and other British universities are busy lowering the standards for black students and students of colour because they do not get enough first-class pass marks. The great days for universities are long gone. So what is the future of universities? I believe the future of universities is the same as that of medieval churches and cathedrals. Rarely used for worship, the cathedrals of Europe and to a lesser extent in the new world have become tourist attractions. Old historic universities will become premier tourist attractions and perhaps be converted into elegant hotels.

It is interesting how we find the Salem witch trials in Massachusetts and similar witch hunts in Europe in medieval times as so incredulous, yet in a similar way they are taking place today. Being removed from electronic media has become the equivalent of being drowned or burnt at the stake. The victims now are predominantly men rather than women of course. All this is evidence of the illusion of academic freedom.

However, the saying "Facts don't care about your feelings" remains true. It was tested in the Middle Ages by King Canute and is now being tested, or about to be tested, by latter day luddites. The results will be no different. Science and technology have been so successful that presently the weak and the stupid hold sway. This has been marginally tested by the recent pandemic and would be sorely tested by another worldwide calamity such as an economic collapse. A miniscule fractional number of people has literally changed the world for billions. This will not be permanent, nothing is.

Constantin Polychronakos[1]

Diversity, Inclusion and Academic Freedom
The Case of Gender Biology[2]

ABSTRACT: As I understand it, academic freedom means that what we publish and what we teach need only be judged for relevance and for support by the evidence base. In addition, it now appears that research must be compatible with institutional priorities. Less clear is where exactly these two guiding principles are expected to clash. In an attempt to understand this, I will reflect on a recent experience that may shed some light here.

TOPICS: feminism and gender mainstreaming; general considerations on suppression of academic freedom; censorship, deplatforming and job harassment.
****

Our university recently circulated an email message whose content I found somewhat strange—for lack of a more tactful word. Or, as a cynic might have corrected me, I ought to have found it strange if I had spent the past decade or two in a coma. The message was a carefully worded reflection on how academic freedom can be reconciled with the university's updated and strengthened policies of diversity, inclusion and equity (DIE). Although said careful wording strategically avoided

---

[1] Professor in the Department of Paediatrics and Human Genetics, McGill University Health Centre, Montréal, Canada. Email: constantin.polychronakos@mcgill.ca
[2] Reprinted (with minor changes) from *Quillete*, 5th April 2021, https://quillette.com/2021/04/05/diversity-inclusion-and-academic-freedom-the-case-of-gender-biology/

specifics, one might be justified to conclude that academic freedom was being presented as some kind of threat to DIE.

The way I understand academic freedom, it means that what we publish and what we teach need only be judged for relevance and for support by the evidence base. An additional test appears now to be proposed—compatibility with institutional priorities. What was less clear is where exactly one was to expect these two guiding principles to clash. Trying to understand this, I reflected on a recent experience I had, that may shed some light here.

I am a paediatric endocrinologist, with teaching duties in the Department of Paediatrics (cross-appointment in Human Genetics), at McGill University in Montréal. For a number of years I had been giving the lecture on DSD, as part of the Reproduction and Sexuality series. The lecture is given to each class of medical students and it addresses a group of rare conditions involving individuals who are born with genital organs that are not clearly male or female. DSD used to stand for "disorders of sexual differentiation" but now the words "difference in sexual development" are increasingly being used to fit the same acronym—"disorders" is felt to be stigmatizing, and "differentiation" is too binary.

A few months before the lecture, I received an email from the Component Chair informing me that, "as you may have heard" (I hadn't), there had been "some controversy" about the lecture. One example was given: the term "ambiguous" was disrespectful and the term "atypical" should be used instead. The Chair was asking if I would meet with the two students who had presented the concerns. I was glad to accept—being advised of one's error is priceless education. Call me naïve, but I did not let myself be distracted by the fact that my question about who exactly these two students represented was ignored and remained unanswered.

The meeting was respectful, civilized and constructive. The students agreed to put in writing their views on the matters we discussed, and I also summarized my responses in writing. I disagreed with many of the points the students brought up, but several others did make me improve the delivery of my lecture and even some of its substance. After the lecture, the two students thanked me for my openness to their concerns. This is why I was surprised to receive an email from the administration, thanking me for my many years of teaching and informing me that I was being replaced—the result of "student feedback". The course organizers placed this feedback in the same category as protestations against "obstetrical violence" in another professor's lecture. My offer to meet my replacement for a brief chat was ignored by the administration. I can only hope that the broader academic community and the public will show more interest in the possible reasons for the decision to silence me. My content was not questioned on grounds of relevance or support by the evidence; could it be that it was considered a threat to DIE?

Let me start with the only one of the students' concerns that is of meaningful substance in caring for DSD individuals: surgery on young infants, to make their genitals conform to a specific sex — indeed a legitimate issue in healthcare ethics. It is typically performed on female infants with the most common single cause of DSD, congenital adrenal hyperplasia (CAH). Because of a genetic defect, these patients' adrenal glands cannot produce adequate amounts of corticosteroid hormones, a life-threatening situation. Instead, they produce abnormal steroids which act as androgens (male hormones). The life-saving and non-controversial treatment is to prescribe the missing corticosteroids in pill form. This restores hormonal equilibrium and allows these newborns to grow into healthy adults. The controversy centres around a surgical procedure called *reduction clitoroplasty*.

In females with CAH, exposure to androgens before birth often makes their clitoris large enough to resemble a penis; their labia majora look like the two halves of an (empty) scrotum, giving the external genitals a male look. Inside, everything is normal female, with perfectly fertile ovaries, uterus, fallopian tubes and vaginal cavity. These individuals, in their majority, seem to grow up to be well-adjusted, fertile females (Dessens et al., 2015; Almasri et al., 2018). The surgery involves removing the shaft of the clitoris, while sparing the glans, where the sensation of sexual pleasure resides. Performing this surgery in infants had been, until recently, standard-of-care (definition: the kind of thing that a doctor could be sued over not doing for a patient). But the purpose is largely cosmetic, in order to put the parents' minds at ease about the gender of the baby and, eventually, help her adjust into the gender identity that is by far the most compatible with her functional reproductive capacity.

In recent years, with broadening societal views on gender conformity and a more rigorous examination of patient autonomy and consent, the procedure has raised concerns. Is it ethical, even legal, to perform irreversible cosmetic surgery on an important body part of an infant, whose function will not be needed until consent age? California and some European countries introduced legislation banning it outright. The legislation didn't pass; largely as a result, I suspect, of opposition by the CARES Foundation, the largest and most credible peer-support organization representing girls and women who have had the procedure, and their families. CARES advocates for a pro-choice view, defending the right of parents to choose.

In recent years, I have been counselling such families about the option to postpone any surgery until consent age. I even point out that a large clitoris may be an advantage for a woman. But, perhaps not surprisingly, I've had no takers so far. In my lecture I presented the matter as an ethical dilemma. Here I was offering an intellectual challenge, to engage my audience's young minds in preparation for the many other kinds of ethical challenges they will face in their careers. But, I have to conclude, nothing short of outright condemnation would have been approved by the unknown (to me) Censors. This I could not do, out of respect for the majority opinion of the procedure's survivors.

Having, now, dealt with the only issue of substance, let us take a look at euphemisms, misconceptions and taboos, typical of current trends that are distorting public discourse.

Semantics: I presented "Disorders of Sexual Differentiation" and "Differences in Sexual Development" as interchangeable, indicating my preference for the former. Does the latter really reflect the sensibilities of DSD persons themselves? Has a *representative* sample of them been polled by the Language Police? These conditions interfere with one fundamental human function—reproduction (not to mention heterosexual intercourse, another function highly valued by a clear majority). The individuals affected come to us as consenting adults asking for counselling and for their healthcare needs (hormones and, yes, surgery). In their list of concerns, the students quoted an Ehrenreich text (Nancy, not Barbara), stating that the stigma coming from calling DSD a "disorder" has the same effect as religion-based genital mutilation—a small example of how far outside a sensible, secular-humanist view of the world some self-appointed justice activists are capable of placing themselves.

Does calling asthma a "respiratory disorder" somehow stigmatize people with asthma and prevent society from embracing, including and equitably treating them? Imagine going to your doctor hoping to receive help, only to be informed that asthma is just a "difference in breathing".

Gender as taboo subject: the students asked me not to include any reference to gender in my discussion of DSD. Gender should be considered elsewhere, in a different lecture by a different lecturer—obviously to completely dissociate it from biology. It did not matter to the Censors that gender is the main preoccupation of the parent–newborn trio we have to deal with as paediatric care providers in DSD cases. My mention, for example, of raising a child as a boy or as a girl represented "outdated and stereotyped conceptions of gender and childrearing". Instead, what should be taught is "raising kids to be who they are and accepting them as such". What I find disturbing here is that the two approaches were presented as incompatible and mutually exclusive: the only way to embrace, include and equitably treat those who do not conform to typical gender identities is to obliterate gender from the rest (vast majority) of society.

In my lecture I clearly made the distinction between social gender (how one is viewed and treated by society, including one's own parents) and gender identity (the gender, if any, that one identifies with). I also taught that we make parents aware of the option of not assigning gender at birth (again, no takers so far). More importantly, to keep an open mind and be sensitive to cues from their DSD child. But none of that was enough. Gender had to be completely expunged from the discourse on sex biology. That gender is an important part of most people's personal identity was presented as a problem. To end gender-based social ills, we must abolish the very concept. Really? Try to explain to a trans person, seeking surgery and hormone treatments so that their anatomy can live in peace with their deeply felt gender identity, that this deeply felt identity is too binary, that it is a social construct or, as Judith Butler proposes, performance in a show.

My statement that DSD is a psychological emergency also drew fire. Was I really proposing that DSD is a life-and-death matter, requiring emergency surgery? Glad you asked. The beginning of their second year is a good time for medical students to learn what an emergency is. The term isn't defined by life, death or, for that matter, surgery. It is a situation where immediate response is called for—reassurance, explanations and counselling in the case of DSD. Imagine a paediatrician responding to the questions, anxieties, misconceptions, religious, cultural or other biases and worst-case fears of the parents of a DSD newborn with: "What, that? Haha, just a difference, not urgent, let us discuss it at the six-month checkup visit!"

Finally, I was expected to talk about the effect of hormones on any other part of the body except the brain. Masculinization of the fetal brain by testosterone is an interesting (but widely misunderstood) phenomenon that needs discussion and whose importance goes beyond caring for individuals with DSD. Do hormones have anything to do with cognitive and behavioural differences between genders?

On the question of cognitive abilities, multiple studies have shown that gender differences are small, buried within the general inter-individual variation, and go in either direction, as subcategories within each type of ability are dissected. Such differences clearly don't explain workplace and career disparities. On the other hand, substantial gender differences in self-declared interests and career preferences have been reproducibly found in study after study. These align with the under-representation of females in fields such as math and engineering, and the underrepresentation of males in the humanities, education and health (including, increasingly in recent years, medical school admissions). In a minimalist summary, men statistically tend to be interested in tools, women in people. Preschoolers choose to play with toy trucks vs. dolls, strongly along gender lines. Social conditioning and attitudes, still lingering after millennia of oppression, may explain some part of this. But how can we be so sure that biology is irrelevant?

In my lecture, I presented the case of females with CAH as a fascinating experiment of nature that can help us answer questions of universal importance. Here is an opportunity to study nurture (almost all girls with CAH are raised as females after a diagnosis is made within days of birth) dissected from its coupling to nature (*in utero* exposure to testosterone). Interestingly, 95% of these individuals are comfortable in the female gender (Dessens et al., 2005), indicating that gender identity has flexibility that can escape fetal exposure of the brain to male sex steroids. On the other hand, this exposure does have measurable effects on interests and preferences, as has unquestionably been demonstrated by a growing body of research on CAH girls. The evidence was recently synthesized by one of its pioneers, Penn State's Sheri Berenbaum, in *Beyond Pink and Blue: The Complexity of Early Androgen Effects on Gender Development* (Berenbaum, 2018). Minimalist summary: CAH girls tend to prefer to play with toy trucks rather than dolls, bucking the play-preference gender polarization observed in preschoolers. Evidence is also accumulating that this apparent effect of fetal hormones tracks into adolescence and adulthood. Fascinating science that, I was hoping, would stimulate some thinking on fundamental questions. But I was not permitted to talk about the biology of gender and, when I refused to abide, I was silenced. Could this affair be, I am now thinking, a test case of limiting academic freedom to protect DIE? Let us examine what is involved.

Will a difference in acronym interpretation really affect the prospects of a DSD person being admitted in a competitive studies programme, or being hired and promoted as faculty? Well… it might, actually. In evaluating grades and track records, equity dictates a reasonable allowance for obstacles that had to be overcome. Substituting "difference" for "disorder" will, if anything, compromise access to such consideration — whether the obstacles stem from the biological reality of DSD or from prejudice by a society still in need of much enlightenment. Or was it, perhaps, knowledge of brain masculinization that needed to be suppressed to save DIE? But by the time an individual applies to a university for studies or for a faculty appointment, an already established track record exists, defining the applicant's position along the broad and widely overlapping male and female bell-shaped curves of interest in the specific field. Gender adds nothing useful to the evaluation—no need to suppress scientifically established knowledge. Knowledge that will make us a little wiser when we use equality of representation in any specific academic field, as a proxy measure for equality of opportunity. And, perhaps more importantly, knowledge that ought to motivate us, as a society, to place a more equitable value on endeavours favoured by each gender.

Perhaps I got carried away. Maybe the censorship I was subjected to had nothing to do with being a threat to DIE. Just, perhaps, another case of spineless university administrations finding it easier to bow to pressure from a small but loud minority.

Finally, this is not a personal grievance. I remain a tenured full professor, and my main academic interest is in the genomics of childhood diabetes, not in DSD. I have more important things to do than teach undergrad courses. It is just sad to see that, beyond beliefs and opinions, it is now established facts that are being censored. Sad to see our institutions of higher learning being led to this kind of neo-obscurantism, in the name of enlightened social attitudes.

References

Almasri, J., et al. (2018) *J. Clin. Endocrinol. Metab.* **103**: 4089–4096.

Berenbaum, S. (2018) *Child Dev Perspect.* **12**: 58–64, PMC5935256.

Dessens, A.B., Slijper, F.M., and Drop, S.L. (2005) *Arch Sex Behav.* **34**: 389–97, PMID 16010462.

Tom Todd[1]

Transgender Activism in Academia

ABSTRACT: Kathleen Stock, Jo Phoenix and Debra Soh all share one thing in common: they believe that one's identity as man or woman is indelibly rooted in biology. But the matter at hand here is not about whether, or to which degree, gender is determined by biological sex (the eternal nature vs. nurture debate), but whether such opinions, theories or even facts should give in to transgender activism or, by contrast, whether any academic research worthy of the name in effect presupposes uninhibited inquiry.

TOPICS: feminism and gender mainstreaming; censorship, deplatforming and job harassment.
****

> Like Saturn, the revolution devours its children. (Jacques Mallet du Pan, 1793)[2]

The cannibalistic terror of Saturn quoted above, in reference to the fate of Danton et al. in the French revolution, originates in the Greek myths surrounding the god Cronus. Cronus was the only child who was prepared to execute his mother Gaia's plan to castrate his father Uranus, in revenge for the latter hiding Gaia's youngest children from her. So, too, would Cronus do all he could to avoid suffering the same fate of being overthrown by his children — by eating them!

Today, this time with female protagonists, we see how the children of the revolution (feminism) are being devoured by its perhaps most radical

---

[1]   Conference organizer, independent campaigner, Hamburg, Germany. Email: info@sciencecensored.com

[2]   From the influential essay *Considérations sur la nature de la Révolution de France.*

expression: transgender activism. This chapter highlights the stories of three of them. The first is Kathleen Stock, professor of philosophy at Sussex University (UK) until she resigned in October of 2021; the second is Jo Phoenix, professor of criminology at the Open University (UK), who resigned her position there on 2nd December 2021; and the third is Dr. Debra Soh (Canada), author of *The End of Gender*, who left academia of her own accord after concluding that she would not be able to freely pursue her line of research.

All share the same basic assumption that one's identity as man or woman is indelibly rooted in biology. The key question here is not whether, or to which degree, gender is determined by biological sex (the eternal nature vs. nurture debate), but whether such opinions, theories or even facts should be suppressed or, by contrast, whether any academic research worthy of the name in effect presupposes uninhibited inquiry — within the confines of law.

This time it is not the "old, white men" but the so-called TERFs, "trans-exclusionary radical feminists", who seem to be the main target of those who claim to be the legitimate defenders of transgender rights. This short chapter will attempt to portray the ordeal of these thinkers and the rationale behind the conflict.

Kathleen Stock

It seems that the academic and public dispute over gender identity issues in the UK, as in Canada (see Jordan Peterson), was also exacerbated by legislation, in this case the UK Gender Recognition Act.[3] In 2017, the Minister of Equalities proposed reforming the act which, in the words of former philosophy professor Kathleen Stock (University of Sussex, UK), would "make it easier for people to 'self-identify' as a particular gender, without any prolonged psychological or medicalised intervention".[4] In this 2018 article, Stock remarked that there was considerable public debate on the "juicy issue" of the conflicting interests of transgender women, on the one hand, and non-transgender women on the other. In academia, specifically philosophy departments, there seemed, by contrast, to be practically no discussion at all.[5]

---

[3] Gender Recognition Act 2004 (UK), *Wikipedia*, https://en.wikipedia.org/wiki/Gender_Recognition_Act_2004

[4] Stock, K., 7th May 2018, "Academic Philosophy and the UK Gender Recognition Act", *Medium*, https://medium.com/@kathleenstock/academic-philosophy-and-the-uk-gender-recognition-act-6179b315b9dd

[5] See her full discussion in the book: Stock, K., 2021, *Material Girls: Why Reality Matters for Feminism*, London: Fleet.

Stock is a "gender-critical" feminist and has in recent years argued that a transgender woman (*viz.* a man identifying as a woman) is, in fact, a man. Gender is, according to her, rooted in a person's biological birth sex; she emphasizes "human sexual dimorphism, its systematic social effects, and problems I perceive with trying to replace talk of biological sex with talk of inner 'gender identity'".[6] Many in government and the transgender community insist, however, that self-identification suffices as the criterion to be legally recognized as a woman. Notwithstanding parliamentary efforts to codify this principle in law, the UK government declined in the autumn of 2020 to do so.

The first of two practical reasons Stock outlines as justification for rejecting self-identification is the concern that men self-identifying as women would gain access to all those areas of public life generally reserved for women only (women's changing rooms, prisons, etc.). Secondly, she believes there is reason to be worried that biologically male transgender women have started to dominate the political arena. In this 2018 article, Stock already asserted her view that people should be able to discuss the "gender critical" viewpoint in the academic world "without fear of making themselves unemployable social pariahs (or worse)".

By October 2021 she would find out just how justified this fear was. As she documented in her written evidence to the UK parliament, her views and her assertion of the right to express these views have been met with radical attempts by the transgender activist community to curtail this right. She and other gender-critical thinkers have in recent months and years experienced: repeated cancellations of events, rejection by academic publishers on ideological grounds, requirements by editors to use gender-sensitive language, threats, assaults, harassment (analogue and digital).

Whereas such occurrences are not necessarily widespread and are clearly the machinations of a radical, "totalitarian" (Stock) minority, Stock believes they represent the tip of the iceberg of a repressive climate at universities that has a demonstrably negative impact on academics' teaching and careers. It was not only the extremists (who glued poster and stickers to walls calling for her resignation), but also the colleagues who over the last few years have been keen to denounce her as "transphobic", that finally triggered her resignation.[7]

---

6   Stock, K., 6th September 2021, Written evidence to UK parliament, September 2021, https://publications.parliament.uk/pa/cm5802/cmpublic/HigherEduc ation/memo/HEFSB11.htm

7   Stock, K., 6th November 2021, "It Wasn't Just the Students…", *Mail Online*, https://www.dailymail.co.uk/news/article-10172813/KATHLEEN-STOCK-reveals-really-like-vilified-beliefs.html

The scale and scope of the protest against her became evident in early 2021 when ca. 600 academics from around the world condemned the British government for recommending her to be awarded an OBE by the Queen. Their argument: she is guilty of "transphobic fearmongering". Despite Stock's clear and evident support for transgender people's rights, these adversaries believe she is "serving to restrict trans people's access to life-saving medical treatments, encourage the harassment of gender-non-conforming people, and otherwise reinforce the patriarchal status quo".[8] They couldn't prevent her being awarded the honour, however.

Further testimony collated by the gender-critical academia network (GCAN)[9] provides evidence of:

- weaponization of university disciplinary complaints procedures against academics;
- pressure by senior staff on colleagues and students to avoid allegedly "transphobic" language ("mother") or topics ("menstruation");
- making access to professional development contingent on ideological conformity.[10]

Finally, it seems that the debate is no longer about gender but about free speech and research. Stock's critics are determined to classify her qualified opinions as harmful and thus intolerable; the obvious and thus almost unnoticed weapon is to pathologize her views by declaring them phobic (i.e. mentally disturbed), a strategy frequently espoused in the past by totalitarian regimes.

Jo Phoenix

Jo Phoenix is a professor of criminology, latterly at the Open University in the UK, a post she resigned in December 2021 to take up teaching at Reading University.[11] Her resignation was also the culmination of years of massive attacks from university colleagues and transgender activists.

---

8 January 2021, "Open Letter Concerning Transphobia in Philosophy", https://sites.google.com/view/trans-phil-letter/
9 Home page, *GC Academia Network*, https://www.gcacademianetwork.org/
10 Stock, K., 6th September 2021, Written evidence to UK parliament, September 2021, https://publications.parliament.uk/pa/cm5802/cmpublic/HigherEducation/memo/HEFSB11.htm
11 Phoenix, J., 11th December 2021, "Constructive Dismissal from The Open University", *Substack*, https://jophoenix.substack.com/p/constructive-dismissal-from-the-open

The conflicts began for her in April of 2019 when she decided to speak publicly[12] about the effect that campaigns for transgender rights had had on freedom of speech, and especially academic debate. Like Kathleen Stock, she sees contradictions between "sex-based" and "trans" rights which lead to a questionable incursion on, for example, "single-sex safe spaces" (women's prisons, etc.). To her mind, the underlying logic in the radical campaigning for transgender rights is a reality game in which a dispute about "the definition of womanhood" was unfolding. She believes this dispute has the effect of dividing people whose "experience of oppression... was based on normative assessments of their capacity to perform gender in specific ways" and as such "served no-one well".

The decision to speak publicly on this issue in 2019 was the result of a conference on the abolition of prisons at her university being cancelled. Activists and several speakers at the conference felt that the organizers (Richard Garside and the Crime and Criminal Justice Society) were too "dangerous" for them to be associated with. The danger they perceived was the support that the organizers had expressed for separate provisioning of trans women in women's prisons.

This activism has, in her opinion, an agenda that goes beyond fighting for trans rights. It is a campaign to deny "difference, fact, reality, expertise and knowledge". It is a campaign that requires of society that it accepts transgender people's rights on the sole basis of their "individual sense of themselves". This she objects to because it is tantamount to denying "the effects of the unequal social structures into which we are born"; it is a reality game that is "perhaps one of the most dangerous games I've seen any so-called radical or progressive movement engage in". The reality that she believes is being ignored, and which she asserts is proven by facts to exist, is the structurally imposed burden of poverty, violence and inequality that women in our society predominantly have to suffer.

This chain of thought was the reason she was harassed for the next two and a half years, deplatformed by Essex University and silenced by her own department at the Open University (OU). Having come from a background with little education and made her way to professorship over the years, she had been very pleased to take the OU job, despite close on 20% less pay, as it meant she could contribute to helping people access quality higher education.

---

[12] Phoenix, J., 15th April 2019, "Effects of Trans Rights Campaigns on Freedom of Speech", *Woman's Place UK Youtube*, https://www.youtube.com/watch?v=eY_fHMkwRnI

The campaigning against Phoenix began after the Essex cancellation of a seminar at that university in December of 2020 and exploded into "hyperdrive" when Phoenix helped establish the Gender Critical Network as an interest group at the OU in June 2021[13] (not to be confused with the GCAN). This network is intended to "reflect on the importance of sexed bodies for health and welfare" and "critique the constraining stereotypes of gender". As a result, 380 academics from all across the OU signed an open letter (one of three) accusing her of being "transphobic". The letter is no longer available online, but its effect was harrowing: Phoenix was later diagnosed with acute PTSD. Consequently, she initiated an employment tribunal case against the OU, on the grounds that the OU had failed to protect her from discrimination. Gender critical views had been deemed earlier in the year by a tribunal to be a "protected characteristic". A crowdfunding campaign for the legal expenses has collected over £90,000 as of December 2021.

Phoenix has also been very outspoken in her criticism[14] of the UK LGBTQ+ organization Stonewall. Like Kathleen Stock, who believes that the Stonewall "Diversity Champions" programme has in part "turned universities into trans activist organisations",[15] Phoenix claims Stonewall "has used its position to make imperialistic incursions into Universities in order to promote its understanding that sex is a 'social construct'".

Stonewall and activists at universities are convinced that trans men and women are literally men and women and that to question this self-identification is transphobic. Hence, "Stonewall promotes a stance on gender identity that reduces the struggles of trans and gender diverse people to the right of individuals to identify *as they choose*", demoting sex-based rights of a sex-class (i.e. women).

Debra Soh

Dr. Soh is most certainly not a radical feminist and would probably not call herself a feminist at all. Moreover, she is currently not as much a high-

---

13 Open University UK, "Gender Critical Research Network", https://www.open.ac.uk/health-wellbeing/research-themes/gender-critical-research-network

14 Phoenix, J., 5th October 2021, "Is it Transphobic to Criticise or be Anti-Stonewall?", *Substack*, https://jophoenix.substack.com/p/is-it-transphobic-to-criticise-or

15 Moorhead, J., 22nd May 2021, "Kathleen Stock: Taboo Around Gender Identity Has Chilling Effect on Academics", *The Gaurdian*, https://www.theguardian.com/education/2021/may/22/kathleen-stock-taboo-around-gender-identity-chilling-effect-on-academics

profile target of attack as Stock or Phoenix, if only because she escaped in good time from the academic arena before suffering the stressful vicissitudes of being mobbed by antagonistic colleagues and activists.

While writing her PhD at York University, Toronto, on paraphilia (abnormal sexual preferences) she began to realize that the progressive narrative encouraging "transitioning" from birth sex to self-identified sex was not a good thing for minors.[16]

At the time (2015) she was using brain-imaging techniques to better understand paraphilias; this gave her insight into the biological substrate of sex, gender and sexual preferences—three dimensions she argues in her recent book, *The End of Gender*, should be separately identified.

Her first public statement in the *Pacific Standard* immediately sparked off a wave of media mobbing, in protest to her statement that "research has shown that most gender dysphoric children outgrow their dysphoria, and do so by adolescence." She had already anticipated trouble but thought that, in the long run, when she would have acquired tenure as a professor, she would be able to survive it.

Her colleagues advised her otherwise and so she took the risk of leaving her academic career to work as a science journalist, publishing her acclaimed book *The End of Gender*, creating a podcast and writing for several press publications.[17]

Conclusions

Perhaps the most succinct and equally alarming statement on transgender issues and education is Debra Soh's thought after her first public appearance: "how strongly gender theory has taken hold of the education system. Children are being recruited as pawns to promote a manner of thinking that serves only adults. Parents can no longer trust that their child's school will teach them a curriculum based in facts."[18]

Whereas the feminist view is that biology provides the justification for claiming spaces to protect women from "patriarchal" males and from infringements on sex-based rights for women in a discriminatory system, another approach is to tackle the problem at the root and discourage early

---

[16] Soh, D., 8th May 2018, "Why Transgender Kids Should Wait to Transition", *Pacific Standard*, https://psmag.com/social-justice/why-transgender-kids-should-wait-to-transition

[17] See her home page for links to podcasts and articles, https://www.drdebrasoh.com/

[18] Soh, D., 2020, *The End of Gender*, New York: Threshold Editions, p. 34, Kindle Edition.

sex "transitioning", and instead promote a natural discovery of sex and gender identity in childhood or adolescence, free of ideology.

A transparent and calm debate of the issues at hand seems to have suffered major setbacks thanks to institutional support for activists whose apodictic claims pre-empt any debate, not least through moral supremacism. Without such a debate, the mythologically pre-emptive violence of Saturn might explode into reality and, in turn, engender a backlash nobody will have wanted.

Andrei Yafaev[1]

#metametoo

Harassment Campaigns in Academia and the Way Universities are Dealing with Them

ABSTRACT: Recent years have seen the emergence of what I would like to call the *#metameetoo* movement, which is a practice of eavesdropping and spying on a male academic in social situations (completely unrelated to work and outside of the working environment), interacting with a female colleague and subsequently reporting it to the male's employer as 'sexual harassment' (often distorting or completely misrepresenting the nature of the interaction) — without checking with the female colleague beforehand or even despite her clear and explicit objections to that course of action. This is also usually done in organized groups — several people colluding to write libellous letters about someone chosen arbitrarily as a target. A typical university administration's response is not to take any action but to use threats of reprisals to force the victim to keep quiet about it and not to do anything about it, in particular to stop the victim complaining about the authors of the letters to their administration. This creates genuinely Kafkaesque/Orwellian situations, naturally very negatively impacting on the victim's ability to perform academically and shattering their feeling of safety.

TOPICS: feminism and gender mainstreaming.
****

[1] Professor of pure mathematics, Department of Mathematics, University College London, UK. Email: andreiyaf@googlemail.com

Introduction

The "#metoo movement" emerged a few years ago, and quickly attracted a lot of attention and controversy. It has largely discredited itself with an increasing number of verifiably false or vexatious allegations, human rights issues, revelations about active members, etc. This "movement" was very often characterized by virulent misandry, anti-male bias and discrimination. It also often leads to the practice of organized mob lynching campaigns on the internet (social media, blogs, etc.) against particular people over allegations which often have never been proven or even investigated. Some high-profile academics have suffered as a result.

A lot has been written about the shortcomings of #metoo and we will not be reiterating it here—a quick Google search will provide an interested reader with all the necessary information and material.

In very recent years, a more dangerous incarnation of #metoo has emerged in academia. I would like to call it "#metameetoo" (my terminology), which presents even more ethical and legal challenges than the original and poses a direct and very serious threat to academics' (of either gender) freedoms, reputation, personal life and ultimately their performance at work.

#metametoo is the practice whereby a certain number of people select a victim—a straight white male, that they have often never met—and start a slander/libel campaign against the individual, accusing him of sexual harassment of unnamed women, without these women's consent and often despite the explicit objections of the women in question to this action. The harassment campaign is usually triggered by a vague rumour or a slander that circulates in the community.

Often, the perpetrators do not know, in fact have never met, the alleged "victims" of "sexual harassment", they often do not even know their names. This sometimes leads to absurd/Kafkaesque situations—for example the victim is being accused of "sexual harassment" of someone he is actually having a romantic relationship with.

Furthermore, the perpetrators of these campaigns attempt to get others to join in, in other words to whip up a lynching mob to cause maximal damage to the victim.

#metametoo is a very severe form of harassment, not only of the direct victim but also of the women who are involved against their wishes. The perpetrators go as far as to contact the victim's university administration and HR (human resources) departments, implicitly (or explicitly) calling for sanctions to be imposed on the victim.

In the next section I describe one particular case with which I am quite familiar. For reasons of confidentiality, I will keep everything anonymous. I can, however, confirm that all of the events described are true and are reported accurately. In the third section I will provide a number of comments, in particular about the way university administrations and human resources deal with such matters.

I genuinely hope this essay will serve a purpose—I would like to appeal to victims of this increasingly widespread form of harassment to speak out. I welcome anyone who has experienced anything similar to get in touch with me to discuss it via email: andreiyaf@gmail.com.

One Case/Instance of #metametoo in Action

In this section I describe the facts of one particular and very characteristic instance of #metametoo in action. The victim is M (Man), a faculty member at a UK university.

Two people, who we will refer to as K and R (a female and a male) with no connection to M's workplace, have colluded to spread false and malicious rumours about M, in particular they have been repeatedly contacting M's administration—his head of department (H, a woman and an ardent woke sympathizer) and the HR department, implicitly calling for sanctions against M.

M has had no previous interactions with these people (save for a very brief interaction with K at a conference), which is why M has no idea why they have chosen him as a target.

No names are mentioned in the letters by K and R (actually R has passed on someone else's letters which makes his actions seem even more bizarre), but it seems that M was accused of "sexual harassment" of three women, one of whom M actually had a romantic relationship with; another is simply a friend and a third is someone M has interacted with casually in a bar after a conference (she was a participant in the conference). All these events have taken place in western continental Europe where such interactions are completely culturally and socially acceptable, in fact considered as a norm. All three women are dismayed by the actions of K and R, have explicitly said so and one has even written to K personally, expressing her dismay at her actions. A very senior and important academic, who knows M very well and knows that these allegations are completely false and grotesque, has emailed R expressing his dismay at R's actions. R has admitted that he did know what he was talking about and that his actions are based entirely on rumours/slanders circulating about M.

The university has taken no action on the false accusations made against M. No investigation was carried out. M has presented ample evidence that the complaints were false and malicious which was dismissed as "irrelevant" since there is "no investigation". The "complainants" (K and R) have not been informed that their "complaints" were not upheld and were not going to be investigated, as would have been appropriate. Instead, they have received a message clearly implying that the university approves of their actions.

The head of Department, H, involved L from HR (a professional "woke enforcing officer") who started threatening M with sanctions in case he complained about the behaviour of K and R to their institutions. Her threats caused M more distress. L failed to provide any acceptable explanation as to why M must not complain. As a matter of fact, no explanation can be provided — in the UK it is illegal to stop someone from complaining. In the UK making a complaint is a statutory right and L's behaviour is a blatant violation of this right.

When M discovered that these people continued their slander campaign against him and have been asking others to join in, M wrote to R personally and subsequently (a few months later) made complaints to their line managers at their institutions.

The three women were angry at being exploited in this manner by K and R. One of them is someone M has a romantic relationship with and who was very upset at being used as a means for attacking M. They have explicitly expressed to K and R that they do not wish to be used in their actions against M.

K has expressed her anger at being complained about to H (M's Head of Department) and H instigated disciplinary action against M on completely false grounds. The HR officer L gave false evidence, which is an actual disciplinary offence according to the university's rules.

The "investigators" into "M's conduct" wilfully wrote false statements in their reports and M was falsely issued with a formal warning, i.e. was formally warned not to complain in the future under threat of further reprisals, including potential dismissal. This is an obvious denial of M's rights. The "investigators" themselves have discarded vital evidence such as letters from two of the women exploited by K and R and letters from other witnesses. They have even ignored the actual content of M's complaints against K and R (which they were apparently supposed to "investigate"). This, too, actually constitutes a disciplinary offence.

M made formal complaints about the way the matter had been handled which were simply ignored by the university's administration and HR. Furthermore, all formal procedures and guidelines in the process have been violated. In particular, H has passed on some sensitive information concerning M's private life, which is a severe violation of regulations and has created an extremely unpleasant atmosphere in the workplace for M. H later claimed that it was an "accident", although it is evident that this was done purely out of spite. M has even contacted the

President of the university directly, complaining and requesting formal action (grievance); his request was denied.

One of the worst aspects of the story is that H and L have effectively communicated to K and R that the university supports their actions and that M will be sanctioned (for opposing them). They have thus effectively joined the harassment campaign against M and the university has tacitly approved this action.

Throughout the process, M has been suffering severe distress and anxiety and has considered seeking medical help; his academic perform-ance has also suffered greatly.

Discussion and Comments

The above is an account of abuse of an academic not just by the perpetra-tors of the smear/harassment/character assassination campaign but also, and most shockingly, by his own institution and his direct management. It is fair to state that in this case administration and HR actively supported the harassment campaign against this academic. The motives for the uni-versity's actions described above are entirely political and have absolutely nothing to do with the conduct of the person we have referred to as "M".

It demonstrates how deeply "woke culture" (which includes arbi-trary/unjustified accusations of "sexual harassment") has permeated uni-versities at all levels and how damaging it is to academics. In the case described above M has been very severely affected by the matter.

It should be emphasized that such behaviour—writing and circulating letters accusing a person of "sexual harassment" of people without the consent of the alleged "victims" and in fact despite their explicit objections—does not just constitute harassment of the accused but also of the women involved. It is hardly necessary to explain why arbitrarily accusing people of "sexual harassment" of those they are actually romantically involved with is very problematic. In the above example, M was accused of sexual harassment of a woman with whom he was, in fact, having an affair. Naturally, both the woman in question and M wanted to keep this fact quiet and are very upset about it coming to light. This could cause her serious personal difficulties, in addition to giving her a reputa-tion for frivolous behaviour that some regard as negative and incompati-ble with "being a serious scientist". This stigma, when forced onto female scientists, is another interesting and important topic but is outside the scope of this essay.

It must be made very clear that the behaviour of K and R constitutes libel/slander, it is illegal and in certain western countries (such as Switzerland or Israel) it is a criminal offence. It must be treated as a genuine offence, potentially criminal, and not as a "service to the community", as they claim.

It should be reiterated that the "complainant" R never had any interactions with M, nor did he meet any of the women he seems to be accusing M of "sexually harassing". Amazingly, for years R has been collecting various slanders and rumours that have been circulating about M and eventually passed them on to his administration, without ever verifying the facts. This, in my opinion (this is just an opinion), could constitute the criminal offence of stalking/criminal harassment under UK law. The point is: the behaviour of K and R is genuinely malicious and should be viewed and treated as such.

The most shocking aspect, though, is not the behaviour of K and R (who are clearly motivated by ego, jealousy, politics, frustration, obsession with power and domination etc…), it is the university's response to their letters. It is university policy that staff should be protected from harassment (this is a statute) and it is HR's duty to implement this policy. In this case, it would have involved assisting M to write a complaint to stop K and R from spreading slanders about him. Instead, HR, as represented by L, have themselves effectively joined in the harassment campaign against M.

HR and related bodies actively encourage everyone (in their own words) "to report unacceptable behaviour wherever they see it", thus actively encouraging and endorsing the kind of harassment described in the previous section. The first obvious question here is: who decides what behaviour is "unacceptable". The only reasonable answer would be: the person on the receiving end of the "unacceptable behaviour". It is not for "an active bystander" (in HR's jargon; in common language: a busybody and a bully) to decide which behaviour is unacceptable. Neither is it for an "active bystander" to police and interfere with other people's private lives.

Furthermore, UK universities have a so-called "dignity at work statement" and it is HR's duty to uphold it. It is evident that being slandered, having one's personal/intimate life put on display and then being punished for complaining is a violation of a person's dignity. Yet, in our case, the university did absolutely nothing in the face of this flagrant violation of its own policies.

Another human rights violation affects the right to a fair trial—these disciplinary hearings are really kangaroo courts where the defendant's defence and supporting evidence is completely ignored and discarded. In the "reports" produced by the "investigators" literally every line is a lie or gross distortion/misrepresentation of the existing evidence.

The notion of "work-related events" deserves particular comment as it directly relates to an academic's (in fact human) right to private life. M was accused by K and R of "unacceptable behaviour at work-related events". The "work-related events" in question are hanging out in late night bars in foreign countries. HR claimed that a night out on the town in a foreign country constitutes a "work-related event" (if it happened during a conference, for example). This is a genuine intrusion into people's private lives. A night out in town is not related to the conference at all. Every conference has a programme which describes which events are related to the conference (including even a social programme); anything outside of it cannot possibly be considered as work-related. Indeed, the whole purpose of a night out with some (selected) participants is to forget about work and relax. The rule of thumb is that a work-related event is any event that employees (or participants at a conference) are invited to and expected to attend. A night in a late-night bar certainly does not fit this definition. An obvious question—"if a night out was a work event, why then can one not claim expenses for it from the university?"—is typically met with silence. It seems that universities progressively control all aspect of academics' lives, including private/romantic/sexual.

As has already been mentioned, this kind of activity has an extremely detrimental impact on women. #metametoo is generally characterized by complete and utter disregard for the views, feelings and desires of the women involved. In our case, one of the women involved (with whom M actually has a romantic relationship) was so upset and depressed by the actions of K and R that she actively contemplated leaving academia. No one paid any attention to her views.

Another, who is a friend of M's, was outraged by the fact that it was assumed, without her consent, that she had been "sexually harassed" and she would not able to deal with the "harasser" herself. Generally, these are talented scientists, who are highly intelligent and confident. It is insulting to them (and they take it this way) that someone, who they do not even know, presumes that they cannot deal with their relations to other people themselves. To reiterate the main point—it is not for individuals completely unaware of people's personal circumstances to police their private life, to dictate how to behave, what to be, etc.

The harassment of M described in the previous section is really a political act. An ideology/system of thought labelled WOKE has progressively and insidiously taken hold in academia over the last decade and has now become the dominant doctrine, its tenets widely accepted like articles of faith. Academics are terrified of speaking out against it.

I was born in the USSR. Although I left that country in 1991 as a child (the regime had essentially already collapsed by that time), my family and relatives have spent most of their lives there and I know a lot about the Soviet regime. In the USSR, anyone aspiring to a serious career in administration needed to join the Communist Party of the Soviet Union, actively participate in a few Party meetings, write a few denunciations and so on. Something very similar is happening now at UK universities. One way to build a career in administration (I am not claiming that it is the only way) is to indicate one's adherence to the Woke Party, write a few bogus reports on suspected dissidents and then become an important manager.

In conclusion: no one should be subjected to harassment of the kind I have described. Such incidences have no place in academia (or else-where), they impact on every aspect of an academic's life, including their professional performance and their social life within academia.

So what needs to be done? It seems to me that the first step would be to make it crystal clear that not only are false allegations unacceptable, but those based on various rumours/slanders that circulate (i.e. vexatious allegations) are equally unacceptable; anyone engaged in spreading lies should be punished. It should be made very clear in officially published policies and guidelines that the onus is on the person who makes the allegations to substantiate them; if they fail to do so, appropriate sanctions should be imposed on them. Universities must never disregard complaints about false allegations and must support both the victim and those involved in those complaints against their will (like the three women in our story). Allegations that are not investigated should de facto be classed as false. This is the presumption of innocence which is a human right. The authors of the allegations must be immediately informed that their complaints will not be investigated and are thus considered false.

"Training events" and publicity (posters, emails, etc…) on sexual (and other forms of) harassment must make it extremely clear that harassment is determined by the perception of the targeted person and not by anyone else. There is a need for a very precise definition of what constitutes a work-related event. With regards to conferences, the only reasonable definition seems to include all events in the official conference programme and all those for which one can claim expenses from one's university.

People experiencing the type of harassment described in this essay should come forward and speak out without shame and without fear of public humiliation/bullying or reprisals from their institutions. No victim of such a harassment campaign should be bullied into suffering in silence.

"Woke" ideology and doctrine are fundamentally anti-intellectual, yet it is in the institutions of higher education and advanced studies that it genuinely holds sway in. Its influence is so strong that, as the above case demonstrates, universities are prepared to breach their policies and even the law, risk media exposure, act dishonestly and unethically with the only purpose of avoiding offending the self-proclaimed "woke activists". A prime example of this is the notorious "Tim Hunt affair" in the UK a few years ago that caused a massive scandal, especially after revelations about the "accuser" came to light. This has genuinely tarnished the reputation of UK academia and the stigma still persists. It seems, though, that no lesson has been learnt and this is cause for concern.

Janice Fiamengo[1]

Let's Imitate Hungary and Make a Bonfire of Women's and Gender Studies[2]

ABSTRACT: Women's and Gender Studies programmes produce and promote ideology rather than science or objective knowledge. In particular, they advance theories of oppression and resistance, often employing a range of different kinds of feminist, Marxist, queer, postmodern, post-colonial, eco-critical and other theories. These theories are, however, rarely subjected to empirical testing. As a result, allegedly scientific courses propagate an unproven theory of misogynistic, discriminatory society and thus create an ideological bias in academia whose primary aim is the promotion of feminist and other agendas.

TOPICS: feminism and gender mainstreaming; general considerations on suppression of academic freedom.
****

In August of 2018, the Hungarian government announced plans[3] to withdraw funding from gender studies programmes at state-funded

---

[1] Philologist, Professor Emeritus Univ. Ottawa, Canada. Email: Janice.Fiamengo@uottawa.ca

[2] Reprinted with minor revisions and with kind permission of *The Rebel Priest*, 15th August 2018.

[3] Williams, T.D., 10th August 2018, "Hungary Discontinues Gender Studies Programs: 'Ideology, Not Science'", *Breitbart*, https://www.breitbart.com/

universities "after determining the programs serve no identifiable purpose and are based on 'ideology rather than science'".

The decision will affect only a small number of students, according to the report, because such programmes are not yet popular or widespread in Hungary. In many parts of the English-speaking world, in contrast, tens of thousands of students take courses and earn degrees in Gender Studies, which is sometimes called Women's Studies, or Women's, Gender and Sexuality studies.

Defunding such programmes in more liberal parts of Europe and North America and Canada would trigger off feminist paroxysms of apocalyptic proportions. But if Hungarian officials are correct that they serve no purpose and are based in ideology rather than science, should we not seriously consider abolishing them?

I have argued for years that the answer to this question is an emphatic and unqualified yes. Evidence drawn from the programmes' own web-sites suggests that, far from serving no purpose at all, they exist to create foot soldiers for feminist social change, mainly by transforming the role of women and greatly enlarging the reach of the feminist state.

Take a look, as one random example, at the two professors who head up the University of Warwick's Centre for the Study of Women and Gender.[4] Both emphasize their involvement in feminist activism. Director Nickie Charles researches how women "through involvement in social movements can bring about social change". Deputy Director Maria Pereira "maintains an active involvement in feminist movements". Gender studies programmes make no pretence of pursuing knowledge for the sake of truth.

On the matter of the content of the courses, the Hungarian government is unquestionably correct. Women's and Gender Studies programmes produce and promote ideology rather than science or objective knowl-edge. In particular, they advance theories of oppression and resistance, often employing a range of different kinds of feminist, Marxist, queer, postmodern, post-colonial, eco-critical and other theories.

While theories are often employed in academic research and teaching, their purpose in legitimate disciplines is to be tested. Feminist theories are not tested except through comparison with other feminist or related (leftist) theories. They are almost never tested against non-feminist (or

london/2018/08/10/hungary-discontinues-gender-studies-programs-ideology-not-science/

4   Center for the Study of Women and Gender, University of Warwick, https://warwick.ac.uk/fac/soc/sociology/research/centres/gender/about/

anti-feminist) theories. The fundamental tenets of feminism — that gender is a social construct and that all major world cultures, especially western cultures, are built on a deep-seated misogyny resulting in the subjugation of women — are not up for debate. These tenets are presented as truths to be learned.

That hundreds of thousands of students across the English-speaking world learn dogma as truth is a staggering testament to the triumph of ideology at institutions of higher education.

A good example of the unproven/unprovable ideological biases of gender theory can be found in the reading material for a course offered at the University of British Columbia in Vancouver, Canada, in 2015 called "Gender, Race, Sex, and Power", described as an introduction to "intersectional feminist scholarship and debate". The required reading on the subject of gender was a chapter called "Introduction to Gender" from a textbook *Language and Gender* by Penelope Eckert and Sally McConnell-Ginet.

The authors of this text are typical of most feminist ideologues in adhering to the theory that gender is a social construct, telling us in the opening pages of the chapter that "the very definition of the biological categories male and female… is ultimately social." Given that anything humans do in language is ultimately dependent on society, of course the labels male and female are in that sense social. But Eckert and McConnell-Ginet mean far more than that.

Eckert and McConnell-Ginet mean that gender is something we "perform" (a very popular word in gender discourse), with little or no basis in biology. They assert that "Labelling someone a man or a woman is a social decision", i.e. it has no natural or biological basis that pre-exists language. Everything in the chapter follows from this key plank of feminist thought, which mandates a consistent downplaying or outright denial of natural, biological differences in male–female nature and development.

Eckert and McConnell-Ginet chronicle what they term the scripting of masculine and feminine identities from human infancy to adulthood. In their argument, un-gendered infants are made into boys and girls by conditioning and modelling; their masculinity and femininity are an effect of cultural programming. The implication throughout the discussion is that boys and girls can and should be re-conditioned and re-modelled at will.

The authors also include a section on what they call the manufacturing of heterosexual desire, which is also not natural, they tell us, but "highly structured and learned" through "dominant socially endorsed images". This claim is also a common plank of gender ideology: in particular, the chapter argues that girls and women are taught to desire men not because it is natural but because girls and women are bombarded from a young age by images of heterosexual romance. The implication is that there is something potentially nefarious about this process, and that girls might be better off learning a different way of being.

The authors also discuss the supposed devaluing of the feminine in culture, claiming that male activities are more highly valued than female activities, and that girls are often told that their femaleness will prevent them from pursuing conventionally male professions and activities. As an example, they claim that a girl will conventionally learn that she cannot be an astronaut when she grows up because she is a girl.

Another section of the chapter emphasizes the pervasive inequalities and injustices that work against women in everything from household chores to the order in which men and women tend to be mentioned in sentences. The emphasis of this section is on the multifarious ways in which girls and women are consistently disadvantaged in relation to boys and men in our society. Such assertions are likely, of course, to produce resentment and anger in female readers who accept that the history of humanity is a history of injustice against their sex.

What is especially notable about the chapter is that it gives no indication that such claims about gender are in any way contentious.

Students aren't made aware of the hundreds of studies that have revealed significant biological differences between men and women. They're not even told that there is a debate on the matter, or that trained scientists have reached a consensus about the biological basis of sex that cannot simply be denied. In fact, readers are given the opposite impression, that the social constructionists have the far more sophisticated case.

It is presented as fact that "Gender is the... process of creating a dichotomy [between male and female] by effacing similarity and elaborating on difference, and where there are biological differences, these differences are exaggerated and extended in the service of constructing gender." Here the authors (reluctantly) admit that there may be some biological basis to sex difference but maintain that it is significantly exaggerated by both researchers and popular commentators.

The authors cite some few scientific studies in support of their position, but no student reading the chapter and being introduced to the idea of gender as a social construct would have any idea that a majority of scientists have come in good faith to the opposite view of the physiological and biological basis of sex difference. For a compendious summation of hundreds of studies of sex differences, see Steven Rhoads' "Taking Sex Differences Seriously".[5]

What is perhaps most shocking in the feminist introduction to gender is the strong suggestion by Eckert and McConnell-Ginet that any researcher who focuses on biological differences between men and women is corrupt. Readers are told, for example, that everyone from scientists to journalists to the reading public has an insatiable appetite for sensationalistic gender news: "Any results that might support physiological differences are readily snatched up and combined with any variety of gender stereotypes in some often quite fantastic leaps of logic. And the products of these leaps can in turn feed directly into social, and particularly into educational policy, with arguments that gender equity in such 'left-brain areas' as mathematics and engineering is impossible."

The authors give no examples of these "fantastic leaps of logic", but the statement tells students in no uncertain terms that whenever they encounter a claim about natural differences between male and female, they can reliably shut their minds to it. They can be certain that "gender stereotypes" and "fantastic leaps of logic" are at work in biased, ideologically driven individuals, probably misogynists who want to prevent women from achieving what they're capable of in mathematics and engineering. It is never admitted that the authors of this chapter, who are not scientists — in fact, they are both linguists — might themselves be choosing their examples and studies to support an ideological position for which there is scant evidence and abundant counter-evidence.

On every major facet of gender knowledge, the chapter opts for feminist orthodoxy over unbiased, research-based discussion, distorting students' understanding by telling them not only that social constructionist theories are true but also that scientific facts about sex difference are false.

Students emerge from such programmes misinformed about the world and filled with a revolutionary zeal as baseless as it is dangerous. Gender and Women's Studies are about as academic or scientific as Tooth Fairy Studies or Yogic Flying or Voodoo Studies. Taxpayers should not be forced to fund these Mickey Mouse courses and students should flee from these fake disciplines like the prophet Elijah fled from the wicked queen Jezebel.

---

5   Rhoads, S.E., 2014, "Taking Sex Differences Seriously", http://sexdifferences. net/

Part II.

Race, Ethnicity

Heather Mac Donald[1]

Conformity to a Lie[2]

ABSTRACT: Since the death of George Floyd, colleges and universities have promised increased diversity spending. Adherence to "diversity" and denunciations of white privilege have been a unifying theme in academia for decades, but never has the struggle against an alleged systemic anti-black racism been so vigorous as today — to the point of pre-emptive self-indictment by university deans and staff. Finally, one needs to ask: what if the racism explanation for ongoing disparities is wrong, however? What if racial economic and incarceration gaps cannot close without addressing personal responsibility and family culture?

TOPICS: Race, ethnicity.
****

Academia's monolithic belief in systemic racism will further erode American institutions and the principles of our civilization.

The lethal arrest of George Floyd in Minneapolis in late May triggered widespread riots and a torrent of contempt for America from virtually every institution in the country. Businesses large and small, the education establishment and the press rushed to condemn the country's purportedly endemic racism, implicitly accusing the majority of Americans of destroying "black lives". Banks and law firms pledged that hiring and promotions would now be even more race-conscious than before. Hundreds of millions of dollars poured forth from corporate coffers into

---

[1]   Thomas W. Smith Fellow at the Manhattan Institute (US), Juris Doctor degree from Stanford University Law School (US), political commentator, essayist and attorney, contributing editor of *City journal*, and the author of the bestseller *The Diversity Delusion: How Race and Gender Pandering Corrupt the University and Undermine Our Culture.* Email: tkupfer@manhattan-institute.org

[2]   This article originally appeared in *City Journal*, Summer 2020, https://www.city-journal.org/academia-systemic-racism

activist groups; the corporate benefactors hoped to dismantle America's white supremacy, they announced.

Colleges and universities also promised increased diversity spending, though in amounts dwarfed by those corporate outpourings. Nevertheless, the academic response to Floyd's death and the ensuing violence will have the greatest impact on the nation's future. Academia was the ideological seedbed for that violence and for its elite justifications; it will prove just as critical in the accelerated transformation of the country.

Fealty to "diversity" and denunciations of white privilege have been a unifying theme in academia for decades, of course. What's different this time is the sheer venom of the denunciations. College presidents and deans competed for the most sweeping indictment of the American polity, rooted in the claim that blacks are everywhere and at all times under threat.

"We are again reminded that this country's 400-year history of racism continues to produce clear and present danger to the bodies and lives of Black people in every part of the United States", wrote Ted Ruger, dean of the University of Pennsylvania law school. Amherst College president Carolyn "Biddy" Martin announced that the "virulent anti-black racism in this country has never NOT been obvious, and yet there are those who continue to deny it." Martin was making a plea, she said, "to white people in particular, to acknowledge the reality of anti-black racism, its long history, and its current force; to recognize how embedded it is in our institutional structures, social systems, and cultural norms; and to assume our responsibility for ending it." UCLA chancellor Gene Block declared that "racism permeates every sector of our society, from education to employment, from housing to health care, from board rooms to court rooms." It was not just name-brand colleges that pumped out sweeping accusations. Queens University of Charlotte, North Carolina, for example, demanded that "our society, systems, and institutions" stop "treat[ing] black and brown Americans violently and perpetuat[ing] deep inequality".

Some presidents hastily crafted a redo of their initial George Floyd statements after their first effort was deemed insufficiently damning of America. Middlebury College president Laurie Patton apologized for not focusing enough on the "root cause and specific harm" of the black community's "profound pain" in her initial letter to the college. "I needed to name the specific and systemic violence experienced by Black people", Patton said. "I now understand that members of our community needed to hear that." Patton's second effort took no chances. The Floyd death was the "result of centuries of entrenched racism in a nation built on and maintained by unjust and inequitable systems of power, including the policies and practices of law enforcement", she wrote.

The self-abasement would have been welcome at any Communist show trial. Holy Cross's president admitted that he had neglected, in his first missive, to "recognize that black women, girls, and boys are impacted" by the "same violence" experienced by black men. "I sincerely apologize", Philip Burroughs wrote, "that my message caused members of our community to feel unseen." The risk of insufficiency still lurked, however. Burroughs tried to ensure against further rebuke with a blanket coverage clause. While he was currently "reflecting both on the past racial history of our country and the continued struggles around racism and racial violence," he said nervously, "I do not want to ignore many other diverse communities that have also been ostracized and dehumanized."

Some presidents apologized even before their racial-injustice statements were found wanting. Duke University president Vincent Price announced: "I cannot as a white person begin to fully understand the daily fear and pain and oppression that is endemic to the Black experience." Only a naïf would think that such sops to the mob would suffice to ward off future assaults. College leaders regularly accuse their own organizations of racism; Yale's Peter Salovey has been a particularly enthusiastic practitioner of the genre. The George Floyd moment, however, brought out the competition. Duke's Price insisted that his university must take "transformative action" to eliminate the "systems of racism and inequality that have shaped the lived experiences of too many members of the Duke community". Middlebury's Patton confessed with punctilious exactitude that racism "happens in our residence halls and in our classrooms, at the tables of our dining halls and in our locker rooms, on our sidewalks, within the offices where we work, and in our town". Biddy Martin announced that Amherst already knew that the college had not done enough to ensure black students' "freedom from racist bias, even racist acts, much less to ensure their sense of belonging and equal ownership of the culture and life of the College". The work that lay ahead "begins, as it must," she said, "with truthfulness when faced with the evidence of our shortcomings".

All such institutional self-accusations by college presidents leave out the specifics. Which faculty members do not treat black students fairly? If that unjust treatment is so obvious, why weren't those professors already removed? What is wrong with an admissions process that lets in thousands of student bigots? In other moments, college presidents brag about the quality of their student body and faculty. Are they lying? Shouldn't they have disclosed to black applicants that they will face "racist acts" and "systems of inequality" should they attend?

Of course, the college presidents were not lying the first time around. American campuses today are the most tolerant organizations in human history (at least toward official victim groups). The claim that colleges are hotbeds of discrimination is a fantasy. Every university twists itself into knots to admit, hire and promote as many black students and faculty as it possibly can, in light of the fierce bidding war among colleges for under-represented minorities.

It has been taboo to hint at the reason that the millions of dollars already expended on campus diversity initiatives have yet to engineer exact proportional representation of blacks in the student body and on the faculty: the vast academic skills gap. Now this truth will be even more professionally lethal to anyone who dares mention it. The highest reaches of the university have declared as a matter of self-evident fact that systemic racism is the defining feature of American society, one that explains every inequality. Fighting against that racism has now officially become colleges' reason for being.

Princeton's president, Christopher Eisgruber, has ordered the school's top faculty and administrators to submit plans on how they will "combat systemic racism within and beyond the University". Every aspect of Princeton will be re-examined with a "bias toward action", Eisgruber said. In June 2020, Eisgruber and the Princeton Board of Trustees set a model for such action by removing Woodrow Wilson's name from Princeton's famed public-policy school. The university had declined to make that change in 2016, in a reasoned analysis that balanced Wilson's service to the university and to the country against Wilson's views on racial segregation. None of the reasons to keep Wilson's name had changed; the new development was Eisgruber's desire to signal his "anti-racism".

The dean of the Jacobs School of Engineering at the University of California, San Diego, pronounced himself "absolutely dedicated" to turning the engineering school into an "anti-racist organization". Doing so "crucially includes unconscious bias work we must do within ourselves", he added. How that work will interact with research on nano-particles and viral transmission, say, was unspecified.

The University of Pennsylvania will fund "impactful projects" by "diverse teams" of students and faculty to eradicate or reduce "systemic racism", President Amy Gutmann has told the "Penn Community". Middlebury's Patton asked the school's "non-Black members" to develop "deeper knowledge about racism, inequality, and the way oppression operates within our culture, within our institutions, and within ourselves". Cornell started offering Zoom sessions on "institutional racism". It was the campus's "collective responsibility" to engage in such conversations. Cornell's bureaucrats also suggested that the Cornell "community" should collectively read *How to Be an Antiracist*, by Ibram X. Kendi, who recently proposed a constitutional amendment holding that any racial inequality is, by definition, the result of racism. Kendi would create a Department of Antiracism to enforce that amendment.

The chairman of the earth and planetary sciences department at the University of California at Davis announced an "anti-racist reading group" for faculty and students. The group's purpose was to confront the "structural racism that pervades" the field of geology. Such structural racism in the study of igneous rocks is apparently so obvious that the chair did not bother to elaborate further. Failure to attend the reading group would undoubtedly count against any faculty member during his promotional review, as a sign of insufficient enthusiasm for "diversity".

The American Mathematical Society declared that "equity, diversity and inclusion" are fundamental to its mission. Mathematicians had an "obligation" to "help create fundamental change", according to the AMS. The American Astronomical Society held colour-coded Zoom meetings, one for white astronomers to "discuss direct actions to support Black astronomers", one for black astronomers to "talk, vent, connect, and hold space for each other", and one for "non-Black people of color to discuss direct actions to support Black astronomers".

An editorial in the journal *Nature* argued that the mission of science should be to "amplify marginalized voices", in atonement for science's complicity in "systemic racism". Nothing was mentioned about the research qualifications of those "voices".

The academy's anti-racist agenda requires different pedagogy. Geology instructors should "specifically confront, in the classroom, the history and relationship of racism and colonialism in Earth Science education, application, and research", advised the UC Davis chair. The head of the political science department at the University of California at Berkeley called on his colleagues to reconsider their "curriculum and teaching agendas" in order to make progress toward "greater diversity and inclusion".

The prevalence of systemic racism in the U.S. is far from an established fact, however. Other credible explanations exist for ongoing racial disparities, including family structure, cultural attitudes and individual behaviour. To declare from the highest reaches of the academy that racism is the defining and all-explaining feature of American society is to adopt a political position, not to state a scientific truth. That political position entails a host of unspoken assumptions about the world, themselves open to debate. In aligning itself with one particular political position, the academy is betraying what Max Weber saw as its mission: to stay assiduously neutral and to teach "inconvenient" facts about the world that undercut received assumptions across the political spectrum. Political action was antithetical to scholarship, Weber argued.

Even before the Floyd riots, universities were notoriously hostile to points of view that challenged the already-powerful campus orthodoxies. Students and professors erupted in sometimes violent rage toward outside speakers who brought nonconforming ideas onto campus. Those few courageous faculty members who dared dispute the racism thesis found themselves ostracized. University of Pennsylvania law professor Amy Wax was denounced by her dean, the aforementioned Ted Ruger, and removed from teaching first-year classes, for mentioning the academic skills gap. Other dissidents from the diversity ideology, like Evergreen State College's Bret Weinstein, were driven out of their jobs. Most freethinking students or professors simply kept quiet, terrified lest they become the next pariah.

Anyone who thought that the intellectual conformity on college campuses could not get worse lacked imagination. In the post-Floyd era, any prospective PhD proposing to study the behavioural components of inequality will find it almost impossible to be admitted to a graduate programme, much less to find a job afterward. A few reckless undergraduates may still push back against the received wisdom, but their numbers will shrink, and the social and professional toll from their obstinacy will be higher. Candidates for the federal bench during the Trump administration have already seen their nominations torpedoed because of undergraduate journalism mocking the pieties of multiculturalism. In the future, the costs of such heresies will rise, and the inhibitions on free thought and speech will grow more crushing.

Each diversity initiative, whether in academia or in business, requires pretending that it was not preceded by a long line of identical efforts. Instead, every new diversity campaign starts with penance for the alleged bias that leads schools and corporations to overlook some vast untapped pool of competitively qualified blacks and Hispanics. Now, the pressure to admit and hire on the basis of race will redouble in force, elevating even less skilled candidates to positions of power throughout society. American institutions will pay the price.

What if the racism explanation for ongoing disparities is wrong, however? What if racial economic and incarceration gaps cannot close without addressing personal responsibility and family culture—without a sea change in the attitudes that many inner-city black children bring with them to school regarding studying, paying attention in class and respecting teachers, for example? What if the breakdown of the family is producing children with too little capacity to control their impulses and defer gratification? With the university now explicitly committed to the racism explanation for all self-defeating choices, there will be little chance of changing course and addressing the behaviours that lie behind many racial disparities. The persistence of inequality will then produce a new round of quotas and self-incrimination—as well as more violence and anger. And the graduates of these ideologically monolithic universities will proceed further to dismantle our civilization in conformity to a lie.

Lawrence M. Krauss[1]

Racism is Real

But Science isn't the Problem[2]

ABSTRACT: Mantras about systemic racism are hard to square with the principles and necessary protocols of academic science. And in any case, overhauling university hiring and promotion aren't the way to address the fundamental underlying causes of racism in our society. The APS and other scientific organizations have adopted dramatic anti-racist posturing in sudden response to George Floyd's homicide and the protests that followed. But in so doing, they risk unwittingly demeaning science and scientists, as well as trivializing the broader and more vicious impacts of real racism in our society.

TOPICS: race, ethnicity; censorship, deplatforming and job harassment; feminism and gender mainstreaming.
****

In his 9th June eulogy[3] for George Floyd, Reverend Al Sharpton said, "What happened to Floyd happens every day in this country, in education, in health services, and in every area of American life." The metaphor goes to the suffocation of hopes, dreams and basic rights among many black Americans, in part because of inequities in American society, and in part because of direct experiences with racism.

Several days later, the American Physical Society (APS), which claims to represent 55,000 physicists working in the United States and abroad, quoted Sharpton's statement in announcing its solidarity with the

---

1   Theoretical physicist, US, retired, previously in Arizona State Univ. (US). Email: lawkrauss@gmail.com

2   Reprinted from *Quillette*, 3rd July 2020, https://quillette.com/2020/07/03/racism-is-real-but-science-isnt-the-problem/

3   9th June 2020, "Rev. Al Sharpton Full Eulogy George Floyd Funeral", *Youtube*, https://www.youtube.com/watch?v=nDxG2jTA2Oc

"#strike4blacklives"[4] campaign. The group declared that "physics is not an exception" to the suffocating climate of racism that Sharpton described; and that the APS would be closed for regularly scheduled business on 10th June, so as "to stand in support and solidarity with the Black community and to commit to eradicating systemic racism and discrimination, especially in academia, and science". And the APS wasn't alone. The strike was embraced by many scientific groups, national laboratories and universities. Throughout scientific disciplines, combating systemic racism has become a rallying cry.

It sounds laudable. But as argued below, mantras about systemic racism are hard to square with the principles and necessary protocols of academic science. And in any case, overhauling university hiring and promotion aren't the way to address the fundamental underlying causes of racism in our society. The APS and other scientific organizations have adopted dramatic anti-racist posturing in sudden response to George Floyd's homicide and the protests that followed. But in so doing, they risk unwittingly demeaning science and scientists, as well as trivializing the broader and more vicious impacts of real racism in our society.

Science is furthered by the development of theories that better explain nature, that make correct predictions about the world, and that may help develop new technologies. A scientific theory that can be supported by rigorous empirical observation, theoretical analysis and experimental results — and which withstands scrutiny and critique from peers — will be adopted by the scientific community, independent of such theories' origins. If the system is functioning properly, the people who develop these ideas and experiments rise in prominence. The nature of the scientific process requires it to be colour-blind, gender-blind and religion-blind.

This means that science can unite humanity in a way that's unmatched by any other intellectual endeavour — for it transcends cultures, languages and geography. Physicists in China and the United States may have vastly different political views and experiences. But at a physics conference, they interact as colleagues. The thousands of physicists who work at the Large Hadron Collider near Geneva, where I've worked in the past, hail from perhaps as many as 100 countries, speaking dozens of languages, and embrace vastly different faiths and political persuasions. Yet they've worked together to build the most complex machines ever devised,

---

4 "June 10, 2020 #Strike4BlackLives", *American Physical Society Sites*, https://www.aps.org/programs/minorities/june10.cfm

behemoths whose millions of separate parts function flawlessly on scales down to less than a millionth of an inch.

The claim that science *per se* is not racist is *not* the claim that no scientists are racist; nor that physicists of colour never experience racism inside or outside of academia. My own PhD supervisor, who happened to be black, advised me that if I rented an apartment in the Boston neighbourhood of Bunker Hill (as I considered doing for a short time), he wouldn't feel safe visiting me. But such personal experiences, awful as they are, don't primarily explain the underrepresentation of minorities in academic departments. The more fundamental problem isn't the culture of science, but rather that many people of colour get driven away long before they might experience this culture in the first place.

Between 1993 and 2005, I was chair of a university physics department in Cleveland, Ohio. The dismal situation in many inner-city Cleveland public schools struck me as a disgrace. At one point, when we renovated our building, I got permission to send some of our older elementary physics equipment to a nearby local, primarily black, public high school. In spite of the special nature of the school, which was for gifted students, it didn't even have enough science textbooks to go around.

When I went to talk to students at a local inner-city school where my ex-wife volunteered, the children asked me what a scientist did. They didn't have the slightest idea of what trajectory they could take to become one themselves, or whether it involved education beyond high school. The topic seemed so alien as to be beyond any of their realistic aspirations. Situations such as this remain common in many areas of the United States. And as long as they persist, there is little likelihood that the demographics of PhD scientists will reflect the underlying population.

During the academic strike called for by the APS, it was emphasized that the proportion of black physicists in national laboratories such as the Fermi National Laboratory in Illinois (where one #strike4blacklives organizer works) is much smaller than the percentage of blacks in the population at large. It was implied that systematic racism in the profession was responsible for this, although no explicit data supporting this claim were presented.

In fact, there is a simpler explanation. There are fewer tenured black physicists at universities and laboratories because there are fewer black PhD physicists. There are fewer black PhD physicists because there are fewer black physics graduate students. There are fewer black graduate students because there are fewer black undergraduates who major in physics. This latter fact is a cause for concern. But the root cause lies in inequities that arise far earlier in the education process. These cannot be addressed by affirmative action policies at the upper levels of practising professional scientists.

In the early and middle decades of the twentieth century, explicit forms of anti-Semitism were ingrained in the culture of many American physics departments. None other than legendary theoretical physicist Richard Feynman narrowly avoided rejection by Princeton because his background was Jewish. The head of the Princeton Physics Department, H.D. Smyth, wrote to a colleague who'd recommended Feynman for graduate school: "One question always arises, particularly with men interested in theoretical physics. Is Feynman Jewish? We have no definite rule against Jews, but have to keep their proportion in our department reasonably small because of the difficulty of placing them [professionally]." (His colleague signalled assent, but added that Feynman's "physiognomy and manner, however, show no trace of this characteristic and I do not believe the matter will be any great handicap".)

How was this endemic anti-Semitism overcome? Thanks to the opportunities afforded by high-quality public education, students such as Feynman were able to shine in university. In spite of his background, he was accepted to Princeton's graduate school, and went on to win a Nobel Prize and become one of the greatest physicists of his generation. This paved the way for another generation of Jewish theoretical physicists, including Sheldon Glashow and Steve Weinberg. As these future Nobelists rose to the top of their profession, anti-Semitism in academic hiring and promotion disappeared.

When I attended the Nobel Prize ceremony in 2004, there was only one female Nobelist on stage. The head of the Nobel committee candidly explained that there was a reason for this: Nobel Prizes usually are given for work done decades ago. And, until relatively recently, there were far fewer women working in the science fields. He indicated his hope that decades in the future, as more women thrive in these professions, their representation on stage at Nobel Prize ceremonies would increase. But he also emphasized that quality, not diversity, would remain the chief factor governing the awarding of prizes, and that diversity would follow organically as the participation of women in each field grew.

Such an approach counsels patience. Unfortunately, the rush to respond to George Floyd's murder by wholesale condemnation of existing disciplines instead serves to encourage new forms of campus bureaucracy. The University of California, Berkeley, which already may have more diversity and equity assurance officers (Poliakoff, 2020) than almost any other public university, for instance, responded to recent protests by announcing the creation of yet another senior administrative post: Executive Director of Civil Rights and Whistleblower Compliance.

Accompanying this movement is the imposition of new demands on junior faculty that can impede their ability to do science, and sometimes serve to prevent departments from hiring the most productive young scientists. Many hiring committees and granting agencies demand equity and diversity statements from young scientists seeking faculty positions. Examples have been published of highly productive scientists whose grants have been rejected not on the basis of science, but because their diversity proposals were insufficiently detailed. "Could Albert Einstein get a job today at the University of California–Berkeley?", asked one *Forbes* columnist recently (Poliakoff, 2020). "Or Enrico Fermi, or Robert Oppenheimer, or John von Neumann? With the University of California's (UC) experiments in diversity screening underway, the answer is that their job applications could stall before a faculty hiring committee reviewed their academic qualifications."

Assistant professors of physics cannot solve racial inequality in our society. The professional responsibility of individual scientists, especially young scientists, is to do the best science they can, and to train their students as best they can. It is not to become part of a social movement, however well-intentioned that movement may be.

As unfashionable as classically liberal ideas have become, I believe that good science is what should govern grant-proposal assessment and faculty hiring, with equal treatment for all, and quality alone being the final discriminator. Yes, the scientific community is part of the broader social fabric, and does not constitute a silo unto itself — which is why, in a democratic society, scientific results should be communicated broadly outside of academia. But this principle should not require that all scientists, especially young scientists, take time out from their research to actively engage in outreach programmes designed to further social goals. These programmes can be useful, and deserve to be encouraged among those with an appropriate interest and aptitude. But they are not to be confused with a scientist's core work.

Part of the current problem arises from a misplaced notion that has become prevalent in the public dialogue about racism. It has been most clearly espoused by historian and National Book Award winner Ibram X. Kendi, who has argued that one is either racist, or anti-racist. Simply being "non-racist" is unacceptable. While Kendi may be a compelling writer, this claim presents a false dichotomy. One might wish to require that anti-racist policies be adopted in law, while at the same time adopting a race-neutral posture in professional contexts. Indeed, I believe that such an approach is central to the work of a scientist.

As my own experience shows, steps taken by academic bureaucrats to actively signal a posture of anti-racism often can be facile or counterproductive. I was chairman of a physics department for 12 years and witnessed several examples in this vein. In one case, our department had an opportunity to recruit an exceptional senior black physicist who was the spouse of a faculty candidate being recruited by another department. Yet my appeals to the diversity gurus at the university fell on deaf ears, because the potential recruit was born in Tobago. For purely geographical reasons, he wasn't on the list of suitably underrepresented minorities. In other words, he wasn't the "right kind" of black physicist.

As is now widely reported, the response of academic and scientific administrators to demands to root out systemic racism in academic science have created an academic environment where free speech and open inquiry — the hallmarks of good scholarship — are being threatened. Recently, a distinguished chemist at a Canadian university was publicly censured by his provost for an article he'd published in a distinguished journal, concerning factors impinging on the success of organic synthesis as a field of research and education. His crime (Krämer, 2020) was having an opinion about merit-based science and the impact of affirmative action policies on university hiring and research procedures. He stated that "each candidate should have an equal opportunity to secure a position, regardless of personal identification/categorization. Hiring practices that aim at equality of outcome [are] counterproductive if it results in discrimination against the most meritorious candidates."

In normal times, such a statement might at most provoke vigorous debate. The same goes for his questioning of "the emergence of mandatory 'training workshops' on gender equity, inclusion, diversity, and discrimination". Yet given the current climate, it was not surprising that this professor was instead censured by his university provost; and the editor of the journal in question removed the paper from its website, apologized for having published it, and suspended two of the journal's other editors. The publication of a special issue of a chemistry journal being published in honour of the author's 70th birthday was cancelled and mention of his body of work was eliminated from another journal.

Last week, the senior VP of research at Michigan State University, a physicist named Stephen Hsu,[5] was removed from his position — despite numerous academics from around the country signalling support for him in an open letter — after a *Twitter* campaign falsely smeared him as a "vocal racist and eugenicist". His crimes? First, his research involved

---

[5] Hsu, S., 19th June 2020, "Pessimism of the Intellect, Optimism of the Will", *Information Processing*, https://infoproc.blogspot.com/2020/06/resignation.html

using computational genomics to study issues that included how human genetics might be linked to cognitive ability. Second, as VP for research, he had supported the peer-reviewed research of an MSU psychology professor who'd studied police shootings, and whose data, analysed by accepted methodologies, supported the idea that there is less statistical evidence for racial bias than is often reported.

Learning and scholarship require an environment in which hard questions can and should be asked, and in which informed research and debate lead us to better understandings of the world around us. If our efforts to combat the underlying racism in society end up marginalizing those who raise sensitive issues and prioritize knowledge over hashtags, the entire basis of higher education will be undermined. Whether such a trade-off is worth it is, at the very least, debatable. But it seems that this kind of debate is no longer allowed.

I freely acknowledge that science as a discipline has its roots in a societal history rife with racism, sexism and religious intolerance. But the same is true for the entire intellectual fabric of modern western society. Will we need to destroy the pyramids because they were built by slaves, or remove the statues of Isaac Newton from physics buildings because of his religious intolerance?

This is where the current movement leads. If the label of systemic racism is universally applied across academic disciplines while we tear down everything that is connected through time to the darkest periods of history, then the legacy of the Scientific Revolution itself risks being lost amid the rubble.

References

Krämer, K. (2020) "Angewandte Essay Calling Diversity in Chemistry Harmful Decried as 'Abhorrent' and 'Egregious'", *Chemistry World*, 9th June, https://www.chemistryworld.com/news/angewandte-essay-calling-diversity-in-chemistry-harmful-decried-as-abhorrent-and-egregious/4011926.article

Poliakoff, M. (2020) "How Diversity Screening at the University of California Could Degrade Faculty Quality", *Forbes*, 21st January, https://www.forbes.com/sites/michaelpoliakoff/2020/01/21/how-diversity-screening-at-the-university-of-california-could-degrade-faculty-quality/?sh=5c48cc181598

Étienne Forest[1] and Tomonori Agoh[2]

Science in Japan versus the West
Lessons to be Drawn?

ABSTRACT: We summarize our lunch discussions over the last 15 years concerning Science in the West and in Japan. We do not fear too much for Asia. However, we see only grim prospects for the West. We think that if the West cannot purge itself of the present postmodernist fallacies, Islam might well do so for reasons that will become apparent in our concluding remarks. The truth, no matter how ugly it may be, how taboo it seems or how uncomfortable it is, must be pursued.

TOPICS: race, ethnicity; diversity, inclusion and equity programmes.
****

As long as you address the question honestly and objectively there is nothing that should be off limits. (Gad Saad, *The Parasitic Mind*, 2020)

An Odd Couple

The authors of this essay are scientists working at the High Energy Accelerator Research Organization in Tsukuba, Japan. This laboratory, known as KEK, is a corporation of the Ministry of Education, Culture, Sports and Technology.

---

[1] Physicist, High Energy Accelerator Research Organization Tsukuba, Ibaraki, Japan; The Graduate University for Advanced Studies Hayama, Kanagawa, Japan. Email: eforest_4816968@hotmail.com
[2] Physicist, High Energy Accelerator Research Organization Tsukuba, Ibaraki, Japan; The Graduate University for Advanced Studies Hayama, Kanagawa, Japan. Email: agoh.tomonori@gmail.com

Forest is originally from Quebec, Canada, and Agoh is from Shimane, now an Ibaraki resident, Japan. Forest was initially educated in Quebec's Catholic educational system, then in a French European "Lycée" in Montreal, then in McGill University and finally in the USA for his graduate studies. Finally, Forest spent 10 years professionally in the post-modernist environment of Berkeley until 1995. Agoh pursued all his studies in Japan. His final degree was a PhD from Tokyo University.

We have two things in common: we use English as our working language, and we are theoretical physicists holding PhDs. What follows is a distillation of our informal exchanges over 15 years sharing lunch.

Exploring, very casually, the differences between Japanese and western culture, we came to some conclusions based in part on the successes of Japan in science and, particularly, technology:

- The scientific method is the only epistemological tool to separate science (correct knowledge) from storytelling and, therefore, it must be protected at all costs in the West and in the rest of the world.

- Western science in non-western cultures, including indigenous cultures trapped in a western country, should be approached like a useful foreign language. Students should be enticed by its technological successes. The philosophical motivations found in western textbooks, which are intrinsic to the "People of the Book", should be explained to non-western students. Translations of western science books into the Japanese language often contain text that is not easily understood by Japanese.

- Attempts in the West to "decolonize" science, which imply that modern science is a tool of oppression, should be fought aggressively. They are part of political movements of a racist neo-Marxist West which equates "whiteness" with the original sin. They do reflect one accurate point: western science is a powerful tool for technology and therefore for power. The Japanese of the Meiji era understood this and adapted the scientific method without its western philosophical/religious baggage.

- We recognize, as stated by some science "decolonizers", that the language and the metaphors used in science books might be obscure to non-Westerners. This problem, as in second language learning, is solved outside science itself. As in second language learning, we claim that the philosophical concepts should be addressed but without touching the scientific method itself. When a person learns a second language, he might be confronted with words that have no equivalent in his mother tongue or obscure metaphors. The solution is not to change the target language but to explain the foreign word and, if necessary, to invent a new word in his native language. In fact, words like "canonical" or "translation" are Christian metaphors no longer understood by most young western scientists: this does not prevent them from learning the underlying mathematical concepts.

- Data collection, which is part of science, can involve indigenous people. This is trivially obvious in the social sciences. But this is also true in fields like pharmacology where new drugs are found in the traditional medicine of even primitive tribes. But only the scientific method permits the synthesizing of the chemicals found in plants used by indigenous people. The alternative is a vile exploitation of the flora and fauna of these people. Indigenous Chinese practices, for example, often result in an attack against endangered species in Africa: killing elephants for the alleged medicinal values of their tusks. Seven tons of elephant tusks were seized in 2019 to satisfy the needs of Chinese "indigenous" medicine.

In brief, western philosophical ideas, grounded in Ancient Greek philosophy and modulated by Christianity, motivated the scientists of the Renaissance to develop modern science and the scientific method. From a western point of view, the scientific method permitted humans to understand nature, the alleged work of God. Humans being fallible, the scientific method can only work if it is accompanied by collegiality, humility and therefore scepticism. Surprisingly, it became clear in the centuries following Galileo that western science also contributed to technology. It is the superior technology of the West that convinced Asians to adopt western science—not the edifice of Christianity, not western philosophy and not western values. The scientific method is precious to Asians as well as it is precious to Westerners and it should not be threatened by postmodernist "decolonizers of science" or "feminist glaciologists" who are, in the words of Professor Gad Saad of Concordia University, "intellectual terrorists flying planes of bullshit in our edifice of reason".

Our Laboratory KEK

If a visitor consults the web page of our laboratory, he is immediately confronted by different messages in English and Japanese.

The English web page of our laboratory

It starts with the following quasi-religious exhortation:

> Aiming for the pursuit of truth.

We notice that the English message is western and central to the scientific enterprise. The sentence implies the existence of a single and unique explanation that science intends to find. Science is the holder of a provisional truth, but the ultimate existence of a unique truth, that must be sought by science, is tacitly accepted by scientists, whether Japanese or other nationals. It is accepted as a working principle especially by Asians, not as "gospel truth" but as a practical *modus vivendi*.

KEK's exhortation fits perfectly with the western belief in universal principles. We can even quote ancient non-Christian sources like Emperor Marcus Aurelius in his "Meditations":

> If our intellectual part is common, the reason also, in respect of which we are rational beings, is common: if this is so, common also is the reason which commands us what to do, and what not to do; if this is so, there is a common law also; if this is so, we are fellow citizens; if this is so, we are members of some political community; if this is so, the world is in a manner a state.

> One universe made up all that is; and one God in it all, and one principle of being, and one law, the reason shared by all thinking creatures, and one truth.

Western people tend to believe in one God, one proper religion which ought to be universal (catholic) and ought to be spread and perpetuated (apostolic). Western people did not tolerate parallel beliefs and, indeed, the history of Christianity is ultimately a history of heresies—heresies which cannot be tolerated and must be constantly fought. Tolerant Christians, of the Protestant, Orthodox or Roman Catholic variety, are not happy with the division of the church because it violates their belief in a universal truth and thus a universal (catholic) church. It goes without saying that Muslims have a similar intolerance built into their religious beliefs.

This intolerance is transmitted to western science. It would be unacceptable for different groups or countries to have their own law of gravity or their own value of π. The search for universal principles, including scientific, legal and human rights principles, seems to be motivated by deep western beliefs. Scientists, in the western tradition, tolerate competing theories out of our collective ignorance: we must work until one theory triumphs via the application of the scientific method. Triumphant theories are not easily overthrown: their acceptance is not a matter of taste like the different forms of Japanese Buddhism or the thousands of *Shintô* cults. And, when they are overthrown, the new theory reproduces all that was correct in the old one: Newton's and Einstein's laws of gravity, for example.

In the West, universal principles extend to human rights and natural law. Under "natural law" the rules of right and wrong are inherent in people and are not created by society or courts. These concepts are also found in Ancient Greece, Islam and in our "woke" postmodernist leftists for whom the lack of universal principles is the universal principle by which they attack the foundational principles of the West. For them, being white/European is the original sin. They are also "people of the book", a book made of the myriad insane papers they publish within the bowels of their DIE- infested academic departments.

For Japanese, western motivations are part of a religious belief which belongs to *Shisô,* the domain of values which in Japan are personal and not the business of the State. Therefore, these western beliefs have no place in the laws of Japan, which are practical constructs to ensure harmony in society. For the Japanese, laws are 100% man-made. The central principle for the Japanese is the maintenance of Harmony in Japan. In fact, in Japanese, the Chinese character for harmony (和), "Wa", is synonymous with Japan, so Japanese beef, "wagyu", literally means harmonious beef. For these reasons, Japanese people can be moral relativists: we decide what is harmonious for Japan and you can do what you want in your country. Incidentally, it is interesting that the Japanese use different Chinese characters when they refer to a human law (法律) versus a law of nature (法則). One has a connotation of regulation and the other of a mechanism.

In summary, Asians have accepted western science and the scientific method on practical grounds. But they do not blindly embrace the philosophical ideas that motivate Westerners to extend this universality to the legal and political aspects of their polities.

The Japanese page of our laboratory

By contrast, our laboratory's Japanese page states:

> Keep Accelerating.
> KEKは2021年に創設50周年を迎えます。
> かがやく未来のために研究活動を走りつづけます。
> [Translation: KEK will celebrate its 50th anniversary in 2021.
> Continue to run research activities for a bright future.]

The first slogan is essentially a meaningless slogan in English. Visitors of Japan will discover the propensity of the Japanese to decorate their surroundings with meaningless platitudes from foreign languages, mainly English since WWII. "Keep accelerating" sounds good but means nothing. As Einstein taught us, it would be more proper to say: "pushing to higher energies."

We should look at the Japanese text rather than the foreign platitude. We are told that we must continue our research activities to ensure a *bright future*. This emphasizes a utilitarian view of science. "Wa" also ensures the tolerance of values if values are kept at home. Buddhism and Shintoism can split into innumerable sects. As of December 2016, 181,098 religious groups were registered by the government for tax benefits. Can one imagine the Kingdom of Isabel "la Católica", Elizabeth I or the Sun King Louis XIV with this kind of tolerance of religious diversity? Keep your values at home, and no one will bother you in Japan. Try to impose them, and you could face brutal persecution: no wonder Christians in Japan are at most 2% of the population.

Thus the *Shisô* of the Japanese cannot justify science easily. However, technology, the production of machines which perform useful tasks efficiently, can justify western science. In Asia, technology is the motivating force which is easy to explain to the average public whose values need not be in sync with western values. Properly channelled for harmony, technology can bring a "bright future".

In the West, we do not need technology to justify science or mathematics. Often scientists and mathematicians are offended by laymen who ask: "Why should I care about the Higgs boson?" or "What is the Poincaré conjecture good for?" The answer is that we do science because we want to know the truth, irrespective of practical applications.

Galileo, Kepler and Newton believed in the apocalypse and the second coming of Christ. They believed that the afterlife mattered most and were not motivated by a "bright future". Man was put on Earth to suffer for the original sin, and later, the gates of Heaven would open: "Blessed are you poor, for yours is the kingdom of God" (Luke 6: 20–23). Science allows us to understand God's true motive and thus, perhaps, open the gates of Heaven for the anointed.

So, in these very innocent welcoming pages of our laboratory, we see subtle differences between Japanese, non-western and western ideas of science.

Difficult Concepts for Forest and Agoh

Quotation from A Brief History of Time *by Hawking*

Forest had stumbled on a paper called "The Concepts of Science in Japanese and Western Education" by Ken Kawasaki (*Science & Education*, Vol. 5 No.1, 1996). It contained the following statements and quotations:

> Nature-associated relations come out both through the Christian inter-pretation of "logos" as God and through its Latin translation as "ratio". Without taking account of the nature-associated relations, non-Western people could not understand the very essence of the following quotation from the concluding remarks in A Brief History of Time.
>
>> However, if we do discover a complete theory, it should in time be understandable in broad principle by everyone, not just a few scientists. Then we shall all, philosophers, scientists, and just ordinary people, be able to take part in the discussion of the question of why it is that we and the universe exist. If we find the answer to that, it would be the ultimate triumph of human reason—for then we would know the mind of God. (Hawking 1988, p. 175)
>
> From the viewpoint of the East, where Christian faith is not embraced, Western science is quite unique in its motive force. We can identify Hawking's motive force with Kepler's.
>
>> It had almost been a mystical urge and a religious preoccupation which had impelled a man like Kepler to reduce the universe to mechanical law in order to show that God was consistent and reasonable—that He had not left things at the mercy even of His own caprice. (Butterfield 1985, p. 166)

It was quite natural for Forest to confront Agoh with that paragraph since Agoh had read Hawking's book *in translation*. And, indeed, Agoh con-firmed, as Kawasaki claimed, that he had not understood Hawking's last chapter. For Agoh, as is the case for most Japanese, this last paragraph of Hawking is within the domain of *Shisô*: it is not an objective statement about *shizen* (nature) but a religious statement with apparently no connection with science.

As for Forest, not claiming to fully understand Hawking, he effort-lessly found a possible explanation for Hawking's remark. Indeed, Forest claimed, as Kawazaki implied, that the essence of Hawking's paragraph is clear for a western person educated in the Christian tradition even if that person is agnostic or atheist. Forest described his thoughts as follows:

> First, we have John Chapter 1, verse 1, which in Koine Greek is:
> Ἐν ἀρχῇ ἦν ὁ λόγος, καὶ ὁ λόγος ἦν πρὸς τὸν θεόν, καὶ θεὸς ἦν ὁ λόγος.
> Following Thomas Aquinas and other late Middle Age theologians, this can be interpreted as:
> In the beginning was Logic/Reason, Logic was with God and God was Logic.

Logic is capitalized to emphasize the Greek definite article "ὁ". Thus, God's creation should be understood via mathematics and logic. If there is a Theory of Everything and, if physicists conclude that this theory is unique (all others failed or are mathematically inconsistent), then the universe is understood via a triumph of human reason and therefore we fully understand the mind of God via reason as John the Evangelist told us. The uniqueness of the correct Theory of Everything is implied by the Evangelist's famous sentence. And, the New Testament could claim, like the Koran, to be the final and complete word of God.

It is remarkable that these thoughts went through Forest's mind faster than it takes him to recall his phone number. The point is not that Forest was correct or more intelligent than Agoh but that his western upbringing led him immediately to a possible explanation for Hawking's conclusion while, in the mind of a non-Westerner, such as Agoh, it remained a perplexing unscientific pronouncement larded with religion.

As is pointed out in the quotation from Butterfield, scientists like Kepler were motivated by the pursuit of the truth, the unique universal truth that motivates "People of the Book". By studying nature, they would discover God. They would confirm that nature obeys laws and that God seldom performs miracles, that is to say, suspends his own mathematical and logical laws.

This is also implied in the foreword for the teachers of *Physics (1), Second Year of High School,* a textbook authorized by the Ministry of Education of Iran and by its religious authorities. We found no woke nonsense in that book. The entire book, including its religious motivations, could be used almost as is by moderately devout Christians (ISBN: 9789640527429—free download in Farsi for the benefit of all students!).

Was mathematics discovered or invented?

Once again, Agoh was surprised to learn that a substantial number of contemporary western mathematicians consider that *all* mathematical concepts, akin to Plato's Forms, exist in the universe independently of humans. The physicist Max Tegmark stated that "all structures that exist mathematically exist also physically." We do not know if Tegmark is religious. The illustrious Paul Dirac was a virulent atheist but held similar beliefs. They are consistent with the western tradition.

Here, the issue is Agoh's amazement that such "religious" beliefs can be held by very smart western scientists as if they were a part of science. Sabine Hossenfelder, Youtuber and author of *Lost in Math: How Beauty Leads Physics Astray,* who considers views like those of Tegmark as outside the purview of science, espouses views quite compatible with Asians.

Japanese apologize to aborted foetuses and laboratory rats?

Here Forest was amazed. If the death of a fetus requires an apology, then homicide was committed. But in Japan issues like abortion and the death penalty are judged primarily on practical grounds. Does the homicide of fetuses and criminals improve harmony as a whole? If so, a compromise must be reached.

Most universities in Japan hold ceremonies to apologize to the spirits of the rats, rabbits and other animals killed in experiments. Japanese scientists, like women who sought abortions, feel that they have sinned for the sake of harmony.

In the West, we need to declare fetuses non-human to permit their killing. We need a religious ceremony, where Her Majesty Queen Elizabeth II inherits from God the right to administer justice, to execute criminals. In Islam, execution needs to be mandated by the Koran. We should not be surprised that the death penalty has been abolished almost everywhere in the West except in the United States and in Islamic countries: very religious countries. The late American conservative Supreme Court Judge Antonin Scalia made the claim that religiosity is an important factor in the maintenance of the death penalty among "People of the Book" ("God, Justice and Ours", Antonin Scalia, 2002). Mai Sato, who is an opponent of the death penalty, states in her book *The Death Penalty in Japan* that religion, values, i.e. *Shisô,* hardly play a role in Japan as regards capital punishment. We should not be surprised.

In the West, sharp boundaries are necessary: animals can be killed, humans cannot, therefore fetuses are not human. The Japanese mind, more practical, abhors clear boundaries. It should be pointed out that in cases of extreme stress, such as war, both Westerners and Japanese are capable of horrible crimes. We are not apologists of Japan nor of the West.

ATM machines?

The president of a local bank in Tsukuba once told an American resident of Japan: *"our ATM machines cannot be used after 5PM and on weekends **to improve service**."*

In a 1943 short film, Joseph C. Grew, US Ambassador to Japan, stated: "The Japanese are as different from ourselves as any people on this planet. The real difference is in their minds. You cannot measure Japanese sense of logic by any western yardstick."

This bank story was, for Forest, a complete absurdity. What kind of idiot could say such a thing?

Given what we said about the Japanese, we leave it as an exercise to the western reader to justify the statement of our bank president! Most

Japanese understand this statement immediately even if they disagree on practical grounds.

Forest, who became Japanese and repudiated his Canadian citizenship after Justin Trudeau's Halloween trip to India, finally understood.

Conclusion: What Should We Do?
De-Westernize Science? Decolonize Science?

The answer for Japanese, Chinese and Korean people is simple: do nothing drastic. Indeed, western science is taught well and, in many respects, East Asian students do better than Westerners in science both in Asia and *in western countries* where they are alleged victims of White Supremacy. According to the 2015 OECD PISA report (Results in Focus), seven of the best countries in science education are East Asian. Japan ranks number 2. The same report states, not surprisingly, that there is little correlation between the epistemic beliefs and the scores. Indeed Japan (#2) and Vietnam (#8) scored poorly on epistemology and Canada (#7) scored high. Many western countries with a high degree of atheism do well. The so-called Anglosphere does well in epistemic belief but that is not reflected in greater aptitudes in science learning. The USA is at position #25 despite a high degree of epistemic belief.

The fact that Japan has less than 2% of Christianity proves that Japan is immune to all the postmodernist religious diseases that presently affect the West. We believe that Japan will reject western postmodernism, wokism, radical feminism, critical race theory, etc. because these are religious beliefs and do not in any way improve harmony or technology. For the Japanese, the western "decolonizers", the radical feminists and the postmodernists are also engaged in a western religion, but a western religion that has no practical value. Indeed, it has its own original sin in whiteness, it is highly racist via intersectionality and critical race theory since it uses these concepts to judge the individual through some immutable features of "his group" and makes laws that are truly discriminatory. But the ultimate question for Asians and Japanese, in particular, is: "Can this new western belief help us build a bridge?"

The Japanese believe in cultural relativism. But the Japanese also believe that Japan belongs to them, and that the Japanese have the right to impose harmony within the archipelago. So Japan can easily reject the new western follies without invoking any fundamental principle. A western person who uses garlic in his house to scare vampires does not need to justify himself to his neighbour, provided he does not force this superstition onto them: Japan is the house of the Japanese. Case closed.

By contrast, western societies, in search of universal values, are in the middle of a culture war where postmodernist activists are blaming the

West for all the sins of mankind. These people have infiltrated academia, schools and, via their pupils, companies and the governments. Prime Minister Justin Trudeau of Canada, who declared Canada void of any core culture, is the lunatic poster boy of all the diseases of the West.

Today scientists in Canada must include Diversity, Inclusion and Equity (DIE) in their research. For example, when applying for an NSERC scholarship (Forest was a recipient in 1982), recipients must now provide a DIE statement in their application covering the entire "Research Process".

Trudeau's government has recently given $163,000 to three Concordia University professors to decolonize light, which is the most precise theory ever devised by mankind and, *summa absurdita*, was initially proposed by an indigenous Japanese, a non-western scientist, Shinichiro Tomonaga.

We wonder if Professor Tomonaga, when he studied in Leipzig in 1937, under the illustrious Werner Heisenberg, had to sign documents showing how his research supported the *Aryanization of Germany*? Certainly not! If anything, he was able to study in Germany because even the Nazis realized that a politicization of the scientific method was dangerous to their murderous regime. Science, in the STEM disciplines, was threatened by National Socialism mainly indirectly: it led to the exile of excellent scientists deemed to have non-Aryan blood.

Western science is so successful precisely because we abandoned our own indigenous legends. We substituted faith in our mythology with the scientific method. In fact, the scientific method is, perhaps, more than human rights, natural law, democracy, etc., the only universal "value" that the West successfully exported to the entire planet.

Incidentally, an indigenous legend can be consistent with the objective world. But, on average, science is not helped by one's own superstitions and legends. This applies to the West as it does to anyone else.

Tycho Brahe made precise measurements of the planets. However, the "Tychonic system" placed the Earth at the centre of the universe. The five known planets were rotating around the Sun while the solar system and the stars were rotating around the Earth. Brahe refused to interpret the absence of parallax as a consequence of the remoteness of the stars, even though this had been argued by Aristarchus of Samos in the third century BC. It is precisely our Judeo-Christian myth of Creation that interfered with Brahe's reasoning. Yet Cree Indian myths, as proposed by our Canadian decolonizers, should be part of science education?

Newton tried to compute approximately the orbits of the Sun and several planets. He concluded, due to an error in his mathematical approach, that the solar system must have suffered instabilities since the Passion of our Lord Jesus Christ. Therefore, God, like a celestial watchkeeper, must re-adjust the orbits. Pierre-Simon de Laplace, minister of police of Napoleon, fixed Newton's calculations and removed the need for God. Had Newton put aside his "indigenous" beliefs, he might have fixed his own calculations, given his mathematical genius.

In the case of Brahe, we see how our indigenous knowledge gives us a scientifically unjustified position. In the case of Newton, it leads us to the God-of-the-gap fallacy.

By the 1880s, Michelson and Morley showed that the Earth could not move with respect to the "aether". Yet, in 1890, nobody claimed, as Tycho Brahe might have done, that this shows conclusively that the Earth is at the centre of the universe. Rather, Galilean-Newtonian relativity had to be abandoned as the most likely hypothesis: western scientists had finally learned to give zero credence to their mythological stories. And now, under the leadership of lunatics like Justin Trudeau, we are to bring back fairy tales in science to help indigenous people and women perform better?

What would have happened if Michelson-Morley's results had been available to Mgr. Berlamine, Cardinal Inquisitor at Galileo's trial? The choice would have been between an immobile Earth and a Galilean relativity with a finite speed of causality which we called now special relativity. A finite speed of causality implies that Man, although made in the image of God, is prevented by Sin and by God's Laws of Nature to reach God! We can easily surmise that both Galileo and Newton would have relinquished their views rather than endanger their indigenous beliefs to such an extent. Einstein's special relativity can be derived from simple Galilean assumptions as shown by V. Ignatowski in 1910. In that context, "c", the speed of causality, is an arbitrary constant that Christian indigenous beliefs would have forced any sixteenth-century scientist to set to infinity.

Clearly, a culture which worships the Sun as a God might have favoured the heliocentric model, but then might have put the Sun at the centre of the universe as well. No matter how you look at it, anyone who believes in an objective reality cannot use his or her myths as a reliable component of the epistemology of science. Talking about *"his or her"*, can there be something more arrogant and geocentric than believing that our gender can determine the laws of nature? That we need a feminist glaciology or astronomy? Aliens looking at us from a distant world would be amazed that we believe that the laws that governed the orbit of their planetary system might depend on the shape of the sexual organs of a biped species on the third planet of an ordinary star system.

In 2021, western professors in the humanities have successfully convinced politicians in Canada that we ought to reintroduce mythology in science via indigenous beliefs. Dr. Linda ManyGuns, associate vice-president of indigenization and decolonization at Mount Royal University in Calgary, Canada, stopped using upper case letters since they are a symbol of hierarchy. Yet the theory of light of Tomonaga is one of the most hierarchical theories ever devised: an edifice built on Maxwell's equation, special relativity, Dirac theory and quantum field theory. As Feynman said: a tapestry woven with a single thread. Feynman expressed in poetic terms what the entomologist E.O. Wilson called *consilience*, a concept explained in Gad Saad's *Parasitic Mind* in relation with "Nomological Networks of Cumulative Evidence". The theory of light, quantum electrodynamics, is the most *consilient* theory of science, the epitome of success.

And that needs decolonizing by these racist and ignorant people protected by our misguided politicians?

Emulating Asia is not a solution for the West. The West, unlike the East, cannot easily function without its "universal" epistemic system. The American philosopher Alan Bloom, the Canadian poet David Solway (*Notes from a Derelict Culture*) and the Quebec nationalist sociologist Mathieu Bock-Côté have warned North Americans of the dangers of multiculturalism and cultural relativism. Bock-Côté talks of "multiculturalisme comme religion politique". Bloom states:

> Science's latest attempts to grasp the human situation — cultural relativism, historicism, the fact-value distinction — are the suicide of science. (*Closing of the American Mind*, 1987)

In fact, our "science decolonizers", our "feminist glaciologists" and the rest of the postmodernist cabal are in a fundamental way western. They want to replace one religion with another. Like the Marxists, their views are fundamentally universal and intolerant. Therefore, they are more akin, for the West, to a cancer than a skin infection. The West will have to fight them to the death or, if incapable of doing so, succumb to another universal doctrine such as Islam. Islam, like chemotherapy, could greatly damage the body, but it will kill the disease. After all, science learning in Iran is not full of nonsense such Rochelle Gutierrez's claim that $2 + 2 = 4$ is a patriarchal concept because algebra is oppressive and too white. Shahid Beheshti University in Tehran, where a former student of Forest studied, is a better safe space against the lunacy and racism of our progressive left than the University of Toronto or Concordia University of Professor Gad Saad.

The West cannot survive without its *Shisô* and so an apocalyptic fight to the finish is perhaps necessary. And if not, God willing, a tolerant Islam might be your only "bright future"!

Neither Forest nor Agoh need to understand the original Chinese motivations behind chopsticks to appreciate that they are an ideal way of eating bony fish. The scientific method is the only tool to pick the objective mechanisms in nature out of the intellectual debris left by our indigenous superstitions.

In Asia, we will continue to build bridges, computers and bullet trains with a youth equipped with the scientific method, whether or not its occidental origins and motivations are fully understood.

Part III.

Diversity, Inclusion and Equity Programmes

Patrick Labelle[1]

The Groundless and Destructive Tenets of DIE

ABSTRACT: The focus of this short text is the increasingly pernicious presence of the DIE (Diversity, Inclusion and Equity) agenda in pure sciences, in particular in academia. Questions addressed will include why scientists are very accepting of this ideology, what is done to promote it and why it is taking away resources from students as well as creating, ironically, more injustice and discrimination.

TOPICS: diversity, inclusion and equity programmes; race, ethnicity.
****

The ideology of DIE (Diversity, Inclusion and Equity) has corrupted all sectors of human activity, including the government, the media, the private sector, the military, the arts, science and even medicine. But its grip is the strongest and the most insidious in the education sector, from grade school to grad school.

One of the core principles of the DIE ideology, borrowed from its close cousin, critical race theory, is that people are divided into oppressors and oppressed, mostly defined through immutable characteristics such as race, gender and sexual orientation. The goal of DIE programmes is then to compensate perceived discriminations against the oppressed by providing them with favoured treatment (sometimes through mandatory school admission or employment quotas).

---

[1] Professor of Physics, Champlain Regional College, Sherbrooke, Quebec, Canada. Email: patrick.labelle@gmail.com

The most shocking, at least to me, is the extent to which this ideology has taken root in academia and in particular in pure sciences, where one would expect that critical thinking skills and rationality would lead to a complete rejection of the deeply flawed foundations of DIE.

As a teacher and researcher in theoretical physics and mathematics, the last ten years have opened my eyes to the fact that academics and researchers in sciences (which I will refer to from now on as scientists, for short) can actually be extremely irrational and easily manipulated when it comes to issues outside of their field of specialization. I have seen again and again people with analytical minds and high IQs abandon all critical thinking in discussions about, for example, climate change, COVID vaccination or DIE.

It seems that scientists fall victim to propaganda more easily than the rest of the population. It might have to do with the fact that people with many years of education have been drilled to idealize academics as being of great intelligence, integrity and honesty, with very few exceptions. Because of this, any ideology presented by other academics tends to be accepted with very little pushback. It makes one wonder how mathematicians and physicists would have fared as subjects of Stanley Milgram's famous obedience experiment.

Another factor is the vulnerability of scientists to peer pressure. This is probably due to them operating in fairly small and very selective cliques. Going against the narrative of the mainstream can quickly lead to ostracism and contempt. This does not only lead to discomfort in the workplace, in science this means lost opportunities to collaborate, present talks, produce papers and obtain grants as well as, if one is not a tenured professor, the very real possibility of losing one's job and seeing one's career destroyed. Scientists are generally incredibly intolerant of differing opinions, in contrast to what one might expect.

The lack of judgment, common sense and critical thought shown by scientists is the most glaring when addressing the issue of DIE where, in contrast with climate change or COVID vaccines, one cannot hide behind an appeal to so-called scientific authorities as an argument. Not only do most scientists not see, or pretend not to see, the lack of rationality behind the DIE ideology, they even refuse to question it, which is a deeply unscientific attitude. It is therefore actually justified to talk about the "cult of DIE" in academia, in the sense that it is based on principles that no one is allowed to criticize or challenge, at the risk of being attacked, ostracized and even fired. To question the foundations of the cult of DIE, and its close parent, critical race theory, is to commit heresy in the eyes of the believers. This is of course antithetical to the very core of the scientific pursuit, which is based on constant questioning.

In my own field of particle physics, the example of Dr. Alessandro Strumia of Pisa University is both frightening and eye-opening. In 2018, this researcher gave a presentation at CERN, the largest physics laboratory in the world, to argue that not only is the field of particle physics not sexist against women but that data on the hiring of professors actually show a bias against men. Professor Strumia included a lot of data and technical analysis based on publication records and job offers to support his claim.

The goal here is not to analyse his presentation but to point out the furious backlash from the entire physics community that ensued. A mob of physicists of both genders proceeded to denounce Strumia and call for his ostracism, in a manner that one would expect more from internet trolls than from intelligent and highly educated scientists. To witness the use of *ad hominem* attacks and cancel culture in a community I used to respect and love was very revealing and deeply disturbing to me. Thankfully Prof. Strumia was not fired (a junior faculty member would probably have had his or her career ended), but the mob and the woke direction of CERN managed to get him banned from this prestigious lab. All for showing data that no one refuted and defending an opinion that the DIE cult would not tolerate.

One can't help drawing parallels with Galileo, another physicist with connections to Pisa who was ostracized for daring to challenge another belief system that, at the time, could not be questioned. The DIE cult has truly brought back the witch-hunts of the Middle Ages.

Before presenting some examples of how DIE has infiltrated science education, it seems important to show why it is irrational and faulty. The first fundamental flaw in the DIE ideology is that it dehumanizes people by focusing on immutable traits rather than on character, skills and talent. The second flaw is that it seeks to correct perceived injustices by creating *more* discrimination and injustice. To exhibit these flaws, consider a *cause célèbre* of DIE, the fight against racism. One might expect that people of different colour or ethnicities would exhibit the same range of interests, goals and skills. Therefore, any disparity between the percentages of various colour or ethnicities present in an organization and in the general population is taken as undeniable proof of systemic racism by the champions of DIE.

The problem is of course that racism is far from being the only possible factor that one must consider. For example, consider professional basketball, where black individuals are disproportionately represented relative to the general population. Indeed, the percentage of black players in the NBA is close to 75% while white players account for only about 18%, which is almost the exact inverse of their proportions in the population.

No one ever suggests the idea that this discrepancy must be due to anti-white racism; everyone agrees that a mix of cultural and genetic differences is responsible.

The same phenomenon plays a role in science. For example, Asians excel in pure sciences, better than any other race. The explanation is likely the same as the explanation for the successes of black people in basketball: a combination of culture and genetics. However, it is very politically incorrect to even mention the possibility of variability of IQ between races, while people have no problem considering that blacks may be on average more athletic than whites. Let me emphasize that IQ measures only a narrow type of skill and that, as I have emphasized in this text, it often does not reflect intelligence in the more general sense, which requires common sense and critical thinking.

But DIE supporters seem unable to consider the effects of culture and genetics when it does not support their narrative. They are akin to someone whose only tool is a hammer and who desperately wants to treat every object as a nail. The nail they see everywhere is discrimination and the tool is DIE programmes. And like a hammer used indiscriminately, DIE is not only inappropriate, it is harmful.

Of course, socioeconomic factors play a significant role in life, and it is absolutely necessary to offer extra help and support to students coming from poor backgrounds. But such help should not be tied to immutable traits such as race. In certain areas, programmes aimed at helping disadvantaged kids would certainly favour specific ethnicities more than others, but the goal should always be to help poor children, not children of specific ethnicities.

Although I normally would never share personal details about my family history, I think it might help give some weight to my arguments. My father died when I was four and my mom, who never remarried, had to raise by herself six children with only a small pension from the military (thankfully, being in Canada, most healthcare was free). We could not afford a house or a car, although we were never left hungry. One of my sisters, the sibling I was the closest to, died when I was twelve due a misdiagnosed blood clot. She was seventeen. My only brother committed suicide when I was seventeen, he was twenty-seven. My mom died of cancer when I was in my first year of graduate school, and I lost another sister a few years later from advanced multiple sclerosis.

I am not mentioning all this to attract sympathy. I am well aware that a lot of people have had much more difficult lives than me. My point is that I never thought, even for a second, that my family history should be relevant in any way to my career. It was clear to me that only my academic performance should play a role in my admission to my undergraduate university or in obtaining the scholarships that allowed me to go to graduate school. Quite the opposite: if my personal life had been a factor, it would have lessened my sense of accomplishment.

But because I am white, proponents of DIE would automatically conclude that I have had a more privileged life than any black or aboriginal person (to give some context, the aboriginals are the most oppressed group in Canada, according to the DIE ideology), more privileged than the life of a kid of any black NBA star earning millions every year. Or, to address other traits targeted by DIE, that (as a heterosexual male) my life was more privileged than any homosexual or transgender person. DIE proponents can reach these conclusions because they do not judge people as individuals, but as members of groups with pre-assigned labels of oppressed or oppressors.

This brings us to the most inexcusable aspect of the DIE programmes: how the means that they promote to correct perceived injustices are actually discriminatory and unjust.

As a concrete example, the law school at a university here in Sherbrooke, Quebec, asks incoming students to specify in their application if they are of aboriginal descent. Calling the law school did not provide any satisfactory explanation, only that it is their policy. It would be naïve to not deduce that race is a factor in choosing who is accepted at that school, where the enrolment is very limited. In plain words, the admission process is almost certainly racist, in the truest sense of the word.

DIE supporters consider their actions virtuous because they, supposedly, aim to correct past injustices and discrimination. What should be obvious is that discriminating against a person for wrongs committed by other people is *never* acceptable. However, the DIE ideology does not see people as individuals but as members of groups compartmentalized according to immutable traits. In the process, they support and implement measures which are themselves the epitome of discrimination.

Clearly, if that law school admits an aboriginal applicant whose record is not as strong as another, Caucasian, student, then discrimination is taking place. DIE proponents usually get upset when presented this argument because, they claim, they are not demanding that people of colour be given special privileges, only that they be treated as well as Caucasians. Of course, if this was an honest argument, there would be no need to mention race (or any immutable trait) in school or job applications.

The only way to really fight racism in all sectors of human activity is to unconditionally and purposefully ignore race in the way people are treated. Supporting any discrimination now with the excuse of fighting against past bigotry is simply creating more injustice.

Of course, defenders of DIE are fiercely opposed to these self-evident truths, as it makes their entire ideology collapse. They can't accept the need for equal treatment of all races, genders and sexual orientations. Part of the reason is their distorted notions of justice. But part of the reason is more down-to-earth and selfish: the DIE proponents have created a whole new industry of self-flagellation that is funded by most institutions, in particular colleges and universities.

Let me use another example from the same university, now in the science programme. This time, the allegedly oppressed category of people that is targeted is the LGBTQ community. While it is probably true that in some circles there are still all sorts of discrimination, the people in academia I have known and worked with over thirty-five years in dozens of universities and colleges are the most non-judgmental and accepting individuals one could imagine. But apparently, they believe that they need to be parented by DIE ideologists.

Which explains the creation by the science programme of a full-time position to implement DIE. I have not been able to find out the salary involved, despite the fact that this is a public university funded completely by taxpayers, but it is safe to say that it must be well above $50,000 a year.

What is the purpose of that position? What can that person do to really help students? I actually contacted her to ask questions about DIE. When I asked what actual practices of the science programme are discriminating, she could not point out any. As all DIE advocates, she could only cite propaganda written by other DIE believers irrelevant to that department. Such a position is a waste of money which could be used to actually help students. Should science departments also hire people to fight discrimination against, say, people suffering from schizophrenia?

So why spend so much money on this person? Is it to remind the faculty and the students in the science departments that discrimination is wrong and people of different skin colour or sexual orientation should be treated equally? An email to everyone a few times a year could accomplish this for free.

The only actual reason this position exists is either that science professors blindly buy into the DIE propaganda, or that they are happy to waste taxpayers' money and deprive students of resources out of the self-righteous need to prove their moral virtue. One thing is for sure: DIE supporters are more than happy to get those jobs.

They are not only wasteful and take money away that would actually help students, DIE programmes actually promote Divisiveness, Exclusion and Inequality based on immutable traits. As such, they have no place in our education system and in our society at large.

Janice Fiamengo[1]

Science Goes to DIE at UC-Berkeley and the Rest of the West

ABSTRACT: Applicants for many positions at UC-Berkeley, and else-where, are required to demonstrate their allegiance to social justice, the principle that wealth and opportunities should be redistributed from members of so-called oppressor groups – mainly white men – to members of so-called oppressed groups – mainly women and people of colour. On a page titled *Berkeley Diversity*, the university states that, "at a time when access and inclusion are unequal", the university is committed to "closing opportunity gaps for our most marginalized groups".

TOPICS: diversity, inclusion and equity programmes; feminism and gender mainstreaming; race, ethnicity.
****

In early 2020, an article in *The College Fix*, "UC-Berkeley Threatened with Lawsuit for Mandatory Diversity Statements in Hiring", reported that a lawyer named Daniel Ortner was considering suing the University of California at Berkeley for forcing job applicants to assent to the equivalent of "loyalty oaths".[2] Alas, it seems that he never got any further than considering it.

---

[1] Philologist, Professor Emeritus University of Ottawa, Canada. Email: Janice.Fiamengo@uottawa.ca

[2] Lexi Lonas, 6th January 2020, "UC-Berkeley Threatened with Lawsuit for Mandatory Diversity Statements in Hiring", *The College Fix*, https://www.thecollegefix.com/uc-berkeley-threatened-with-lawsuit-for-mandatory-diversity-statements-in-hiring/

Applicants for most academic positions at UC-Berkeley, and elsewhere, are required to demonstrate their allegiance to social justice, especially to the principle that opportunity and reward should be redistributed from members of so-called oppressor groups — mainly white men — to members of so-called oppressed groups, mainly women and people of colour. On a webpage titled *Berkeley Diversity*, the university states that, "at a time when access and inclusion are unequal", Berkeley is committed to "closing opportunity gaps for our most marginalized groups".[3]

The article about the possible lawsuit is well worth reading not necessarily because it portends the imminent end of diversity statements, but for what it shows about the explicit intention of many university departments to weed out white male applicants from job searches in order to increase racial and gender diversity on faculty. The process has been going on for decades, as scholars such as Nathan Glazer[4] and Martin Loney[5] have documented, and it could be argued that the diversity statement — which allows candidates to clarify precisely how they are "marginalized" — is merely a more subtle instrument in a now well entrenched and richly funded levelling project.[6]

A close look at the instructions about diversity statements shows that, in addition to excluding white men from applicant pools, diversity statements have the added purpose of purging non-left-wing individuals, including women and people of colour, from college campuses.

An advertisement for a professor position in the Astronomy Department[7] at UC-Berkeley provides abundant evidence that many job competitions today are far less focused on academic qualifications than on demonstrated commitment to the principles of diversity, inclusion and equity (DIE).

Although the word excellence does appear in the job ad, it is mentioned in such a way as to be closely linked to ideological conformity. We

3   UC Berkeley, Division of Equity and Inclusion, *Berkeley Diversity*, https://diversity.berkeley.edu/about

4   Nathan Glazer, 1987, *Affirmative Discrimination, Ethnic Inequity and Public Policy*, Cambridge, MA: Harvard University Press.

5   Martin Loney, 1998, *The Pursuit of Division: Race, Gender, and Preferential Hiring in Canada*, Montreal and Kingston: McGill-Queen's University Press.

6   Jesse Stiller, 7th January 2020, "School Gets Nearly $1 Million from NY State University Budget for 'Diversity' Hires", *Campus Reform*, https://www.campusreform.org/?ID=14178

7   "Job #JPF02260: Assistant, Associate or Full Professor — Department of Astronomy — Division of Mathematical and Physical Sciences — UC Berkeley", Open Recruitments University of California Berkeley, https://aprecruit.berkeley.edu/JPF02260

are told that: "Diversity, equity, and inclusion are core values at UC Berkeley and the Department of Astronomy. Our department strives for excellence by fostering a community of faculty, students, and staff who share our commitment to these values."[8]

One might ask how a commitment to diversity etc., whether admirable or not, would have anything to do with excellence in astronomy. No argument is made in support of the statement, and no argument will be made about this article of faith in social justice dogma.

The job ad says nothing about whether there are other core values of UC-Berkeley: nothing about a commitment to scientific objectivity or academic freedom or the unfettered pursuit of knowledge. Instead, it assures readers that the university is "responsive to family needs of faculty" and mentions that "Applications from women and candidates in other underrepresented groups are especially encouraged." It also stresses that the University of California is an "Equal Opportunity/Affirmative Action Employer".

So far, there is nothing here that hasn't been the case for decades. But the advertisement doesn't stop at such formulaic statements, going much further in various hyperlinked pages to make clear how extensively the diversity mandate now governs the academic selection process.

The outline of the position requirements explains that all candidates must submit a "Statement on Experience and Plans Regarding Advancing Diversity, Equity and Inclusion". This statement requires the applicant to demonstrate "your understanding of these topics, your record of activities to date, and your specific plans and goals for advancing equity and inclusion if hired at Berkeley".

In a linked document entitled "Support for Faculty Candidates",[9] prospective job candidates are informed that their diversity statement will be evaluated according to three main criteria: 1. their ability to articulate diversity concepts, including their command of demographic data related to diversity in higher education; 2. their track record as advocates, ideally including "multiple examples of action from undergraduate through current career stage", and 3. their "concrete goals, plans, and priorities" for advancing diversity at UC-Berkeley. Candidates are told that "A typical strong statement is two to three pages in length, and includes specific, detailed examples and descriptions."

---

8   "Statement of Diversity", Department of Astronomy of University of California Berkeley, https://astro.berkeley.edu/about/diversity-and-climate/

9   Berkeley Office for Faculty Equity and Welfare, "Support for Faculty Candidates", https://ofew.berkeley.edu/recruitment/contributions-diversity/support-faculty-candidates

Clearly, this is not about pledging that you are well-intentioned person who supports equal opportunities for all, or even that you're an enthusiastic member of the Democratic Party committed to social justice activism.

This is about showing that you have fully embraced in word and deed the arcane and often extremely subjective, non-scientific and even demonstrably false and bigoted theories of intersectional feminism. Candidates are explicitly told that they will be expected to apply social justice criteria to their teaching, especially in "mentoring and supporting the advancement and professional development of underrepresented students or postdocs". Even candidates' own research subjects should preferably have a social justice angle. Candidates are encouraged to highlight "research focused on underserved communities".

A further linked document from the Berkeley Office for Faculty Equity and Welfare entitled "Support for Faculty Search Committees"[10] provides copious detail about how a hiring committee should rate applicants by making the diversity statement the primary evaluative standard.

This document lectures the old fogies in the department that although they may have been hired at a time when all that mattered was whether or not they knew their academic subject, those days are long gone. "While faculty who were hired years ago may not have been evaluated in this way", the statement notes, Berkeley is now *exclusively interested* in hiring "excellent contributors to advancing equity and inclusion for all".

If you're not sure how a zeal for combating white privilege or promoting indigenous or female ways of knowing can aid in understanding the origins of the universe or the lifespan of a quasar, that's your problem. All members of the search committee, which must include "women and underrepresented minorities", should be "actively committed to advancing equity and inclusion at Berkeley".

The web document advises hiring committees to be unwavering in monitoring ideological compliance amongst applicants. No matter how brilliant a candidate, no matter how extensive their record of achievements, no one should be considered for a job, according to this document, if they are not politically on board: search committee members are advised to "Consider creating a cut-off score" for assessing the diversity statement "below which a candidate would not move forward in the search process... regardless of their scores in other areas". Search

---

[10] Berkeley Office for Faculty Equity and Welfare, "Support for Faculty Search Committees", https://ofew.berkeley.edu/recruitment/contributions-diversity /support-faculty-search-committees

committees are further advised to guard against a "tendency to rationalize an anemic record in advancing equity and inclusion if the candidate's research is stellar". In other words, it is wrong to justify "an anemic [SJW] record" on the grounds that the young candidate has been focusing all of his or her energies on being a brilliant astrophysicist.

Berkeley even provides specific examples of how diversity statements should be scored from 1, least impressive, to 5, most impressive, making clear that a candidate who writes simply that all people should be treated equally will be rejected from the application process as insufficiently informed and engaged. To reach the acceptable 4–5 score, according to this Marxist manual of mind control, a candidate must "demonstrate sophisticated thinking about the underrepresentation of groups in academia and structural barriers to success (e.g., racism, sexism, homophobia, etc.)".

The candidate must also have a robust record of social justice activism, ideally extending back to undergraduate days, and a detailed plan for equity activism if hired. The hiring document mentions that "for example, a new assistant professor may plan to undertake one major activity within the department…, conduct outreach to hire a diverse group of students to work in their lab, seek to mentor several underrepresented students, and co-chair a subcommittee or lead a workshop for a national conference."

One might well wonder how the newly hired faculty member will be able to contribute at all to astronomy research at Berkeley, given how busy that person will be organizing anti-racism workshops and recruiting diverse students for their lab and for collaborative work with other academics. A friend of mine has informed me that two tiers are being created in astronomy departments, one for the regular academics, mostly men, who pursue astronomy research, and the other for social justice warriors who spend their time conducting bias surveys and giving talks about diversity.

It's also hard not to notice that the new hire will be pressured, if not in fact required, to see students and collaborators not primarily as individuals — whether appropriately talented or not — but as faceless members of designated groups, valuable not for their potential as scientists but for adding a much-needed black or brown or female or gender non-conforming face to the lab. Will that obsession improve research excellence at Berkeley? Will it lay the groundwork for future cutting-edge scholarship? It's hard to see how.

One might ask whether there is any evidence for the much-touted connection between excellence and ethnic and gender diversity. As an astrophysicist friend of mine has noted, "China and Japan are doing pretty well in STEM without any diversity. The moon landing was not the product of diversity, and neither were discoveries in electromagnetism, thermodynamics, quantum physics, or general relativity." One study published in *Nature Communications* in June of 2018 did find that a more ethnically diverse set of authors had overall a 10% higher chance of producing a highly-cited paper than a team that was more homogeneous.[11] But it's far from clear that the fact of ethnic diversity was itself the necessary and sufficient condition for the more-cited research; there might well have been other factors, such as that the more ethnically diverse teams had members with larger scientific networks, leading to more citations.

What we do know is that in the absence of any scientifically sound evidence of the benefits of racial and gender diversity, enormous public money and energy are being poured into the social justice vision, not just at Berkeley or in California as a whole, but all across the western world, as universities abandon their commitment to individual ability in favour of political correctness. In 2018, Vanderbilt University's Center for Teaching website affirmed that "Increasingly, institutions of higher education are becoming more intentional and programmatic about their efforts to embrace principles of inclusion, equity, justice, and diversity throughout campus life."[12] And in 2019 the *Chronicle of Higher Education* reiterated that "More Colleges are Asking Scholars for Diversity Statements."[13]

A 2019 article by influential astronomer and professor at the Australian National University, Lisa Kewley, in the journal *Nature Astronomy* is titled "Diversity and Inclusion in Australian Astronomy."[14] Predictably, it celebrates the plethora of diversity initiatives, policies, surveys, reports and action plans, including many female-only astronomy job positions, and calls for much more to be done for women and minorities. Thirty years ago, senior astronomy professors would have been expected to write articles for *Nature* about scientific discoveries. Now

---

[11] Bedoor K. AlShebli, Talal Rahwan and Wei Lee Won, 2018, "The Preeminence of Ethnic Diversity in Scientific Collaboration", *Nature Communications*, 9, https://www.nature.com/articles/s41467-018-07634-8/

[12] Sara L. Beck, 2018, "Developing and Writing a Diversity Statement", Vanderbilt University Center for Teaching, https://cft.vanderbilt.edu/guides-sub-pages/developing-and-writing-a-diversity-statement/

[13] Sarah Brown, 2nd January 2019, "More Colleges are Asking Scholars for Diversity Statements: Here's What You Need to Know", *The Chronicle of Higher Education*, https://www.chronicle.com/article/more-colleges-are-asking-scholars-for-diversity-statements-heres-what-you-need-to-know/?cid2=gen_login_refresh&cid=gen_sign_in

[14] Lisa J. Kewley, 2019, "Diversity and Inclusion in Australian Astronomy", *Nature Astronomy*, 3, https://www.nature.com/articles/s41550-019-0954-1

they devote themselves to social justice, and create conditions to force others to do the same.

How long all of this can continue is far from clear, but the fact is that diversity is not a whim of one whacky California college. It is the wave of the future, lavishly funded, seemingly unstoppable, largely immune to criticism, and determined to sweep away everything in its path, including the research pre-eminence and even research soundness of the scientific institutions of the west. They're popping the corks on the champagne bottles in South Korea, China, Japan and India. Even the lawyers, it seems, can't save us now.

Martín López Corredoira[1]

Reflections on the Statement

"The International Astronomical Union (IAU) Has a Clear Ideology about Inclusion that Has to Be Accepted by All its Members"[2]

ABSTRACT: IAU (the most important association for astronomers worldwide) states that the organization has a clear ideology about inclusion — in particular about the promotion of gender parity in astronomy across the world — that has to be accepted by all astronomers who are members of the organization. What happens if an astronomer is not a feminist? Should an astronomer be a feminist in order to be a member of IAU? These questions have not been replied to by the General Secretary of IAU. This should not be allowed if we aim to follow the basic principle of political neutrality of these institutions — paid for with the taxes of all citizens of all ideologies, a high proportion of them probably not feeling represented by these *diversity, inclusion and equity* committees. From a professional point of view, the claims and demands of social justice warriors are not the province of scientists.

---

[1] PhD in Philosophy, PhD in Physics, staff researcher at Instituto de Astrofísica de Canarias, Tenerife, Canary Islands, Spain. Email: martin@lopez-corredoira. com

[2] Reprinted from *Science 2.0*, 8th August 2020, https://www.science20.com/ martin_lopez_corredoira/reflections_on_the_statement_the_iau_has_a_clear_i deology_about_inclusion_that_has_to_be_accepted_by_all

TOPICS: diversity, inclusion and equity programmes; feminism and gender mainstreaming.
****

There are epochs in which science, academia and all intellectual activities are constrained by an ideological system to create monsters at the beck and call of political or religious agendas within totalitarian regimes that repress the free development of ideas. One of the most remarkable examples in the history of science is the prosecution of heliocentric ideas at the time of Galileo, because they contradicted Catholic Church dogmas. Nonetheless, one does not need to go so far back in time to find this kind of repression, or even worse examples. An example from the twentieth century in the former Soviet Union and other communist countries is the campaign led by Lysenko, and supported by the Stalin himself, against genetics and Darwin's natural selection and in favour of Lamarckism, in which more than 3,000 mainstream biologists were dismissed or imprisoned and numerous opposing scientists were executed. Marxism-Leninism postulated universal and immutable laws of history, only changeable by evolution and revolution, which was at odds with Darwin's concept of random mutations being able to transform sub-sequent generations, perceived as bourgeois pseudoscience with strong liberal contents.

The intrusion of political ideology into scientific development is also evident today in western countries in many aspects. Some topics of discussion may contain political elements but can still be argued on scientific grounds, such as global warming. However, other topics are just impositions of dogma in which any scientist daring to challenge them is directly damned to ostracism, especially those who compare the characteristics of different human groups and challenge the central dogma of democracy that all human beings are equal (and have equal rights, but this is not a scientific topic, whereas the first is).

Among such topics, the imposition of a gender ideology[3] has been particularly aggressively pursued in recent years, both in scientific contexts and in the social organization of working environments in science. Indoctrination talks have become the norm, along with con-gresses on gender and science, in which only arguments in favour of the

---

3   López Corredoira, M., 19th November 2018, "Gender Ideology in Science: The New Dogma and the New Witch Hunt", *Science 2.0*, https://www.science20.com/martin_lopez_corredoira/gender_ideology_in_science_the_new_dogma_and_the_new_witch_hunt-235318

new ideology are accepted, all discrepant views being rejected or censored. For the ideologists of feminism in science, their own point of view is unassailable, and ostracism and witch-hunts[4] are meted out to those who dare to challenge them. Even women — who are supposed to be defended by feminism — suffer ostracism and obstacles to progress in their careers when they do not agree the leftist-feminist ideas. Paradoxically, the lemmas of *inclusion* carry hidden implications of *exclusion*: women and many historical minorities in science are overprotected and given advantages, but only so long as they openly endorse leftist ideology. This is similar to the solidarity of the Catholic Church some centuries ago towards certain weak collectives, who were offered help provided that they converted into Catholicism, otherwise they were treated as scum.

We no longer burn heretics and the Soviet Union is dead; some countries still respect in some degree the laws that allow and protect academic freedom. In my country, Spain, article number 20 of our Constitution is quite explicit about it and is similar in spirit to article 19 of the Universal Declaration of Human Rights of the United Nations. Therefore, I think there is legal basis to support a fight against ideological impositions, at least theoretically; although, in practice, sectarian behaviour in many academic departments, usually biased and externally pressured by political agendas on which funding depends, do not make such opposition easy. As scientists, we are faced with a powerful force that we cannot dominate. The only thing we can do is observe and experiment, and analyse the phenomenon through its reactions. I do this from my position as a staff scientist in an astrophysics research centre.

One of my experiments was as follows: given the chance offered by the Diversity and Inclusion Working Group of IAU (*International Astronomical Union*; the most important association for astronomers worldwide) to send ideas for new subtopics, I sent a proposal with the following rationale:

> I would like to propose the following subtopic within the Diversity and Inclusion Working Group: "**Ideological inclusion**". For this item, I propose to analyze within our astronomical community the cases of discrimination or exclusion for people with some political, religious, philosophical ideas away from the majorities. It is our moral and legal obligation to watch over the neutrality of our institutions against non-scientific ideologies that try to become dogmas. At present, indeed, there are many documented cases of ostracism/bullying in our community related to it. Paradoxically, extreme

---

4   López Corredoira, M., 23rd November 2017, "Feminism in Science: Towards a New Witch Hunt?", *technology.org*, https://www.technology.org/2017/11/23/feminism-in-science-towards-a-new-witch-hunt/

defense of "diversity and inclusion" programs carries implicitly sometimes "exclusion and lack of diversity" and lack of freedom of expression for individuals who do not share the political ideas usually associated to the first lemmas. But we pursue a society where everybody is welcome (within legality, of course), and in which only the merits of a CV and potentialities for research should be taken into account in the distribution of jobs, conferences,… in astronomy. Christian or Muslims or atheists, leftists or rightists, materialists or mentalists, feminists or non-feminists, etc. all of them should have a place in a plural society, and exclusion because of the ideology should be discouraged.

This proposal was rejected, of course. Indeed, I did not expect anything else from the feminists of IAU hiding behind the shield of *inclusion*. They want their ideology to be the only one with no possible discussion of their dogmas. However, the reply surprised me because it contained the recognition of a fact that is not usually recognized explicitly. This was the reply from the Chair of Executive Committee Working Group Astronomy for Equity of IAU:

> We regret to inform you that the Working Group's OC has rejected the proposal. The IAU has a clear ideology about Inclusion that has to be accepted by all its members. In particular, its Strategic Plan 2020–2030,[5] states that *"The IAU strives to be an inclusive organisation within which all astronomers, regardless of nationality, ethnicity, religion, gender, sexuality, or disability, are welcome at all activities. Astronomy as a whole is enriched when there is a diverse body of astronomers, who bring a variety of perspectives, ideas, and approaches to the field. Gender equality is a particular focus of the IAU, since men have largely dominated the field of astronomy… The IAU will continue to promote gender parity in astronomy across the world."* Therefore, the IAU cannot include any ideologies that contradict these principles, and so we cannot approve the creation of an Ideological Inclusion subgroup whose goal is to include all ideologies.

I had not talked about introducing new ideologies into IAU policy, but respecting individuals with different ideologies. Anyway, I find the answer interesting. The statement that "The IAU has a clear ideology about Inclusion that has to be accepted by all its members" attracts my attention. This recognition of an ideology behind the IAU programme was unexpected. Was it a *lapsus*—a Freudian *lapsus*, I would say—in which true intentions are revealed that are supposed to be hidden? Anyway, this statement may be interpreted as:

---

5   "IAU Strategic Plan 2020–2030", International Astronomical Union, https://www.iau.org/static/administration/about/strategic_plan/strategicpl an-2020-2030.pdf

1. IAU is not a neutral organization from a political point of view; because there are different points of view about the topic of inclusion in different political orientations. IAU is not a political organization, so I wonder where the rights to establish an official political ideology stem from. This kind of organization dedicated to research or education "cannot" be attached to any political ideology. It is not their mission. In particular, the mission of IAU is promoting astronomy, not promoting certain political ideologies. So, with this statement, it looks that they are adopting an illegal promotion of ideologies, which is now common practice in academia and scientific research.

2. Even more surprising is that an ideology "has to be accepted by all its members". Do they mean that a member that does not follow this ideology should leave the organization? This would be a case of discrimination of members because of ideological orientations. According to the Rules of Human Rights of United Nations, no individual may be rejected from an organization dedicated to research and education due to ideological orientations, and, of course, this member cannot be "forced" to change his/her ideology.

I have also read the statutes and rules of IAU[6] and point 22 of the rules explicitly states: "The Union strongly supports the policies of the International Council for Science (ISC) as regards the freedom and universality of science. Participants of IAU sponsored activities who feel that they may have been subjected to discrimination are urged, first, to seek clarification of the origin of the incident, which may have been due to misunderstandings or to the cultural differences encountered in an international environment. Should these attempts not prove successful, contact should be made with the General Secretary who will take steps to resolve the issue." Within this context, I would understand that no scientist can be discriminated against on political or ideological grounds (within legal limits, of course). And there is no justification for forcing astronomers to accept a given ideology different from their views, in particular the fashionable one of *feminism*.

What happens if an astronomer is not a feminist? Should an astronomer be a feminist in order to be a member of IAU? This is the question that I transmitted to the General Secretary of IAU — responsible for

---

6   "Statutes & Rules", International Astronomical Union, https://www.iau.org/administration/statutes_rules/

clarification of IAU policy to IAU members (and I am a member of this organization)—together with a request for clarification of the statement "The IAU has a clear ideology about Inclusion that has to be accepted by all its members." Probably, the Working Group Astronomy for Equity of IAU was not very fortunate in this choice sentence, and this should be either emended or better explained. I might have also misunderstood, so I asked the IAU General Secretary (in 2020: Teresa Lago) to tell me whether she agrees with that statement and, if so, to clarify its meaning to me. I wrote an email to the General Secretary of IAU in April 2020; no answer. I wrote again by email one month later; no answer. A third time was tried in July 2020 through a registered/certified electronic fax,[7] so an official communication has arrived to the General Secretary of IAU and, if the message was not read or answered, it cannot be argued that the notification to read the message was not received. Result: again, no answer.

A proverb says "Silence gives consent." In this case, we could interpret the silence of IAU on my questions as consent for interpretation in terms of imposition of dogmas associated with ideas that have nothing to do with either science or nature. To speak clearly and without circumlocutions: the situation is such that liberal-progressive leftists form a majority in academia[8] and particularly in most scientific research areas, and they have decided to convert research centres and universities into media for distribution of political propaganda and proselytism. Many minority rightists also follow the imposed stream under the pressure of giving their acquiescence or being excluded. This should not be allowed if we aim to follow the basic principle of political neutrality of these institutions—paid for with the taxes of all citizens of all ideologies, a high proportion of them probably not feeling represented by these diversity, inclusion and equity committees. From a professional point of view, the claims and demands of social justice warriors are not the province of scientists. If some researchers have a leftist ideology, they should keep it to themselves, and not use their professional status to propagandize it.

Solutions to remove leftist propaganda from putative neutral institutions have been suggested, including the abolishment of offices of

---

7   Registered/certified electronic fax, 6th July 2020. To: Prof. Maria Teresa Lago, IAU-UAI Secretariat, 98-bis Blvd. Arago, F-75014 Paris, France. From: Martín López Corredoira, Instituto de Astrofísica de Canarias, C/.Vía Láctea, s/n, E-38205 La Laguna, Tenerife, Spain. https://corredoira.000webhostapp.com/PDF/BurofaxE_IAUJuly2020.pdf

8   Magness, P.W., 25th September 2018, "The Reason for the Leftist Hegemon on Campus", *American Institute for Economic Research*, https://www.aier.org/article/the-reason-for-the-leftist-hegemon-on-campus/

diversity, inclusion and equity.[9] Proposals to suppress gender studies[10] because of their political bias have also been suggested. As a matter of fact, this solution has been adopted in countries like Hungary.[11] However, in most western European countries and the US, we are far from adopting such measures and it will be a long time before we can get rid of this ideological brainwashing. Maybe another solution would be declaring scientific research institutes and academic departments as ideological associations, such as political parties or religious organizations like the Catholic Church. However, in such a case, taxpayers should honestly be given the option to assign part or none of their taxes for such politico-scientific enterprises, such as is done with Catholic Church in Spain,[12] which receives state funds proportional to the number of individuals that tick the appropriate box of the taxes form.

The point here is not whether certain points of feminism are worth being considered or not, but whether scientific research centres are the right places to discuss them. Many political ideas and proposals may be worthwhile, but it is not the mission of scientists to discuss ideologies, but to observe nature and interpret those observations with models built with an objective methodology. Some scientists think we must join the social revolution, following the trends in other areas of the society, but they are usually awkward in their argumentation, becoming charlatan politicians rather than well-trained scientific minds.

Let us discuss another sentence given by the committee of IAU. They say in their Strategic Plan 2020–2030: "Gender equality is a particular focus of the IAU, since men have largely dominated the field of astronomy... The IAU will continue to promote gender parity in astronomy across the world." This is comparable to the statement: fishes

---

[9] Perry, M.J., 17th February 2020, "Higher Education Has Been Hijacked by Leftist, Ideological Interests: Portland State University Professor Spells Out Five Ways to Fix it", *American Enterprise Institute*, https://www.aei.org/carpe-diem/higher-education-has-been-hijacked-by-political-interests-portland-state-university-professor-spells-out-five-ways-to-fix-it/

[10] See the chapter "Let's Imitate Hungary and Make a Bonfire of Women's and Gender Studies" by Janice Fiamengo in this book.

[11] Williams, T.D., 20th August 2018, "Hungary Discontinues Gender Studies Programs: 'Ideology, Not Science'", *Breitbart News*, https://www.breitbart.com/europe/2018/08/10/hungary-discontinues-gender-studies-programs-ideology-not-science/

[12] Bedoya, J.G., 21st February 2020, "Catholic Church Gets a Record €284m of Donations from Spanish Taxpayers", *El País*, https://english.elpais.com/society/2020-02-21/catholic-church-gets-a-record-284m-of-donations-from-spanish-taxpayers.html

have largely dominated the seas, while mammals have been a minority; therefore, we have to promote equality and parity by killing the excess of fishes and throwing more mammals into the sea, even if they cannot swim. Certainly, this comparison with marine life is an exaggeration, since women on average can adapt their lives to any job much better than mammals to water, but the point to make here is not the adaptation, but the ridiculousness of the conclusion that in cases where we find under-representation of a group in proportion to their population we must force parity: the equality of fishes and mammals to adapt to ocean life, or the equality of men and women in their preference to choose a STEM job. No doubt there is much to discuss about the topic, but it is not a principle. Nowhere in nature is it written that men and women have statistically the same interests in life and should be ~50% represented in any job; for instance, nurses are usually >90% women, and only fanatics of gender ideology would defend that 50% of them should be men.

Of course, we may agree that equality of rights is a good principle, as it is already established in the laws of all civilized countries, but claiming that 50% of astronomers should be women is fruit of ideological fanaticism and is neither a legal duty nor amenable to scientific analysis. It is ideology in its purest state, an ideology that is producing damage to the career prospects of many scientists: many good male scientists do not get positions in some centres, or get to give talks at conferences, under the excuse of increasing the ratio of women; and many excellent female scientists are having their careers devalued because of the assumption that they got positions, not through merit, but because of a scheme to reach parity quotas of women in the system. As a matter of fact, statistical analyses[13] show that in the 1950s women and men in science got the same productivity and impact in their works with much lower ratios of women than today, but in the 2000s both average productivity and impact of women in research are around 35% lower than for male researchers, owing to the difference in length of career and other factors. It seems that in the past the selection of researchers was done in a better way than it is nowadays.

Is gender parity more important than professional merit? That is the question. Certainly, we should support any defence of equality of conditions in the selection of researchers, independently of gender, race, *ideologies*, etc. — only merit and potential capabilities should count, and we

---

13 Huang, J., Gates, A.J., Sinatra, R. & Barabasi, A.L., 2019, "Historical Comparison of Gender Inequality in Scientific Careers Across Countries and Disciplines", *arXiv*, 1907.04103, https://arxiv.org/abs/1907.04103

should reject any kind of discrimination (also the discrimination against men implicit in gender quotas). Promoting gender parity is immoral and moreover illegal in terms of discrimination, and it is worrying that official institutions within science are adopting it as part of their priorities in their agendas.

One wonders what the next crazy idea of extreme leftists within science in the name of equality of all human beings will be. Should we exclude Jewish people because they are overrepresented in science and Nobel Prizes in proportion to their population? Should we expel most Europeans and US citizens from science because they are only 10% of the world population and are overrepresented in science? Should we offer 20% of all scientific positions worldwide to black African researchers because they are underrepresented?

Or should we fight for a science free of ideologies and political agendas, a science where only the importance of scientific discoveries counts and not political correctness? I think this is much more reasonable, much more representative of the scientific spirit.

Philip Carl Salzman[1]

The Death of Merit and the Race to Mediocrity in Our Increasingly Marxist Universities[2]

ABSTRACT: From the 1960s, teachers and educational institutions increasingly adopted Marxism and feminism ideologies that redefine western liberal democracies as systemic oppression by an elite class of white people and males who victimize suffering females and people of colour. These ideologies switched the liberal concept of individual equality before the law and equality of opportunity into the socialist concept of equality of outcome or result, and equality of collective census categories of sex, race, sexuality and ethnicity. In order to achieve equal demographic "representation", ideas of achievement, merit, excellence and potential were scrapped, and "diversity, inclusion and equity" implemented by giving special preferences and benefits to the statistically underrepresented.

TOPICS: diversity, inclusion and equity programmes; race, ethnicity; feminism and gender mainstreaming.
****

---

1   Professor Emeritus of Anthropology, McGill University, Canada. Email: philip.carl.salzman@mcgill.ca
2   Reprinted from *PJ Media*, 28th May 2019, https://pjmedia.com/columns/philip-carl-salzman/2019/05/28/the-death-of-merit-and-the-race-to-mediocrity-in-our-increasingly-marxist-universities-n120276

The television series *The Enemy Within* begins by informing the viewer that there are 100,000 foreign spies in the United States working to undermine and destabilize America. China has sent hundreds of thousands of students to America to gain maximum access (Hansson, 2019) to the West's advanced knowledge and technology, some through education alone, some through espionage.

While the foreign threat is real and serious, it pales beside the internal threat represented by the North American education complex. There are 756,900 teachers and professors in Canada, and 5.2 million in the U.S. Almost all of these professors and teachers are daily resolutely and relentlessly attacking western culture, rejecting American culture, and advocating cultural Marxism.

How did this come about? During the 1960s and 1970s, two converging social movements transformed the culture of education (Salzman, 2018d). One was the adoption of Marxism by a wide range of North American university professors in the social sciences and humanities. The other was the widespread adoption of feminist theory. Together, Marxism and feminism redefined North American society as a hierarchy of oppression, with white, patriarchal capitalists at the top, and poor lesbians of colour at the bottom. All citizens were redefined as members of racial, economic, gender, sexual and ethnic classes, with people of white oppressing people of colour, males oppressing females, rich oppressing poor, heterosexuals oppressing LGBTQ++, Christians and Jews oppressing Muslims and so on. This approach is called "social justice" theory.

Following the Marxist prescription of class conflict, feminists attack males as "toxic" (Salzman, 2019a), and people of colour and their "woke" allies attack whites (Salzman, 2019e) as having unearned "privilege" and being oppressors. But that is only the beginning. "Social justice" theory attacks the most basic concepts of American culture and western civilization.

The liberal principle of equality of opportunity is replaced by equality of result or outcome (Salzman, 2017). This means that, instead of the allocation of opportunities and benefits on the basis of merit derived from demonstrated achievement, opportunities and benefits must be allocated evenly across the categories in each field: gender, race, sexuality, ethnicity, by means of statistical representation in every organization and position according to statistical representation in the general population. This means in practice, according to the "equity, diversity, and inclusion" slogan, there must always in the U.S. be 50% or more females, 13% African Americans, 16% Hispanics, and at least some LGBTQ++, some

Muslims, some other people of colour, some poor and homeless, some uneducated and some mentally ill.

According to "social justice" theory, ideas such as "merit" and "achievement" are male, white supremacist ideas, used to ensure the unfair dominance of white men. "Social justice" requires equal category representation. For example, the prime minister of Canada, Justin Trudeau, who is a great advocate of "social justice", appointed females to make up 50% of his cabinet (Ditchburn, 2015). His justification? "Because it is 2015." But females made up only 27% of the Liberal caucus, which means that 50% of cabinet members were selected from 27% of the caucus, while only 50% of the cabinet were selected from 73% of the caucus. If we assume that capability and potential are distributed equally among males and females, how likely is it that the strongest candidates in achievement, merit and potential were selected? For Trudeau, gender trumped achievement and merit, "because it [was] 2015". But, as is par for the course, even this has not satisfied feminists, who demand (Anderssen, 2015) the most powerful ministries for females.

"Social justice" allocation of opportunities and benefits is well represented in the U.S. and Canada by programmes of so-called "affirmative action", in which people are selected, not because of their merit or potential, but because of their ethnicity, gender, sexuality and/or race. In other words, underperforming, weak students are admitted to universities, and funded, because their sexuality, or race, or gender, is statistically "underrepresented" in relation to their presence in the general population. Although this practice was outlawed by a binding referendum in the state of California, the University of California has found "workarounds" (Kidder and Gándara, 2015) to advance racial "diversity".

And, although the Supreme Court of the United States has imposed serious restrictions on racial preferences, Ivy League universities have proceeded with them cavalierly, for which they have been investigated by the Department of Justice, and currently face court challenges (Krislov, 2018).

McGill University, in its "Open Call" (McGill, 2019) for Canada Research Chair applications, claims that "Chairholders are nationally recognized as exceptional researchers and innovators in their discipline." But, "for the purpose of a nomination for a Canada Research Chair in the October 2019 round, preference will be given to qualified applicants who self-identify as a person with a disability or as an Indigenous person." In actual choices, for McGill, disability and ethnicity count more than achievement, merit and potential. And note that you do not actually have to be disabled or Indigenous, but merely to "self-identify" as disabled or Indigenous. Even in our top universities, identity is regarded as more important than facts. I suppose that, in this competition, U.S. Senator Elizabeth Warren, a.k.a. Fauxcahontas, would be given preference as "Indigenous", as she has in previous employments.

A side note, "social justice" is a disease of the educational sector, not the population at large. In the U.S. the public does not like or support "affirmative action" and gender and racial quotas. According to a 2016 Gallup poll (Jaschik, 2016), 63% of Americans say race or ethnicity should not be considered in university admissions, and 66% say gender should not be considered. Among African Americans, 57% say race and ethnicity should not be considered, and a plurality of Hispanics, 47%, say the same. In a follow-up 2019 Gallup poll (Jaschik, 2019), 73% of Americans say that race should not be considered in university admissions. 62% of African Americans say that race should not be considered, and 62% of Hispanics say the same. 81% say that gender should not be a factor.

It appears that Americans increasingly oppose "social justice" racial and gender preferences. Note that while "social justice" advocates are pushing for representation on the basis of races, gender, sexuality and ethnicity, they have no concern with the representation of public opinion. In fact, the one kind of diversity that they oppose is diversity of opinion. Only "social justice" views are acceptable; contrary views are vilified as "hate speech".

In fact, the educational "social justice" bulldozer plows ahead. The latest ill-conceived initiative is by the College Board, producers of the Scholastic Aptitude Test (SAT), the results of which are considered in college university admissions. The College Board is alarmed that, while Asian Americans do best on the SAT exams, and white Americans score average, Hispanics and African Americans score low. So, to correct that, in the hope of having equality of result for the racial groups, the Board has invented an "adversity" assessment, giving high scores for negative social, economic and other conditions, and giving low scores for beneficial social, economic and other conditions. This would allow admissions officers to explain away poor SAT scores. As one critic (Margolis, 2019) puts it, "Tests only discriminate against those who don't know the answers... The last thing we need is an artificial 'adversity score' to tip the scales in favor of those who don't know the answers."

The reality is that, while minority students with strong backgrounds do reasonably well in university, students with weak backgrounds and levels of achievement, admitted to university for "social justice" reasons, do poorly (Sander and Taylor, 2012), and are harmed by being put into a position that they are ill prepared for. But the overall effect of "social justice" admissions and hiring is the dumbing down of universities and of the U.S. and Canada. Just as world competitors, such as China, ramp up their academic and research achievement, North American universities are catering to "identities", and raising subjectivity—"everyone has their own truth"—above objectivity, truth and reality. This is a deep dive into decadence.

"Social justice" has one simple explanation for differing results among gender, racial and other categories of people: discrimination. But the evidence does not support this explanation. Some unpopular minority groups are highly overrepresented (Salzman, 2018e) in prestigious educational and professional positions, which is a result of their family and community cultures, and cannot be attributed to discrimination against the majority. At the same time, we know that underperforming and "underrepresented" (Salzman, 2019c) minorities have serious internal family and community problems (Pilgrim, 2019), such as single-parent families and a high crime rate. Finally, the evidence shows that "underrepresentation" is in many cases the result of preferences and choices (Salzman, 2019b), not discrimination.

"Social justice" teachers, professors and administrators who dominate our schools and universities do not stop with preferred "equity, diversity and inclusion" admissions and hiring. Rather, they aim to discredit western civilization and American and Canadian society because they were founded and built by white men. The great literary and philosophical works of western civilization are no longer read because they are the creations of "dead white men".

It is offensive to "social justice" advocates, particularly feminists, that white men invented western culture, science and technology (Salzman, 2018b).

"Social justice" educators, which means just about all educators, see their job as discrediting those white men. Western civilization, America and Canada are framed as oppressive hierarchies of gender and racial injustice, with no saving graces. The Founding Fathers of the U.S., and John A. Macdonald, the first prime minister of Canada, are dismissed as slave-holding, anti-Indigenous evil villains, who sinned by living in the nineteenth rather than the twenty-first "social justice" century, and whose statues should be torn down (CBC News, 2018), and names erased.

The Constitution of the United States is now rejected by "social justice" professors because it is the work of slaveholders (Gordon-Reed, 2018). Slavery in the United States is a trump card of "social justice" theorists, who frame it as the original sin (D'Souza, 1995) of America which taints everything else. What they neglect is that slavery was the basis of ancient civilization, and a worldwide historical phenomenon; was a major institution in ancient Greece and in Rome; was a major social fact in Africa, where African slave raiders and traders, in addition to keeping slaves for local use, provided the slaves for the North Atlantic slave trade; in the Middle East where Muslims slavers raided Africa for over a thousand years, and where the Islamic State in the twenty-first century, up to 2018, enslaved "infidels", turning the females into sex slaves; in North Africa, where Muslim slave raiders sailed north as far as Ireland to capture tens of thousands of white Europeans to be sold into slavery; while in India "untouchable" quasi-slaves were half of the population; and in Russia serfs performed the same functions. It was white men in Europe who made slavery redundant by inventing science, modern agriculture and the industrial revolution, raising productivity through the work of machines, so that slave labour was no longer desirable. Furthermore, anti-slavery movements among white Europeans and white Americans led to the banning of the North Atlantic slave trade, policed by the Royal Navy, and the emancipation of the slaves in the Caribbean and the American South. Estimates are that at least 360,000 Union soldiers (Holzer), almost all white, died in the Civil War that led to emancipation.

"Social justice" subjectivity and advocacy (Lindsey et al., 2019) have replaced the search for reality and truth in schools and universities. Objectivity is viewed as a tool that straight white men use to suppress females, people of colour, and those of various sexualities. Today, in universities, identity is the most important "reality", and everyone has their "own truth". If you argue along with science that men and women are biologically different, you are rejected as sexist. If you argue along with science that men cannot be women and women cannot be men, you are rejected as a transphobe. If you argue that African American culture has serious problems, you are rejected as a racist. If you argue that there is discrimination in favour of, not against, females, you are rejected as a sexist. Research and evidence on such matters are suppressed (Salzman, 2018c). There is not just peer pressure against views contrary to "social justice" fantasies, but these views are actively suppressed by administrators, the many "equity, diversity and inclusion" officers (Salzman, 2019d), whose job is to suppress them.

Once equality of opportunity, merit and competition are denounced as white male tricks to maintain supremacy, or as toxic masculinity, it is only logical to reject capitalism and differential distribution of assets, or inequality, and to advocate for socialism. This is no surprise for Marxists, whose sights were aimed at capitalism from the beginning. But the jihad against capitalism has been taken up by "social justice" advocates generally. According to a 2019 poll (Bedard, 2019), "77 percent of Democrats believe that the country would be 'better off' if it were more socialist."

Of course, most American professors (Richardson, 2018) are Democrats, and many are Marxists (Salzman, 2018a). Many university departments declare themselves anti-capitalist. This statement from the Ryerson University (Toronto) School of Social Work is one that most schools of social work and education would agree with:[3]

> School of Social Work is a leader in critical education, research, and practice with culturally and socially diverse students and communities in the advancement of anti-oppression/anti-racism, anti-Black racism, anti-colonialism/decolonization, Aboriginal reconciliation, feminism, anti-capitalism, queer and trans liberation struggles, issues in disability and Madness, among other social justice struggles. Our vision is to transform social structures into more equitable and inclusive social, economic, political, and cultural processes of society.

Apparently, the school has not noticed the abject failure of socialism in the USSR, China, North Korea, Cambodia, Cuba and Venezuela to provide security and prosperity. Nor the hundred million murdered by those societies in implementing socialism. Nor does it seem to have noticed that capitalism in developed societies has brought levels of prosperity to the average person beyond the imaginings of kings and queens in the past.

Our school teachers and university professors have been doing their best to discredit and destroy liberal individualism, freedom, merit, the search for objective truth, western civilization, American and Canadian culture, and capitalism, all contrary to the views of the American and Canadian public. This is an ambitious agenda but, through the magic of "social justice", they have made great progress in shaping the minds of pupils and students, and our future doctors, lawyers, bureaucrats and legislators, if at the expense of objectivity, science and truth. In a competitive and dangerous world, they lead us to ever increasing mediocrity and vulnerability.

References

Anderssen, E. (2015) "We Have a Record Number of Female MPs, but Hold the Applause", *The Globe and Mail*, 20 October, https://www.theglobeandmail.com/life/we-have-a-record-number-of-female-mps-but-hold-the-applause/article26887164/

Bedard, P. (2019) "2020 Poll: 77 Percent of Democrats Back Socialism, but Most Voters Don't", *Washington Examiner*, 25 February, https://www.

---

3   "About the School of Social Work", Ryerson University, Toronto, Canada, https://www.ryerson.ca/social-work/about/

washingtonexaminer.com/tag/donald-trump?source=%2Fwashington-secrets%2F2020-poll-77-dems-back-socialism-but-most-voters-dont

CBC News (2018) "John A. Macdonald Statue Removed from Victoria City Hall", 11 August, https://www.cbc.ca/news/canada/british-columbia/john-a-macdonald-statue-victoria-city-hall-lisa-helps-1.4782065

Ditchburn, J. (2015) "'Because it's 2015': Trudeau Forms Canada's 1st Gender-Balanced Cabinet", *CBC*, 4 November, https://www.cbc.ca/news/politics/canada-trudeau-liberal-government-cabinet-1.3304590

D'Souza, D. (1995) "We the Slave Owners", *Policy Review*, 1 September, https://www.hoover.org/research/we-slave-owners

Gordon-Reed, A. (2018) "America's Original Sin: Slavery and the Legacy of White Supremacy", *Foreign Affairs*, January/February, https://www.foreignaffairs.com/articles/united-states/2017-12-12/americas-original-sin

Hanson, V.D. (2019) "Chinas's Brilliant, Insidious Strategy", *National Review*, 14 May, https://www.nationalreview.com/2019/05/china-strategy-build-economic-military-technological-superiority/

Holzer, H. (no date) "Civil War Casualties: Casualties Numbers and Battle Death Statistics for the American Civil War", *Historynet*, https://www.historynet.com/civil-war-casualties

Jaschik, S. (2016) "Poll: Public Opposes Affirmative Action", *Inside Higher ED*, 8 July, https://www.insidehighered.com/news/2016/07/08/poll-finds-public-opposition-considering-race-and-ethnicity-college-admissions

Jaschik, S. (2019) "Most Americans Say Colleges Shouldn't Consider Race", *Inside Higher ED*, 4 March, https://www.insidehighered.com/admissions/article/2019/03/04/survey-finds-most-americans-say-colleges-shouldnt-consider-race

Kidder, W.C. and Gándara, P. (2015) "Two Decades After the Affirmative Action Ban: Evaluating the University of California's Race-Neutral Efforts", *Education Testing Service, Measuring the Power of Learning, The Civil Rights Project*, https://civilrightsproject.ucla.edu/research/college-access/affirmative-action/two-decades-after-the-affirmative-action-ban-evaluating-the-university-of-california2019s-race-neutral-efforts/Kidder_PIC_paper.pdf

Krislov, M. (2018) "What Will the Harvard Case Mean for Affirmative Action?", *Forbes*, 3 December, https://www.forbes.com/sites/marvinkrislov/2018/12/03/harvard-case-explainer/?sh=3f82e72d3be0

Lindsay, J.A., Boghossian, P. and Pluckrose, H. (2019) "Academic Grievance Studies and the Corruption of Scholarship", *Areo*, 10 February, https://areomagazine.com/2018/10/02/academic-grievance-studies-and-the-corruption-of-scholarship/

Margolis, M. (2019) "Killing Education: SATs to Add 'Adversity Score' to Address 'Wealth Disparity' in Results", *VIP*, 16 May, https://pjmedia. com/news-and-politics/matt-margolis/2019/05/16/killing-education-sats-to-add-adversity-score-to-address-wealth-disparity-in-results-n65891

McGill University (2019) "Canada Research Chair Open Call", 21 May, https://www.mcgill.ca/provost/files/provost/attachment_a._crc_open_c all_final.pdf

Pilgrim, N. (2019) "PILGRIM: Black Culture is in Dire Need of Reform", *Daily Caller*, 22 May, https://dailycaller.com/2019/05/22/pilgrim-black-culture-reform/

Richardson, B. (2018) "Democratic Professors Outnumber Republicans 10 to 1: Study", *The Washington Times*, 26 April, https://www.washingtontimes. com/news/2018/apr/26/democratic-professors-outnumber-republicans-10-to-/

Salzman, P.C. (2017) "Diversity Replaces Merit at Canadian Universities", *Frontier Center for Public Policy*, 28 July, https://fcpp.org/2017/07/28/ diversity-replaces-merit-at-canadian-universities/

Salzman, P.C. (2018a) "Are Our University Professors a Fifth Column?", *Frontier Center for Public Policy*, January, https://fcpp.org/wp-content/ uploads/EF21UniversityProfFifthColumn.pdf

Salzman, P.C. (2018b) "It's Time to Fight for Western Civilization", *Minding the Campus*, 6 June, https://www.mindingthecampus.org/2018/06/06/ its-time-to-defend-and-protect-western-civilization/

Salzman, P.C. (2018c) "How 'Social Justice' Warriors Kill Free Thought", *Minding the Campus*, 2 October, https://www.mindingthecampus.org/ 2018/10/02/how-social-justice-warriors-kill-free-thought/

Salzman, P.C. (2018d) "What Happened to Our Universities?", *Minding the Campus*, 31 October, https://www.mindingthecampus.org/2018/10/31/ what-happened-to-our-universities/

Salzman, P.C. (2018e) "Why Do Some Succeed?", *Frontier Center for Public Policy*, 15 December, https://fcpp.org/2018/12/14/why-do-some-succeed/

Salzman, P.C. (2019a) "The Toxic Mission to Reengineer Men", *Minding the Campus*, 15 January, https://www.mindingthecampus.org/2019/01/15/ the-toxic-mission-to-reengineer-men/

Salzman, P.C. (2019b) "Feminists Assault Science", *Frontier Center for Public Policy*, 23 January, https://fcpp.org/2019/01/23/feminists-assault-science/

Salzman, P.C. (2019c) "Why Do Children of Some Minorities Have Weak Academic Performance?", *Frontier Center for Public Policy*, 2 February, https://fcpp.org/2019/02/02/why-do-children-of-some-minorities-have-weak-academic-performance/

Salzman, P.C. (2019d) "Commissars in Our Universities", *Frontier Center for Public Policy*, 27 April, https://fcpp.org/2019/04/27/commissars-in-our-universities/

Salzman, P.C. (2019e) "The War Against White People", *Minding the Campus*, 29 April, https://www.mindingthecampus.org/2019/04/29/the-war-against-white-people/

Sander, R. and Taylor, S. Jr. (2012) "The Painful Truth About Affirmative Action", *The Atlantic*, 2 October, https://www.theatlantic.com/national/archive/2012/10/the-painful-truth-about-affirmative-action/263122/

Part IV.

Censorship, Deplatforming and Job Harrassment

Alessandro Strumia[1]

Why Discussing Gender and STEM is So Dangerous

ABSTRACT: I describe my experience, as an example of the troubles that happen when discussing scientific results on gender and Science, Technology, Engineering, Mathematics (STEM) beyond the boundaries imposed by political correctness. Moving to the wider context, I interpret these troubles as symptoms of a serious illness of current academia and society.

TOPICS: censorship, deplatforming and job harassment; feminism and gender mainstreaming; race, ethnicity; general considerations on suppression of academic freedom.
****

I. Particle Physics and Gender

When the Large Hadron Collider (LHC) started in 2010, I wanted to be at Conseil Européen pour la Recherche Nucléaire (CERN) because it had to be an historical moment, in one way or another. LHC could open a golden era for high-energy physics, by discovering new physics such as super-symmetry expected by most colleagues. Or it could end the field, by discovering only the boson predicted by Higgs half a century earlier (a possibility known among physicists as a "nightmare scenario"—Cho, 2007). After the Higgs discovery the dust settled, and the result was a nightmare: no new physics while the discovery potential of the LHC was almost over.

CERN was in a doubly difficult position, as it had reached at the same time the bottom of its scientific interest (scientists started being attracted

---

[1]   Physicist, Fauglia, Italy. Email: astrumia@icloud.com

by other fields) and the peak of its mediatic visibility (that started attracting people with extra-scientific interests, see Kass, 2014, for a gender-related example). Instead of attempting a Rubbia-style scientific innovation, CERN started discussing a far-future, huger 100-km collider that needs huger money and thus good public relations.

This happened while many western leftists moved to identity politics, with its cancel culture and systemic victimization narratives (see e.g. Rozado et al., 2021). CERN got a "diversity office", its director attended Bilderberg, Davos, G7 meetings, "progressive" causes started impacting science. For example, while inviting experts to a physics workshop, we were informed about a new rule: gender quotas (now partly formalized in CERN).[2] In 2018, CERN organized the "1st workshop on high energy theory and gender", while accidentally I had data to perform the basic checks that CERN could have done before hosting allegations that physics discriminates against women. Indeed, I had co-authored a bibliometric publication (Strumia et al., 2019) using the InSpire database about papers and authors in fundamental physics worldwide from 1970 to now. Checks with bibliometric data showed no bias in hires against female researchers in fundamental physics.

We discussed how one could carefully present these results and survive: minimize the impact by stating aseptic numbers? Restrict comments to the usual lip service to those who decide what is "offensive"?

But next, I remembered that the former Harvard president Summers, the former Harvard physicist Motl, and the former Google engineer Damore got into trouble for mentioning Higher Male Variability (HMV) as a possible factor behind gender gaps in STEM. In the polemics that followed, most media said that HMV is a discredited concept. I checked my data, finding distributions with roughly the same average and a higher variability among male physicists. Seeing hints of this universal biological phenomenon made the bibliometric study scientifically interesting (it was no longer just descriptive sociology), but it also meant that surviving was no longer possible. Part of sociology rests on the Blank Slate paradigm, refusing scientific input from biology. HMV indicates that biology plays a role in generating a group difference, violating a political ideology endorsed by most media and even scientific institutions. HMV was proposed by Darwin, who proposed evolution too. In Darwin's

---

2   CERN Diversity and Inclusion Policy, https://diversity-and-inclusion.web. cern.ch/about/cern-diversity-policy. CERN Gender in High Energy Theory, https://genhet.web.cern.ch

times, evolution was politically incorrect; now HMV is politically incorrect.

Damore tried to be careful and moderate, but this did not save him. A mathematician, Hill, wrote a scientific paper about HMV, that was cancelled twice (see references in Strumia, 2021). So I considered that either I self-censor or I am the next on the list, because being non-conforming to gender ideology is not allowed.

If I get attacked, would CERN resist? I remembered when, someday in 2016, CERN LGBT associations put posters everywhere (more LGBT posters than physics posters, more posters than at a gay pride) and prompted an international media storm against the homophobic CERN because a few posters were defaced. CERN "strongly condemned" this, instead of explaining that a few people over-reacted to an exaggeration and that CERN hosts people from multiple cultures. In 2012, the CERN director wrote that diversity can be achieved "without the need for groupings or associations that foster separateness" (Mayor, 2016), but now the situation was different.

After a battle with the mirror, I chose not to self-censor, expecting that it will be my last day at CERN. I had no strong motivation to remain at CERN at any cost, expecting that discoveries were likely over. As a theorist, I can work with small resources. As a physicist, I am less dependent than a social scientist on current ideologies. Finally, I work in Italy where the intolerance of political correctness is above the level reached in the anglosphere.

Then I feared the risk of talking but ending up censored and disappearing in silence. To avoid a useless sacrifice, I chose to present the data and their interpretation in an explicit way, replacing lip service with the prediction of which political area will attack me.

CERN colleagues saw nothing bad in my talk and believed that my last sentence "hope to see you again" was a joke. After the talk, I privately warned them that they might soon have to say otherwise, and I moved back to Italy with half of my stuff.

After that, activists managed to start a storm, CERN issued a press release according to which "everyone is welcome… regardless of… beliefs", but suspended me while investigating whether my 30-minute talk might have violated internal rules, such as the "obligation to exercise reserve and tact", "reserve in expressing personal opinions" and "communications to the public". In the meantime, CERN cancelled my slides, my audio and my video. This backfired, because some people had downloaded my slides and put them on their websites; the word "cernsorship" was trending on social media.

Some politicians and their syndicates wanted me suspended/fired/ cancelled, forgetting that in the past their political area defended workers. Some newspapers attacked me as "sexist" for mentioning gender differences in interests, while at the same time publishing horoscopes tied to female interests. Most comments of their readers were positive. I started receiving a few emails per minute, largely supportive. Some warned me that people targeted by activists and media usually back down, wrongly believing that this stops the attacks. Others suggested I open a subscription for legal defence. I declined, but later I got into trouble for not having sued newspapers that falsely attributed a few sentences to me.

Various scientists wrote to me, sharing their expertise in relevant topics of biology and psychology, confirming that what I had mentioned as the likely explanation of gender gaps in STEM—the combined effect of gender differences in interests and HMV—is not discredited science. Instead, there is an industry of activists that work on media to paint real science as discredited and their ideology as science. A thesis at Padua University examined my talk, finding its science sound.

Attending the CERN workshop, I got the impression that my results were in conflict with previous literature on gender and STEM: I later became aware that the allegations of discrimination in physics and other fields were not supported by data in many previous scientific publications that found results similar to mine. The anomaly was not my talk, but the fact that all other talks discussed only one point of view. CERN cancelled the diverse talk while proclaiming "CERN stands for diversity".

CERN kept investigating my 30-minute talk for months, preventing me from attending the physics workshop I co-organized. CERN colleagues did not mobilize the workshop to support me (although they did so two years earlier to support a physicist at CERN who was arrested and later sentenced for plotting Islamic terrorism—Butler, 2016). One day I went to CERN to bring back the other half of my stuff. CERN is surrounded by fences and private police, and they finally had something important to do: protect scientists from "offensive" data. After meeting colleagues outside CERN, it was late and snowing, so I stopped at a hotel for truck drivers. Talking with them confirmed that "outside of certain university departments, virtually everyone believes that there are physical and psychological differences (on average) between men and women" (Cofnas, 2020).

Finally, CERN lifted the suspension, deciding that there was no basis for starting proceedings at which I could have defended myself. In the meantime, my contract had expired. CERN restarted the mediatic mess with a new press release on Women's Day (a few years earlier, CERN had chosen a silent style when the director of its theory division disappeared).

At this point, I could have returned to CERN as a visitor, but I no longer wanted to be subject to rules that restrict free speech using vague, subjective language. Instead, I started defending myself by opening the website https://alessandrostrumia.home.blog. Indeed, lies about my slides had backfired, but the audio of my talk had been cancelled, allowing for lies such as "Strumia's presentation went far beyond the content of his slides and was even more sexist and offensive", "Strumia... in a talk at CERN... insulted Prof. Giannotti". CERN refused to send me the file with the audio of my talk, but I got hold of a private recording, and I was now free to put it online, to show the falsity of such allegations.

The worst attacks come from those countries where identity politics and political correctness is a big problem. Some mostly American physicists opened a *"Particles for Justice"* (P4J) blog (P4J, 2018) addressed to my "superiors", attacking me with false statements and reiterating the hegemonic viewpoint on gender and STEM. Some physicists described the scientific mistakes in P4J in two independent texts, but both remained anonymous "for fear of losing my career" (Areo, 2018). Somebody else questioned the orthodox view during a free debate in a physics department in Australia, leaving an anonymous paper. A colleague wrote to me from CERN using an anonymous email. Thanks, anonymous body. One young physicist openly invites colleagues to avoid mixing politics with science and to tolerate dissent, but he gets routinely cancelled (for a recent example see Chu, 2021).

I wrote a scientific paper with my data on gender and physics, and submitted it to the preprint bulletin *arXiv* in 2018. Usually, *arXiv* accepts preprints in one day, but mine was rejected, on the grounds that it had not been published. My paper is now published on *Quantitative Science Studies*, a bibliometric scientific journal (Strumia, 2021). This shows that a normal scientific debate remains possible, at least outside physics. I re-submitted my published paper to *arXiv*, and it was rejected again with the reason that it "is on a topic not covered by arXiv or that the intended audience for your work is not a community we currently serve". I wonder if *arXiv* now serves a political community, as *arXiv* accepted politically correct but scientifically incorrect preprints on the same topic, including a heated reply to my paper (Ball et al., 2021). Some journalists criticized my paper after reading only its title, getting its content 100% wrong. This was to be expected. Less expected was somebody capable of attacking my paper while getting even its title 100% wrong (Greco, 2019)!

A few more papers about gender and STEM by other authors got cancelled (see references in Strumia, 2021): can we trust science operating under such social pressure?

Every year, some activists discuss on social media how to get me fired. So far, they stopped at posters. I kept doing physics (*Web of Science* wrote to me that I am in their "Highly cited researcher — 2020" list), away from CERN that discovered no new physics.

My little problems exemplify the big problem: a part of the scientific community capitulated to a political ideology that rejects free speech and the scientific method. Let's move to the elephant in the room.

II. Politics and Gender

Pourquoi mourir pour Danzig? Because gender and STEM has little to do with gender and STEM. Free speech about this topic is not free because gender is one of the Trojan horses of identity politics that is damaging science and society.

These politics try to attract the votes of selected groups using victimization narratives, dividing people in a caste system of oppression, rejecting the principle of non-discrimination, seeking aggressive "positive" discriminations to make more equal than others those groups elevated to the status of "victim".

These politics want to replace "equality" with "equity". They sound the same, but they are not. I am in favour of the former, which means *equal opportunities*: fairly considering people based on individual merit irrespective of their political opinion/religion/sex/race, etc. I am against the latter, which means discriminating based on race/gender/etc. to get *equal outcomes,* irrespective of personal merit. Many scientific institutions introduced quotas and positions reserved for women or other "minorities".[3] Furthermore, those who apply for discriminatory positions presumably accept their political rationale, so these positions indirectly create political discrimination, too.

By weaponizing group differences, identity politics broke the silent agreement on avoiding discussion of group differences. In my opinion, the correct answer to discriminatory affirmative actions (allegedly aimed at compensating for discrimination) is free research and free speech (are

---

[3]   My 2018 talk at CERN listed early examples in physics and was cancelled and dubbed "fake news" on the CERN conference website. One of the colleagues who signed is now hired in a position for women only, and this kind of explicit discrimination is now routine. CERN indicated in a five-year plan the goal of increasing the proportion of women by 1% per year (see previous footnote).

alleged discriminations real?), together with the moral obligation to treat people as individuals. As P4J claim that my "arguments are morally reprehensible", let me compare their approach with mine.

I followed this approach: first find out what is true (some gaps seem mainly due to group differences, rather than to discrimination). Based on the findings, one can next make ethical judgments (don't use group differences to justify discrimination against people). This time-honoured approach originally resulted in scientific institutions with freedom of research and excellence, at the expense of group equity.

According to the P4J approach, we should first decide what is ethical (equal outcomes among groups, according to identity politics) and next, based on this decision, judge what is true (group differences are reprehensible and cannot exist). We see the result: elite institutions that discriminate to get politically correct demographics, sacrificing excellence and free speech.

Many colleagues prefer to avoid these topics and be apolitical. But this is no longer possible: professors in many North American universities must now sign "diversity statements". Applicants can get excluded for not showing "ideological/political conformity" (Coine, 2019). I would write that "the most qualified person should get the job", but this can now be considered a micro-aggression (Volokh, 2015). The greatest physicist of the last half century, Steven Weinberg, told a colleague that he wrote: "I will seek out the best candidates, without regard to race or sex." The colleague comments: "he might be one of the only academics who could get away with that" (Aaronson, 2021). The same colleague recognizes the existence of currently unspeakable "truths" and justifies his silence by comparing the situation in current U.S. academia to the former Soviet Union, where some scientists built private bubbles of decency, feeling that there was no point in fighting impossible battles (Aaronson, 2017). I understand why others make the same comparison, although being fired is less bad than being imprisoned in a gulag.

Although I had only spoken about gender, P4J wrote that I was "belittling the ability and legitimacy of scientists of color". P4J introduce race because the real issue behind gender and STEM is identity politics. Indeed, in 2020 the P4J physicists proclaimed the first "strike" in the history of physics, to end "white supremacy" in physics.[4] Furthermore, the main P4J author wrote a paper with the title "White Empiricism: The

---

4   Their term "strike" is imprecise, as real strikers don't get paid. P4J members who believe they got their positions thanks to "privilege" could voluntarily resign, opening space to minorities in a non-discriminatory way.

Racialization of Epistemology in Physics", with claims things such as: "Black women must, according to Einstein's principle of covariance, have an equal claim to objectivity" (Prescod-Weinstein, 2020). In Europe, the idea that race is upstream of physics was abandoned after *Deutsche Physik*, but U.S. academia now offers courses such as "Black Holes: Race and the Cosmos" (MacDonald, 2021).

These are typical manifestations of the ideology known as *applied postmodernism*. Around the year 2000 the American physicist Alan Sokal warned that postmodernism was spreading in academia, publishing the book *Intellectual Impostures* and the hoax *Transgressing the Boundaries: Towards a Transformative Hermeneutics of Quantum Gravity*. Recently, multiple hoaxes got published (Lindsay et al., 2018), while scientific papers have been deemed "controversial" and cancelled. The humanities have been conquered, STEM is under attack, and U.S. physicists no longer openly say that relativistic covariance and black holes have no connection to race or gender.

To conclude, I argue why postmodernism is especially toxic for science.

This ideology started in the '60s when western Marxists realized that no class revolution was going to happen: they extended Marxian conflict theory from class to identities such as gender and race (Hicks, 2004). After decades of accidental historical evolution, class got dropped and race became dominant in the USA. Unlike the U.S. Civil Rights Movements, this ideology divides humans into oppressors and oppressed in irreconcilable conflict. In the past half century, social barriers have largely been removed worldwide: we now see that some differences disappeared, others grew or remained (gender in STEM is one example). Instead of rethinking social constructivism, a political constituency tightened this ideology, insisting that any difference must be due to remaining hidden discrimination, stereotype threat, unconscious bias, systemic racism, micro-aggressions, nano-aggressions. As usual, "the most radical forms of activism often emerge after demands for reform have been met" (Kronen, 2021).

This resulted in this postmodernism that denies individuality, liberal universalism, objectivity and views reason as western power over oppressed minorities. Consequently, postmodernism rejects the scientific method, meritocracy, free speech (see Pluckrose & Lindsay, 2020; Saad, 2020). Its activists don't recognize the universal value of science and treat it accordingly. Many scientific results, and the very existence of science as a way to seek objective universal truths, are incompatible with postmodernism. Science emerged after religious wars by finding a common ground in objectivity, and thus occasionally finds truths considered offensive by somebody. Unlike past episodes (heliocentrism, creationism, etc.), now science conflicts with the internalized ideology of the academic elite. So we now have academic mobs that use political methods rather than reason and scholarship to impose an ideology that cannot stand liberal scrutiny and condemns all other views as "systemic XXXism". In the anglosphere, about 1/3 of PhD students support cancelling dissenters and discriminating based on political ideas (CSPI, 2021).

Most waves of craziness come and go without causing serious damage. Except when they capture institutions and use power to stay.

The strong political imbalance in western academies became a problem when many western leftists turned to this illiberal, authoritarian ideology: more political diversity would have allowed more warning voices. If scientific institutions fail, science risks becoming another form of covert political activism. We used to have elder, accomplished scientists in charge of scientific institutions. But now various institutions put people in charge from politically correct demographics, who actively implement the political ideology that favoured them, believing it's a universal value.

Outside academia this is considered as a partisan political ideology, supported by one side and considered toxic by the other side: recent laws in the USA and elsewhere aim at keeping (parts of) this ideology out of public schools. Given the decreasing public confidence in higher education (GALLUP, 2018; PEW, 2019), politicized scientific institutions risk getting involved in future political battles. Institutions that rely on public funds are particularly at risk of getting involved in processes that will likely be more chaotic than beneficial.

References

Aaronson, S., 2017, "The Kolmogorov Option", https://www.scottaaronson.com/blog/?p=3376

Aaronson, S., 2021, "Steven Weinberg (1933–2021): A Personal View", https://www.scottaaronson.com/blog/?p=5566

Aero, 31st October 2018, (anonymous) "Gender Controversy Comes to Physics: A Response to the Statement Against Alessandro Strumia", *Areo Magazine*, https://areomagazine.com/2018/10/31/gender-controversy-comes-to-physics-a-response-to-the-statement-against-alessandro-strumia. See also: anonymous, "Justice for Strumia", https://web.archive.org/web/20190809221134/https://justiceforstrumia.org

Ball, P., Britton, B., Hengel, E., Moriarty, P., Oliver, R.A., Rippon. G., Saini, A. & Wade, J., 2021, "Gender Issues in Fundamental Physics: Strumia's Bibliometric Analysis Fails to Account for Key Confounders and Confuses Correlation with Causation", *ArXiv*, https://arxiv.org/abs/2106.15255

Butler, D., 2016, "LHC Scientists Bring Conference to Deported Physicist", *Nature,* https://www.nature.com/articles/nature.2016.21155

Cho, A., 2007, "Physicist's Nightmare Scenario: The Higgs and Nothing Else", *Science,* **315**: 1657, https://science.sciencemag.org/content/315/5819/1657

Chu, Y.Z., 2021, *Twitter,* https://twitter.com/Yi_Zen_Chu/status/141154233 1132547083

Cofnas, N., 2020, "Research on Group Differences in Intelligence: A Defense of Free Inquiry", *Phyl. Psych.*, **33**.

Coyne, J., 2019, "Life Science Jobs at Berkely Give Precedence to Candidates' Diversity and Inclusion Statements", https://whyevolutionistrue.com/2019/12/31/life-science-jobs-at-berkeley-with-hiring-giving-precedence-to-diversity-and-inclusion-statements

CSPI, 2021, Report no 2. "Academic Freedom in Crisis: Punishment, Political Discrimination, and Self-Censorship", https://cspicenter.org/reports/academicfreedom

GALLUP, 2018, Jones, J.M., "Confidence in Higher Education Down Since 2015", https://news.gallup.com/opinion/gallup/242441/confidence-higher-education-down-2015.aspx

Greco, P., 11th November 2019, "La primavera, al femminile, della fisica", *il BoLive,* https://ilbolive.unipd.it/it/news/primavera-femminile-fisica

Hicks, S.R.C., 2004, *Explaining Post-modernism,* New York: Scholargy Publishing.

Kass, I.W., 2014, "Rich, White Men at the Top of CERN", *KILDEN Information and News About Gender Research in Norway.*

Kronen, S., 28th May 2021, "Black Lives Matter and the Psychology of Progressive Fatalism", *Quillette,* https://quillette.com/2021/05/28/black-lives-matter-and-the-psychology-of-progressive-fatalism

Lindsay, J.A., et al., 2nd October 2018, "Academic Grievance Studies and the Corruption of Scholarship", *Aero Magazine,* https://areomagazine.com/2018/10/02/academic-grievance-studies-and-the-corruption-of-scholarship

MacDonald, H., 2021, "Down a Black Hole", *City Journal,* https://www.city-journal.org/cornell-black-hole-class-racializes-astronomy

Mayor, L., 3rd March 2016, "Where People and Particles Collide", *Physics World.*

P4J, 2018, *Particles for Justice,* https://www.particlesforjustice.org/statement-sexism

PEW, 2019, Parker, K., "The Growing Partisan Divide in Views of Higher Education", https://www.pewresearch.org/social-trends/2019/08/19/the-growing-partisan-divide-in-views-of-higher-education-2

Pluckrose, H. & Lindsay, J., 2020, *Cynical Theories*, Durham, NC: Pitchstone Books.

Prescod-Weinstein, C., 2020, "Making Black Women Scientists Under White Empiricism: The Racialization of Epistemology in Physics", *Journal of Women in Culture and Society*, https://www.journals.uchicago.edu/doi/full/10.1086/704991

Rozado, D., Al-Gharbi, M. & Halberstadt, J., 2021, "Prevalence of Prejudice-Denoting Words in News Media Discourse: A Chronological Analysis", *Social Science Computer Review*, doi: 10.1177/08944393211031452

Saad, G., 2020, *The Parasitic Mind: How Infectious Ideas are Killing Common Sense*, Washington, DC: Regnery Publishing.

Strumia, A., 2021, "Gender Issues in Fundamental Physics: A Bibliometric Analysis", *Quantitative Science Studies*, **2**: 225, https://doi.org/10.1162/qss_a_00114. See also Strumia, A., 2021, "Reply to Commentaries about Gender Issues in Fundamental Physics: A Bibliometric Analysis", *Quantitative Science Studies*, **2**: 277, https://doi.org/10.1162/qss_c_00120

Strumia, A. & Torre, R., 2019, "Biblioranking Fundamental Physics", *Journal of Infometrics*, **13**: 515, https://www.sciencedirect.com/science/article/abs/pii/S1751157718301512?via%3Dihub

Volokh, E., 16th June 2015, *Washington Post*, https://www.washingtonpost.com/news/volokh-conspiracy/wp/2015/06/16/uc-teaching-faculty-members-not-to-criticize-race-based-affirmative-action-call-america-melting-pot-and-more

Jordan Peterson[1]

Cambridge University Rescinds My Fellowship[2]

ABSTRACT: Professor Jordan B. Peterson requested a visiting fellowship at the Faculty of Divinity in Cambridge (UK), and an initial offer has been rescinded after a further review, signalling a solidarity with the diversity-inclusivity-equity mobs. Members of Cambridge University Student Union thought that his work and views were not representative of the student body and as such they did not see his visit as a valuable contribution to the university, but one that works in opposition to its principles. Professor Peterson replies here to these arguments.

TOPICS: censorship, deplatforming and job harassment; general considerations on suppression of academic freedom.
****

I visited Cambridge University in November of 2018, during my *12 Rules for Life* book tour, one stop of which was the city of Cambridge, where I spoke publicly at the venerable Cambridge Corn Exchange.[3] While there, I had lunch and dinner and various scheduled conversations with a good number of faculty members and other interested individuals who came in for the occasion, and we took the opportunity to speak with a welcome frankness about theological, philosophical and psychological matters. I

---

[1] Professor of Psychology, Univ. of Toronto, Canada. Author of the bestseller *12 Rules for Life: An Antidote to Chaos*. Email: jordanbpeterson@gmail.com. Social media of Jordan Peterson: Twitter: @jordanbpeterson, Instagram: @jordan.b.peterson, Youtube: https://www.youtube.com/user/JordanPetersonVideos, Website: jordanbpeterson.com

[2] This article was originally published in the blog of Jordan Peterson on 20th March 2019: https://www.jordanbpeterson.com/blog-posts/cambridge-university-rescinds-my-fellowship/.

[3] Cambridge Corn Exchange, https://www.cambridgelive.org.uk/cornex

also recorded two *Youtube* videos/podcasts: one with the eminent philosopher Sir Roger Scruton,[4] presented by The Cambridge Centre for the Study of Platonism,[5] and another with Dr. Stephen Blackwood,[6] founding President of Ralston College,[7] a university in Savannah, Georgia, preparing for launch.

I was also invited to address[8] the student-run Cambridge Union,[9] the oldest continuously running debating society in the world — a talk which was delivered to a packed house (a relatively rare occurrence) and which, despite being posted only four months before I write this text, is now the second-most watched of their 200 total videos. I'm mentioning this for a very particular purpose: CUSU, the Cambridge University Student Union[10] (not to be confused with the aforementioned Cambridge Union), pinned to their *Twitter* account the rescindment announcement three minutes before (!) the Faculty of Divinity did so, and in a spirit of apparent "relief". *The Guardian* cited the following CUSU statement:[11]

> We are relieved to hear that Jordan Peterson's request for a visiting fellow-ship to Cambridge's faculty of divinity has been rescinded following further review. It is a political act to associate the University with an academic's work through offers which legitimise figures such as Peterson. His work and views are not representative of the student body and as such we do not see his visit as a valuable contribution to the University, but one that works in opposition to the principles of the University.

It seems to me that the packed Cambridge Union auditorium, the intelligent questioning associated with the lecture, and the overwhelming number of views the subsequently posted video accrued, indicates that

---

[4] 15th December 2018, "Sir Roger Scruton/Dr. Jordan B. Peterson: Apprehending the Transcendent", *Youtube*, https://www.youtube.com/watch?v=XvbtKAYd cZY

[5] "Cambridge Centre for the Study of Platonism", Faculty of Divinity, Univeristy of Cambridge, https://www.divinity.cam.ac.uk/researchareas/projectsandclusters/ccsp

[6] 21st February 2019, "Our Cultural Inflection Point and Higher Education: JB Peterson/Stephen Blackwood", *Youtube*, https://www.youtube.com/watch?v=nlgG8C1GydA

[7] Ralston College, https://www.ralston.ac/

[8] 4th November 2018, "Jordan Peterson | Cambridge Union", *Youtube*, https://www.youtube.com/watch?v=_bRDbFU_lto&t=1s

[9] The Cambridge Union, https://www.cus.org/

[10] Cambridge SU, https://www.cambridgesu.co.uk/

[11] Marsch, S., 20th March 2019, "Cambridge University Rescinds Jordan Peterson Invitation", *The Guardian*, https://www.theguardian.com/education/2019/mar/20/cambridge-university-rescinds-jordan-peterson-invitation

there a number of Cambridge students are very interested in what I have to say, and might well regard my visit "as a valuable contribution to the University". I also have to say, as a university professor concerned with literacy, that the CUSU statement offered to *The Guardian* borders on the unintelligible, perhaps even crossing the line (as so much ideological-puppet-babble tends to): what in the world does it mean that "it is a political act to associate the University with an academic's work through offers which legitimise figures such as Peterson"? And who could write or say something of that rhetorical nature without a deep sense of betraying their personal conscience?

In any case: in November of 2018, when I was in Cambridge, I began discussions with one of the faculty members (whom I had met briefly before, in London) about the possibility of entering into a collaboration with the Cambridge Divinity Faculty. I enjoyed the conversations I had at Cambridge immensely. I learned a lot about Biblical matters that had remained unknown to me in a very short time. This was of particular relevance to me, but also perhaps of more broad and public import, because of a series of lectures on the Biblical stories of Genesis I prepared, delivered live (at the Isabel Bader Theatre in Toronto) and then posted on *Youtube*[12] and in podcast form.[13]

Since their posting, beginning in May of 2017, these lectures have received about 10 million hits (as well as an equal or greater number of downloads). The first lecture, on the first sentence of Genesis, has, alone, garnered 3.7 million of those, which makes it the most well-received of all the talks I have ever posted online. I have received correspondence in great volume from religious people all over the world, Jews, Christians, Buddhists and Muslims alike—and an equally large number from atheists —all telling me that my psychological take on the Genesis material resonated very strongly with their faith, or that it helped them understand for the first time the value of these stories. You can see this for yourself by reading the comments on the *Youtube* channel, which are remarkably civilized and positive, by modern social media standards. I don't think there is another modern religious/psychological phenomenon or happening that is genuinely comparable. It's also the case that my books, *12 Rules for Life* and *Maps of Meaning*, both rely heavily on Judeo-Christian thinking, and are predicated on the idea that the stories that make up such

12 Peterson, J.B., 2017–2021, "The Psychological Significance of the Biblical Stories: Genesis", *Youtube*, https://www.youtube.com/watch?v=f-wWBGo6a 2w&list=PL22J3VaeABQD_IZs7y60I3lUrrFTzkpat

13 "The Jordan B Peterson Podcast", https://www.jordanbpeterson.com/podcast/

thought constitute the bedrock of our civil, peaceful and productive society. The former has now sold three million copies (one million in tongues other than English), and will be translated into 50 languages; the latter, a much older book, was recently a *New York Times* bestseller in audio format. This volume of interest is clear indication of the widespread cross-cultural appeal of the work that I am doing.

In the fall, I am planning to produce a series of lectures on the Exodus stories. I presume they will have equal drawing power. I thought that I could extend my knowledge of the relevant stories by spending time in Cambridge, and that doing so would be useful for me, for faculty members who might be interested in speaking with me, and to the students. I also regarded it as a privilege and an opportunity. I believed (and still believe) that collaborating with the Faculty of Divinity on such a project would constitute an opportunity of clear mutual benefit. Finally, I thought that making myself more knowledgeable about relevant Biblical matters by working with the experts there would be of substantive benefit to the public audience who would eventually receive the resultant lectures.

Now the Divinity school has decided that signalling their solidarity with the diversity-inclusivity-equity mob trumps that opportunity – or so I presume. You see, I don't yet know, because (and this is particularly appalling) I was not formally notified of this decision by any representative of the Divinity school. I heard about the rescinded offer through the grapevine, via a colleague and friend, and gathered what I could about the reasons from social media and press coverage (assuming that CUSU has at least something to do with it).

I would also like to point out something else. As I already noted, the Divinity Faculty (@CamDivinity) tweeted their decision to rescind,[14] consciously making this a public issue. This is inexcusable, in my estimation, given (1) that they did not equally publicize the initial agreement/ invitation (which has to be considered an event of equal import) and (2) that they implied that I came cap-in-hand to the school for the fellowship. This is precisely the kind of half-truth particularly characteristic of those who deeply practise to deceive, as the fellowship offer was a consequence of mutual discussion between those who invited me to Cambridge in July

---

[14] 20th March 2019, "Jordan Peterson Requested a Visiting Fellowship at the Faculty of Divinity, and an Initial Offer Has Been Rescinded After a Further Review", *Twitter*, https://twitter.com/CamDivinity/status/1108352122779774 977

and my subsequent formal request, and not something I had dreamed up on my own.

It's not going to make much difference to my future, in some sense. I have more opportunities at the moment than I can keep track of, let alone (let's say) capitalize on. It's a complex and surreally fortunate position to occupy, and I'm not taking it for granted, but it happens to be true. In the fall, therefore, I will produce the lectures I plan to produce on Exodus, regardless of whether they occur in the UK or in Canada or elsewhere, and they will attract whatever audience remains interested. But I think that it is deeply unfortunate that the authorities at the Divinity school in Cambridge decided that kowtowing to an ill-informed, ignorant and ideologically-addled mob trumped participating in an extensive online experiment in mass Christian and psychological education. Given the continued decline of church attendance, the rise in atheistic or agnostic sentiment, the increasing irrelevance of theological education and the collapse in interest in such matters among young people, wiser and more profound decisions might have been made.

You see, it matters whether people around the world understand these ancient stories. It deeply matters. We are becoming unmoored, because we no longer share the structure these stories undergird. This is psychologically destabilizing. It's producing a pathological and desperate nihilism that is increasingly common and, at the same time, a pronounced proclivity for the ideological certainty that mimics but cannot replace true religious belief. Both consequences are bound to be, as the evidence certainly indicates, divisive and truly dangerous.

I think the Faculty of Divinity made a serious error of judgment in rescinding their offer to me (and I'm speaking about those unnamed persons who made that specific decision). I think they handled publicizing the rescindment in a manner that could hardly have been more narcissistic, self-congratulatory and devious.

I believe that the parties in question don't give a damn about the perilous decline of Christianity, and I presume in any case that they regard that faith, in their propaganda-addled souls, as the ultimate manifestation of the oppressive western patriarchy, despite their hypothetical allegiance to their own discipline.

I think that it is no bloody wonder that the faith is declining (and with it, the values of the West, as it fragments) with cowards and mountebanks of the sort who manifested themselves today at the helm.

I wish them the continued decline in relevance over the next few decades that they deeply and profoundly and diligently work toward and deserve.

P.S. I also find it interesting and deeply revealing that I know the names of the people who invited me, both informally and formally, but the names of the people who have disinvited me remain shrouded in exactly the kind of secrecy that might be expected from hidden, conspiratorial, authoritarian and cowardly bureaucrats. How many were there? No one knows. By what process did they come to the decision (since there were obviously people who wanted me there)? No one knows. On what grounds was the decision made? That has not been revealed. What role was played by pressure from, for example, the CUSU? That's apparently no one's business. It is on such ground that tyranny does not so much grow as positively thrive.

P.P.S. Here's something from Vice-Chancellor Professor Stephen Toope[15] of the University of Cambridge that's worth consideration, in the current context (the described "openness" is apparently part of the university's declared strategic initiatives regarding (what else) equality and diversity (bold mine):

> One very specific aspect of... openness is being inclusive, and open to diversity in all its forms — **diversity of interests and beliefs**, of gender, of religion, of sexual identity, of ethnicity, of physical ability.

---

[15] "Race Equality at Cambridge", University of Cambridge, https://www.race-equality.admin.cam.ac.uk/university-diversity-fund

David Benatar[1]

Disinviting an Academic Freedom Lecturer[2]

ABSTRACT: Academic freedom at South African universities, and especially at the country's (and the continent's) leading university, the University of Cape Town (UCT), has been increasingly threatened since 2015. While there are many examples to illustrate this claim, arguably the most ironic is the deplatforming of a speaker invited to give the 2016 academic freedom lecture! Flemming Rose had been invited by UCT's Academic Freedom Committee to deliver this lecture. The invitation was subsequently withdrawn by UCT's Executive. In this article, written at that time, I respond to and reject the arguments advanced to justify the disinvitation.

TOPICS: censorship, deplatforming and job harassment; general considerations on suppression of academic freedom.
****

The irony should be lost on nobody. A speaker invited to give the annual academic freedom lecture at the University of Cape Town (UCT) has been prevented by the University Executive from giving that lecture.

In March 2015, the Academic Freedom Committee at UCT decided to invite Flemming Rose, a prominent defender of freedom of expression, to

---

1   Professor in Philosophy Department, Director Bioethics Centre, University of Cape Town, South Africa.
2   This article was original published with a different heading: David Benatar, 22nd July 2016, "UCT: A Blow to Academic Freedom", *Politicsweb*, https://www.politicsweb.co.za/opinion/uct-a-blow-against-academic-freedom

deliver the 2016 TB Davie Memorial Lecture, which was due to take place on 11th August.

As the culture editor of the Danish newspaper the *Jyllands-Posten*, Mr. Rose had published some drawings and cartoons depicting Mohammed. The purpose of this exercise was to establish the extent to which artists were self-censoring. The question had arisen following a number of European instances of self-censorship pertaining to Islam. One of these occurred when the author of a children's book about the life of Mohammed had had difficulty finding a willing illustrator because artists indicated they were fearful. Mr. Rose wrote to members of the association of Danish cartoonists, asking them to "draw Mohammed as you see him". Twelve illustrations, not all of them depicting or targeting Mohammed, were published on 30th September 2005. Among those lampooned by the cartoons were the author of the children's book, the leader of a Danish anti-immigration party and the *Jyllands-Posten* itself. Nevertheless, two Danish Muslim clerics used the publication of the cartoons to incite international violence in early 2006. These reactions galvanized Mr. Rose, and he became a prominent advocate of free speech.

It is unsurprising that Mr. Rose's unrepentant publication of the Mohammed illustrations makes him a controversial figure. However, it is precisely such a person who is a barometer of how much freedom of expression we enjoy. Everybody is willing to tolerate some speech. The real test of freedom of expression occurs when people are asked to tolerate the speech of those whose ideas they do not like. On that test, the University of Cape Town has shown that it does not have the robust commitment to freedom of expression that it says it has.

In explaining the University Executive's decision to override the Academic Freedom Committee's invitation to Mr. Rose and to disinvite him, the Vice-Chancellor, Dr. Max Price, makes the obligatory affirmation of "our commitment to the right to academic freedom and freedom of expression".

As all those who seek to curtail freedom do, he is quick to qualify this commitment by noting that "[l]ike all fundamental rights... the right to academic freedom is not unlimited." Of course, there is a sense in which academic freedom and freedom of expression are appropriately limited. Dr. Price notes that, according to section 16(2) of the South African constitution, the right to free expression does not extend to "(a) propaganda for war; (b) incitement of imminent violence; or (c) advocacy of hatred that is based on race, ethnicity, gender or religion, and that constitutes incitement to cause harm."

These restrictions are reasonable, at least if we interpret them appropriately. Thus, what is ominous about a reminder that a right to freedom of expression is not unlimited is that it is commonly used to segue into a justification of an unjustifiable limitation. That is exactly what Dr. Price does. He provides justifications that fail to meet any of the above criteria.

The justifications he provides are listed under three headings. One might presume that each heading would correspond to a different reason. However, he regularly slips from the titular reason to another. Irrespective of how they are classified his justifications fall short.

The first purported reason is that the lecture would provoke conflict on campus. It is not clear what Dr. Price means by "conflict". In elaborating, he refers to "protest and disruption" and then to the likelihood that the lecture will "divide and inflame the campus".

Many events at UCT are protested against, and yet that has appropriately not been thought good reason to cancel them. The prospect of protest is not a reason—even under the South African Constitution—to limit freedom of expression. Instead, protest, on condition that it is peaceful and does not prevent the expression of those against whom the protest is being held, is itself a form of expression, and thus to be protected.

Nor does the prospect of disruption indicate that the potentially disrupted expression exceeds moral (or legal) limits. Disruption might be indicative merely of the disrupters' intolerance, and thus one has to show on other grounds that the limits are exceeded. If one cannot show this then the disruption itself exceeds the limits of acceptable protest. UCT has proved very ineffective at prohibiting such forms of (illegal and immoral) protest, which makes the prohibition of (legally and morally) "protected" speech all the more curious.

Moreover, the campus is already divided—about all sorts of matters. If a view's likelihood to cause division were grounds for prohibiting it, then Dr. Price's own letter should be prohibited for it too will divide the campus. If his letter does not *inflame* the campus, that is only because the people who disagree with him on this matter are unlikely to cause a conflagration.

The second reason for disinviting Mr. Rose is "security". The Vice-Chancellor tells us that he and the University Executive are "convinced" that the lecture "would lead to vehement and possibly violent protest". The mere vehemence of the protest is beside the point, and thus we are left here with the conviction that there will *possibly* be violence.

There are two problems with this argument. First, we have been provided with no evidence that violence is likely to result from Mr. Rose's lecture (even though the Academic Freedom Committee specifically requested such evidence). Second, if a lecture results in violence, it does not follow that the lecture itself exceeds the moral or legal limits of freedom of expression. If it did follow, then those willing to respond violently will have a *de facto* veto on any ideas they dislike.

Put another way, there is a difference between "incitement" to violence and a violently intolerant response to a speaker or the expression of an idea. Speech constitutes incitement to violence when the speech aims to elicit the violent behaviour of those who then act violently. If the content of the speech does not seek violence, then it is not incitement. Your violent reaction to my expressing an idea does not mean that I have incited you. It means you have resorted to violence when you should not have done so.

The expectation of a violent reaction may sometimes require somebody to desist from expressing the idea that will be reacted to violently. However, in the rare cases that this is true, the reason for being silent is not that one's right to freedom of expression has exceeded its limits. Instead, one's right is being violated by those threatening violence. Perhaps Dr. Price and his colleagues have this position in mind. If that is the case, then they should unequivocally acknowledge that academic freedom and freedom of expression are being violated. Dr. Price does gesture at such a possibility, but it is obscured by his more extensive (but flawed) implied argument that Mr. Rose's lecture would fall foul of the Constitution's limits on freedom of expression.

When legitimate speech has to be curtailed because of a threat of violence, limiting the speech has to be seen as a temporary measure until the threat is neutralized. Dr. Price's attempt to defend the position of those opposed to Mr. Rose's speaking encourages rather than neutralizes that threat. Dr. Price's energies should be focused on condemning those who threaten violence rather than on veiled condemnations of Mr. Rose. He is thus ill-placed to invoke an "imminent violence" defence of the Executive's decision.

The third purported reason for disinviting Mr. Rose is that bringing him to campus "might retard rather than advance academic freedom on campus". Here Dr. Price's "doublespeak" reaches full-throttle. He wishes to restrict academic freedom in order to advance it.

He says that we "know that many within our universities don't feel safe to engage, which undermines the spirit of mutual tolerance and understanding". He asserts that this is "a deeply worrying situation which all adherents of academic freedom should find disconcerting, and ultimately unacceptable". However, he asks rhetorically whether progress will be made "by inviting somebody who represents a provocatively... divisive view". Because the Academic Freedom Committee's brief is to defend academic freedom on campus, he implies that in sticking to its invitation to Mr. Rose it is in breach of its brief.

Dr. Price is not explicit about who "feel unsafe to engage". It is unlikely to be campus revolutionaries and those who will resort to violence, for their very actions suggest that they feel very safe. It is much more likely that Dr. Price is referring to campus liberals who have either been cowering or, if outspoken, under constant attack—without a public word of support from the University Executive. (If Dr. Price is referring to this group, then the fact that he does not identify them as such is another indication of just how politically dangerous it has become to express sympathy with them.)

Thus, it seems that we are being told that we must restrict the speech of those serious about freedom of speech in order to protect those same people's freedom of speech. That is exactly the wrong response. Instead, the University should be standing firm on freedom of speech and teaching those who do not already know that this value extends (most crucially) to people with provocative and even divisive views.

There is a fourth reason running, as a thread, through Dr. Price's argument for disinviting Mr. Rose. This takes the form of impugning Mr. Rose, although in a slippery way. Thus, Dr. Price *refers* to accusations of bias and bigotry that are buttressed by the claim that "the *Jyllands-Posten* had previously refused to publish cartoons that mocked Christ, on the grounds that this would offend its readers, and also said that it would not publish cartoons about the Holocaust." In fact, the *Jyllands-Posten* has published several cartoons ridiculing Jesus. It has also published anti-semitic and Holocaust-mocking cartoons—not because it endorsed them, but so that their readers could see for themselves what, for example, was being published in the Arab and Iranian press. Mr. Rose is at pains to emphasize that publication does not constitute endorsement.

Dr. Price also says that "Mr. Rose is regarded by many around the world as right wing, Islamophobic, someone whose statements have been deliberately provocative, insulting and possibly amount to hate speech." Dr. Price quickly adds that "[n]o doubt all these claims can be contested." This is exactly why it is not sufficient to trot out those accusations as a basis for disinviting. For example, there are those who have said that Edward Said, who in 1991 gave the TB Davie lecture without disruption, was an anti-semite and terrorist sympathizer. It is easy to make such accusations but harder to make them stick. Anybody wanting to *disinvite* a speaker because they are not a suitable "chosen champion of the University of Cape Town to deliver its symbolic and prestigious TB Davie public lecture on academic freedom" will have to make the accusations stick. In fact, the accusations against Mr. Rose, to which Dr. Price refers, are utterly groundless. Mr. Rose's commitment of freedom of expression is a deeply principled one and has resulted in his defending the anti-democratic speech of fundamentalist Muslims.[3]

Almost all of the arguments that Dr. Price musters could be advanced, *mutatis mutandis*, against giving a platform for the many Israel-bashers who speak on campus. These speakers are typically selective in their moral outrage, cause division and hostility between different groups, and risk "diminishing, rather than bolstering, the opportunities for proper and mutually respectful intellectual and institutional engagement". Moreover, they occur against a background of millennia of anti-semitism. This is not to say that anti-Israel speakers should be banned from campus, but rather that the selective application of the arguments to some speakers is revealing.

The one argument that does not apply to anti-Zionist speakers is the argument about violence. The University Executive have had grounds for confidence that campus Zionists will not engage in violent, disruptive protest. We can only hope that that remains the case and that other parties learn the bounds of acceptable protest. The University Executive should be helping them learn that rather than pandering.

The decision to disinvite Mr. Rose is not the only way in which freedom of expression has been limited recently at the University of Cape Town. It is, however, the most obvious and the least deniable example. During the Apartheid era, the torch of academic freedom was extinguished. It was only rekindled with the advent of democracy. It is now time to extinguish it again, and to keep it extinguished at least until Mr. Rose delivers the lecture he was invited to give.

Postscript

The Academic Freedom Committee's criticism of UCT Executive's decision to disinvite Mr. Rose was its last act. Its term of office came to an end shortly afterwards. When the committee was reconstituted for the next term of office, its members were (largely) either hostile to academic freedom or at least pliant in the face of such hostility. This explains why the reconstituted Academic Freedom Committee has not taken a stand against any of the subsequent violations of academic freedom at UCT. It also explains why proposals from members of the university to have Mr. Rose invited again were passed over. Instead, the new Academic Freedom

---

[3] Flemming Rose, 12th May 2016, "Denmark Sacrifices Free Speech in the Name of Fighting Terror", *Politico*, https://www.politico.eu/article/denmark-sacrifices-free-speech-in-the-name-of-fighting-terror-muslim-religion-europe-integration-imams/ (accessed 19 July 2016).

Committee invited the likes of Mahmood Mamdani who, in his "academic freedom" lecture, defended the disinvitation of Mr. Rose.[4] UCT has reached the point where its Academic Freedom lecture is used to justify restrictions on academic freedom.

---

[4]   For more on this see: David Benatar, 7th August 2017, "The Academic Freedom Farce at the University of Cape Town", *Index on Censorship*, https://www. indexoncensorship.org/2017/08/academic-freedom-farce-university-cape-town/; David Benatar, 10th October 2017, "Mahmood Mamdani Continues the Academic Freedom Farce", *Politicsweb*, http://www.politicsweb.co.za/opinion/uct-the-academic-freedom-farce-continues

Dorian Abbot[1]

MIT Abandons Its Mission

And Me[2]

ABSTRACT: I am a professor who just had a prestigious public science lecture at MIT cancelled because of an outrage mob on *Twitter*. My crime? Arguing for academic evaluations based on academic merit. This is the story of how a cancellation is carried out, why it should worry all of us, and what we can do to stop this dangerous trend.

TOPICS: censorship, deplatforming and job harassment; race, ethnicity.
****

I have been a professor in the Department of the Geophysical Sciences at the University of Chicago for the past 10 years. I work on topics ranging from climate change to the possibility of life on extrasolar planets using mathematics, physics and computer simulation.

I have never considered myself a political person. For example, a few days before an election I go to *ISideWith.com* and answer the policy questions, then I assign my vote using a weighted draw based on my overlap with the candidates. It's an efficient algorithm that works perfectly for a nerd like me.

But I started to get alarmed about five years ago as I noticed an increasing number of issues and viewpoints become impossible to discuss on campus. I mostly just wanted to do my science and not have anyone yell at me, and I thought that if I kept my mouth shut the problem would

[1] Geophysicist, Associate Professor at the University of Chicago, USA. Email: dorian.abbot@gmail.com
[2] First published by Bari Weiss's substack *Common Sense* on 5th October 2021, https://bariweiss.substack.com/p/mit-abandons-its-mission-and-me

eventually go away. I knew that speaking out would likely bring serious reputational and professional consequences. And, for a number of years, I just didn't think it was worth it.

But the street violence of the summer of 2020, some of which I witnessed personally in Chicago, and the justifications and dishonesty that accompanied it, convinced me that I could no longer remain silent in good conscience.

In the fall of 2020, I started advocating openly for academic freedom and merit-based evaluations. I recorded some short *Youtube* videos[3] in which I argued for the importance of treating each person as an individual worthy of dignity and respect. In an academic context, that means giving everyone a fair and equal opportunity when they apply for a position as well as allowing them to express their opinions openly, even if you disagree with them.

As a result, I was immediately targeted for cancellation,[4] primarily by a group of graduate students in my department. Whistleblowers later revealed[5] that the attack was partially planned and coordinated on the Ford Foundation Fellowship Program listserv by a graduate student in my department. (Please do not attack this person or any of the people who attacked me.)

That group of graduate students organized a letter of denunciation.[6] It claimed that I threatened the "safety and belonging of all under-represented groups within the department", and it was presented to my department chair. The letter demanded that my teaching and research be restricted in a way that would cripple my ability to function as a scientist. A strong statement[7] in support of faculty free expression by University of

---

3   Abbot, D.S., "My Perspective on the Controversial Events of 11/13/20–11/15/20", https://drive.google.com/file/d/1J_vf46R100Q84PBcScdoD0Z7Q VfKC7gy/view

4   Abbot, D.S., 5th February 2021, "'More Weight': An Academic's Guide to Surviving Campus Witch Hunts", *Quillette*, https://quillette.com/2021/02/05/more-weight-an-academics-guide-to-surviving-campus-witch-hunts/

5   "Whistleblower Emails Reveal Partisan Rot at Ford Foundation, that Gets 'Nonpartisan' Tax Perks", *Karlstack*, https://karlstack.substack.com/p/whistleblower-emails-reveal-partisan

6   Members of the Department of Geophysical Sciences Community at the University of Chicago, 20th Novermber 2020, Letter to the Department of the Geophysical Sciences Faculty, https://docs.google.com/document/d/1fCOez NmxmaeVLSirrYp9y2nzy7m9Yr-rgPulwW-eNDw/edit

7   Zimmer, R.J., 29th November 2020, "Statement on Faculty, Free Expression, and Diversity", Office of the President of the University of Chicago,

Chicago President Robert Zimmer put an end to that, and that is where things stood until the summer of 2021.

On 12th August, a colleague and I wrote an op-ed in *Newsweek*[8] in which we argued that Diversity, Inclusion and Equity (DIE) as it currently is implemented on campus "violates the ethical and legal principle of equal treatment" and "treats persons as merely means to an end, giving primacy to a statistic over the individuality of a human being". We proposed instead "an alternative framework called Merit, Fairness, and Equality (MFE) whereby university applicants are treated as individuals and evaluated through a rigorous and unbiased process based on their merit and qualifications alone". We noted that this would mean an end to legacy and athletic admission advantages, which significantly favour white applicants.

Shortly thereafter, my detractors developed a new strategy to try to isolate me and intimidate everyone else into silence: they argued on *Twitter* that I should not be invited to give science seminars at other universities and coordinated replacement speakers. This is an effective and increasingly common way to ratchet up the cost of dissenting because disseminating new work to colleagues is an important part of the scientific endeavour.

Sure enough, this strategy was employed when I was chosen to give the Carlson Lecture at MIT[9] — a major honour in my field. It is an annual public talk given to a large audience and my topic was "climate and the potential for life on other planets". On 22nd September, a new *Twitter* mob, composed of a group of MIT students, postdocs and recent alumni, demanded that I be uninvited.[10]

It worked. And quickly.

On 30th September the department chair at MIT called to tell me that they would be cancelling the Carlson Lecture this year in order to avoid controversy.

It's worth stating what happened again: a small group of ideologues mounted a *Twitter* campaign to cancel a distinguished science lecture at

---

https://president.uchicago.edu/from-the-president/announcements/112920-free-expression

8   Abbot, D.S. & Marinovic, I., 8th December 2021, "The Diversity Problem on Campus | Opinion", *Newsweek*, https://www.newsweek.com/diversity-problem-campus-opinion-1618419

9   "Upcoming Lecture: October 21 2021, 7pm, Hybrid — Location TBA", https://drive.google.com/file/d/13RjCdMbhrwH0EyyvYLq25NEpC83tvpTU/view

10 *Twitter* sample, https://drive.google.com/file/d/13Xd01jH1UAJ4yQ2Xt5py OFwjRcyIudOG/view

the Massachusetts Institute of Technology because they disagreed with some of the political positions the speaker had taken. And they were successful within eight days.

The fact that such stories have become an everyday feature of American life should do nothing to diminish how shocking they are, and how damaging they are to a free society. The fact that MIT, one of the greatest universities in the world, caved in so quickly will only encourage others to deploy this same tactic.

It has become fashionable in some circles to claim that "cancel culture is just holding people accountable." I challenge you to read the material that led to the attacks against me and find anything that would require me being held "accountable". What you will find instead is the writing of a man who takes his moral duty seriously and is trying to express his concerns strongly, but respectfully. You may agree with some of my positions and disagree with others, but in a free society they cannot be considered beyond the pale.

I view this episode as an example as well as a striking illustration of the threat woke ideology poses to our culture, our institutions and to our freedoms. I have consistently maintained that woke ideology is essentially totalitarian in nature: it attempts to corral the entirety of human existence into one narrow ideological viewpoint and to silence anyone who disagrees. I believe that these features ultimately derive from the ideology's abandonment of the principle of the inherent dignity of each human being. It is only possible to instrumentalize the individual in order to engineer group-based outcomes within a philosophical framework that has rejected this principle. Similarly, it is easy to justify silencing a dissenter if your ideology denies her individual dignity. Clearly, wokeism has not reached a terrible nadir of destruction yet, but the lesson of history is that we need to name and confront totalitarianisms before they cause disaster, while it is still possible to do so.

This issue is especially important to me because my wife and I are expecting our first child in January. We all need to decide what type of country we want our children to grow up in. Do we want a culture of fear and repression in which a small number of ideologues exert their power and cultural dominance to silence anyone who disagrees with them? Or do we want our children to enjoy truth-seeking discourse consisting of good-natured exchanges that are ultimately grounded in a spirit of epistemic humility?

If you want the latter, it's time to stand up and so say. It's time to say no to the mob, no to the cancellations. And it's time to be forthright about your true opinions.

This is not a partisan issue. Anyone who is interested in the pursuit of truth and in promoting a healthy and functioning society has a stake in this debate. Speaking out now may seem risky. But the cost of remaining silent is far steeper.

Thanks to Princeton Professor (and friend of Common Sense[11]) Robby George, Dorian Abbot's cancelled lecture will be hosted by the James Madison Program in American Ideals and Institutions[12] on the day it was scheduled to be given at MIT: October 21 at 4:30 PM EST. It will be free to the public via Zoom and you can register at this https://jmp.princeton.edu/events/climate-and-potential-life-other-planets. We hope you'll tune in.

***

By now we have run many pieces about the epidemic of groupthink and cowardice in higher education. Many of you are rightly wondering: what can I do? I asked Dorian for his advice. Here's what he recommended:

Administrators: Never give in to a mob. Rewarding bad behaviour encourages more of it. You, more than anyone else, have the power to put an end to cancel culture by simply ignoring demands made by a mob. Be aware that it's easy to gather a large number of signatures for just about anything by revving up a *Twitter* mob, and that many of the signatories of letters of denunciation may have felt intimidated into signing.

Faculty: Cancellation tactics work by isolating the target and fostering an atmosphere of fear. You can help by joining together with others committed to academic freedom. I recommend organizations like AFA,[13] FIRE,[14] Heterodox Academy[15] and ACTA.[16] If you are ever tempted to join a cancellation mob, remember that you could be the next one on the chopping block. Finally, get the Chicago Principles,[17] the gold standard

---

[11] Weiss, B., 12th January 2021, "The Great Unraveling", *Common Sense*, https://bariweiss.substack.com/p/the-great-unraveling

[12] James Madison Program in American Ideals and Institutions, Princeton University, https://jmp.princeton.edu/

[13] Academic Freedom Alliance, https://academicfreedom.org/

[14] Foundation for Individual Rights in Education, https://www.thefire.org/

[15] Heterodox Academy, https://heterodoxacademy.org/

[16] American Council of Trustees and Alumni, https://www.goacta.org/

[17] Free Expression, The Univeristy of Chicago, https://freeexpression.uchicago.edu/

for academic freedom, and a statement insisting on political neutrality of the university, like the Kalven report,[18] adopted on your campus.

Students: Don't participate in social media mobbings or sign letters of denunciation. Publicly encourage friends with dissenting viewpoints to speak out, whether you agree with them or not.

Parents: Take into consideration a university's commitment to academic freedom when you are helping your child decide which school to attend. Ask if the university has adopted the Chicago Principles. Consider the FIRE free speech rankings.[19] Tell university officials that this is something that is important to you.

Alumni Donors: Tell your alma mater that freedom of conscience, freedom of expression and academic freedom are supremely important to you. Ask what protections for free speech are in place and whether the school has endorsed the Chicago Principles. Make your gifts conditional. Stop giving if administrators do not robustly defend these principles.

Trustees: Hold the administrators you appoint responsible for upholding academic freedom. If they refuse, replace them.

Lawmakers: Add stipulations to funding for both public and private universities that require that academic freedom and political neutrality be strictly observed.

Citizens: Make sure your lawmakers know that you want the research you pay for to be untainted by ideology.

---

[18] The Kavlen Committee, November 1967, "Report on the University's Role in Political and Social Action", The University of Chicago, https://provost.uchicago.edu/reports/report-universitys-role-political-and-social-action

[19] FIRE (Foundation for Individual Rights in Education) free speech rankings, https://rankings.thefire.org/

Gerhard Amendt[1] and Tom Todd[2]

Denunciation as a Weapon of Censorship

ABSTRACT: In April of 2018 Dr. Gerhard Amendt organized an independent international scientific conference on family and domestic violence, sponsored by a private donor. Its aim was to introduce professionals in the field to the scarcely known decades of research that showed how domestic violence is a symmetrical phenomenon, perpetrated equally by both sexes. Massive protests by the student and LGBTQI community forced the organizers to hire expensive security personnel and ask for police protection to ensure the conference could proceed. The media and even political parties aided in denouncing and discrediting the conference.

TOPICS: censorship, deplatforming and job harassment; feminism and gender mainstreaming.
****

In Germany, as in so many other countries of the West, public debate on IPV (intimate partner violence) or domestic violence is still dominated today by the narrative: 90% of victims of domestic violence are women. This blame-and-shame assertion persists despite an overwhelming body of at least 30 years of academic research, clearly demonstrating that such violence is at least in half the cases bilateral and in the other half more frequently perpetrated by the female participant.

It was high time to publish some of this material in German. Consequently, Gerhard Amendt produced a translation of *Family Interventions*

---

[1] Professor emeritus of Gender and Generation Research, University of Bremen, Germany. Email: amendt@uni-bremen.de
[2] Conference organiser, independent campaigner, Hamburg, Germany. Email: info@sciencecensored.com

in Domestic Violence[3] and followed this up by organizing a conference[4] on the topic with internationally renowned researchers in April of 2018.

The troubles began before International Women's Day 2018, in Bockenheim — Frankfurt's once left-wing working-class district. Anybody going to their car found a pamphlet under its windscreen wipers. A note had been stuck to one of the buildings' front doors stating that a "homophobe" was running a publishing house there. This campaign was announced by the *Antifa* as a contribution to the worldwide Women's Day. The residents were not sure what to make of it.

Everything became more volatile when the publication *Merkurist Rhein-Main* began to report about a conference at the Frankfurt Goethe University organized by 'homophobes' at which, it was alleged, compulsory treatment for homosexuals was to be promoted. This assertion was quickly adopted by the Green Party. They claimed that Prof. Gerhard Amendt, the scientific director of the conference "Handling Conflicts without Violence", belonged to the circle of highly controversial "therapists of homosexuals" and that he described homosexuality as "perverse". This quickly escalated into a media tsunami. Local and nationwide newspapers such as the *Frankfurter Rundschau*, the *Frankfurter Allgemeine Zeitung*, the news and TV programme *Hessenschau*, the Social Democratic Party (SPD), the Lesbian and Gay Federation in Germany (LSDV), the Students' Union Executive Committee (ASTA) of Frankfurt University and several other media outlets — all proclaimed to know that Amendt was a "healer of gays", practised at an institute that propagated compulsory treatment of homosexuals or endeavoured to make their life harder in other ways. Without checking any of the facts, many of these organizations consequently demanded that the university cancel the rental contract for the conference.

In response, Amendt and Todd (co-organizer of the conference) issued a press release on the 28th March 2018 systematically rebutting the false claims about the conference. Amendt further demanded in an interview with the local TV website on 29th March 2018 that the Hesse state broadcaster desist from political denunciation. This convinced President Professor B. Wolf enough for her to refrain from calling for the conference to be cancelled.

---

3   *Family Interventions in Domestic Violence: A Handbook of Gender-Inclusive Theory and Treatment*, Editors: John Hamel & Tonia Nicholls, https://www.amazon. de/-/en/John-Hamel-LCSW-ebook/dp/B0084YQJYU/ref=sr_1_1

4   Congress "Handling Conflicts without Violence: Effective Means of Prevention. 13–15 April 2018, Frankfurt/Main, Germany", https://familyconflict. eu/en/

But that was not the end of it. We received a letter dated 28th March 2018 that threatened censorship of the conference (with the help of two unnamed people for whom anonymous tickets were requested). The president reserved the right "to cancel the event at any time should you [Professor Amendt] or your guest speakers' statements contradict our values", but took no action in the end. In any event, the letter was tantamount to admitting that she had been taken in by a canard.

The president had brought the university's own specific principles and values into play: "especially [those] of diversity and equality of the sexes and freedom of sexual self-determination". In other words, academic freedom and the freedom of expression were made conditional on adherence to a political agenda. Specific values thus replaced the guaranteed freedom of science and free speech. Although this is now nothing unusual at many universities, both in Germany and in the USA, the blunt threat of censorship was.

Meanwhile this has grown to become a worrisome trend. Gender-feminist ideology or critical race theory do not allow any criticism of diversity groups' grab for power. And they undermine rights guaranteed by the constitution. Demands were made for a woman's right to kill her violent husband to prevent her psychotic breakdown. Her subjective judgment alone would preclude any court decision and invalidate criminal liability for murder in self-defence. The case of John Bobbitt, whose wife cut off his penis in 1993 because of sexual dissatisfaction, is a drastic example. German feminists, too, celebrated it as female empowerment.

In view of the blatant threats against the conference, we preferred to react to the president's letter sarcastically. Given several years of preparation and the financial risk, we could not risk the conference failing. The president's written threat caused lawyers to shake their heads over its legal incompetence and illegal propositions and was met with dismay by the speakers from the USA, Israel and Britain.

The conference, in its preparatory phase as well in its proceedings, was never about homosexuality or compulsory therapy—and not even about violence in homosexual relationships where violence, especially among lesbians, is a major problem that is inadequately dealt with. Rather, it was the first attempt to move the debate about intimate partner violence from the realms of obscurity onto a solid footing of facts from international research. New evidence on domestic violence was to be presented by scientists specialized in relevant research. Research has now established that violence is committed equally by men and women, but not necessarily within each individual relationship. In some relationships, violence is initiated by the woman or the man alone. However, violence in relationships is always a mutual process and its dynamic involves on both sides' anger, disappointment, feelings of powerlessness and the mutual fear of losing control over the other — to name only the major psycho-dynamics that contribute to personal conflicts ending in violence. This can entail both verbal and physical injuries, which in turn can lead to further violence. Establishing the guilt in criminal proceedings of one or the other parties in cases of severe violence cannot cover up the need for both to work through the complex dynamics. Either they manage to cope by themselves, or they require external support. Only the most severe psychopathologies are an exception. That said, women have a higher chance of incurring severe injuries when men hit back because of their greater muscle power. Even though men and women hit each other with equal frequency, women incur more severe injuries in altercations due to their physical inferiority.

Acknowledgment of equally distributed violence is met in Germany still today by radical and even violent opposition — as the disruption of the conference demonstrated. Particularly the persistently hostile attitude of the German Federal Ministry of Family Affairs (BMFSFJ) towards men impedes such acknowledgment — all the more so as most media have for years been replicating allegations of the collective body of evil men with-out admitting the facts. Almost all journalists in this country refuse to acknowledge that the frequency of violent acts is symmetrically distributed in relationships. Government-financed research institutions adhere to an implicit order to deny international research results, and even domestic research results that do not fit the prejudice that only men are violent are suppressed and neither presented at scientific conferences nor published. Many researchers know this all too well. They fear sanctions through equality bureaucracies, gender studies and feminist groups who label men as culprits and aim to keep alive an either/or polarity: men are evil, women are good. Consequently, many hesitate to publish their research findings. Quite a few refrain completely from continuing their research in this political minefield. Especially political parties on the left battle tenaciously to keep international research findings out of the media and public TV. Those who do not succumb are in danger of being labelled as *homophobic, populist, anti-feminist, woman-hater* or *extreme rightist* and ultimately being cancelled.

At Frankfurt University, the demonization of the conference started with the president being taken in by fake news. The university's inadequate examination of the accusations and hostilities brought against the academic head of the conference served to fan the flames of his critics. Minorites that felt subjectively offended resorted to political sabotage. A false fire alarm set off by activists delayed the opening of the conference and another nightly alarm at the hotel hosting the speakers forced a temporary evacuation. The conference was able to continue only under massive police protection called in by the university and with the help of expensive security guards paid by the organizers.

Eventually, almost all the above-mentioned media and political parties signed a cease-and-desist declaration or had to accept a temporary injunction by the media chamber at the district court which subsequently was accepted as a final settlement. Lastly, the local Lesbian and Gay Federation in Germany (LSDV), Hesse, was deemed by the court to have violated Prof. Amendt's personality rights, thus rehabilitating him. All assertions were found to be unproven allegations and diatribes that violated his personality rights.

In this irrational search for those guilty and in need of punishment, it was not surprising to hear anti-Semitic reactions which were meant to deflect from any criticism of sexual minority groups. Whatever the confused motivation behind all of this, one email thread abruptly stated surprisingly:

> The speakers are for the most part Jews (at least Amendt, Dekel and Winstock).

This anti-Semitic attitude fell on fertile ground. This is all the more frightening as a university, whose duty to rationality forms the basis of its legitimation and productivity, renounced its ability to influence irrational reactions and instead descended into the murky waters of a mix of negligence, political correctness and collusion with demonstrators. Yet President Birgitta Wolf did not leave it at that. Several months after the conference, pieces of circumstantial evidence appeared that she intentionally stoked anti-Semitism in order to stop criticism of gender studies, diversity politics and extreme variants of gender-feminism.

Three months after the conference on 16th July 2018, Wolf—in her role as President of the Goethe University—vehemently attacked Amendt in the *Frankfurter Neue Presse*.[5] She questioned his status as an academic. She said the conference was at the "level of pub talk" and based on "insufficient science". She attempted to use her position as university president to destroy his reputation.

The interview was remarkable in that the issue was no longer the fake news reports alleging compulsive treatment of homosexuals, originally at the heart of the media tsunami. Suddenly, the central questions of the

---

5   https://familyconflict.eu/wp-content/uploads/Frankfurter_Neue_Presse_16Juli2018.pdf

conference had become the focus, *viz.* how often do men and how often do women exert physical violence? How can the generational replication of parental violence be avoided? What traumatizing consequences for children arise from witnessing parental violence? Which methods applied in the USA and Israel could render our public health policies more efficient? Answers to these questions could put an end to revolving-door counselling and replace it with evidence-based methods. These are all questions whose answers are decisive not only for establishing whether efficient help for violent partners can be provided but also whether a responsible public health policy against interpersonal violence ought to be developed.

In order to further thwart this debate, the president dismissed the conference as *pub talk*. This is remarkably courageous for someone who did not attend the conference and who, as a business economist, has at best only a layman's knowledge of the matter.

What is the source of this strange partiality with which she violated a public institution's obligation to neutrality? Apparently, she slipped as president of the university into the role of speaker for those who seek to deny the socio-political relevance of violent conflict in relationships and families. Significantly, in so doing she toes the line of the German Federal Ministry for Family Affairs (BMFSFJ), which is the major sponsor of research projects at several institutes and controls their field of work. Recipients of grants are the Robert Koch Institute (RKI), the Deutsches Jugendinstitut (DJI), Deutsche Arbeitsgemeinschaft für Jugend- und Eheberatung (DAJEB) with almost 16,000 counselling centres, most of the gender study departments and quite a few women's shelters. They all reject the notion of symmetrically distributed violence as the empirical basis for preventive and curative intervention. Instead, this insight is viewed as an attack on women and as recrimination. The price for this denial of reality is high as it fails to contribute anything to the reduction of violence. Rather, it encourages intergenerational perpetuity. Men and women are being denied the assistance that would help them and their children to be spared the shattering experience of violent episodes.

The conference stood for the breakthrough of important research findings that could enable more efficient public health policies. It not only focused on research findings and new intervention methods, but also questioned the ideology and the political model of a society polarized by gender identity.

As an alternative to the prevailing polarization model, the relationships between men and women are increasingly accessible to research and helpful intervention. It will become increasingly difficult for the organizations mentioned above to suppress this alternative. This will expose their limited relevance for the organization of gender relations and show that in the long run research findings cannot be suppressed. By attacking critical research findings with accusations of homophobia or by the president of the university accusing Amendt of propagating "anti-Semitism and racism", nobody is going to prevent growing enlightenment. This, however, seems to have been Wolf's explicit intent. This was not the only occasion on which she demonstrated her fickle attitude towards academic freedom. So it came as no surprise that she was not re-elected as university president.

In the end, we see the ongoing battle between polarized gender politics that pit men and women against each other as a historical substitute for the conflict of labour and capital, on the one hand, and the struggle to assert evidence-based research on the other. For as long as federal policy continues to endorse female victimology, we will fail to implement strategies of conflict resolution that empower couples to jointly overcome violent outcomes in their relationships.

Peter Boghossian[1]

My University Sacrificed Ideas for Ideology
So Today I Quit[2]

ABSTRACT: Boghossian was assistant professor of philosophy at Portland State University for ten years. In September of 2021 he resigned his position. In this letter to the Provost at Portland State he details the reasons. He sought to create the conditions for rigorous thought in his courses, to help students gain the tools to hunt and furrow for their own conclusions. He describes how, despite this attempt to provide impartial courses, his work was constantly sabotaged, thus making it impossible for him to continue.

TOPICS: censorship, deplatforming and job harassment; race, ethnicity.
****

Dear Provost Susan Jeffords,

I'm writing to you today to resign as assistant professor of philosophy at Portland State University.

Over the last decade, it has been my privilege to teach at the university. My specialties are critical thinking, ethics and the Socratic method, and I teach classes like Science and Pseudoscience and The

---

[1] Philosopher and pedagogist, Assistant Professor of Philosophy at Portland State University for over 10 years, later resigning from that university for limiting free speech, US. Email: erisapple@protonmail.com

[2] First published by Bari Weiss's substack *Common Sense* on 8th September 2021, https://bariweiss.substack.com/p/my-university-sacrificed-ideas-for

Philosophy of Education. But in addition to exploring classic philosophers and traditional texts, I've invited a wide range of guest lecturers to address my classes, from Flat-Earthers to Christian apologists to global climate sceptics to Occupy Wall Street advocates. I'm proud of my work.

I invited those speakers not because I agreed with their worldviews, but primarily because I didn't. From those messy and difficult conversations, I've seen the best of what our students can achieve: questioning beliefs while respecting believers; staying even-tempered in challenging circumstances; and even changing their minds.

I never once believed — nor do I now — that the purpose of instruction was to lead my students to a particular conclusion. Rather, I sought to create the conditions for rigorous thought; to help them gain the tools to hunt and furrow for their own conclusions. This is why I became a teacher and why I love teaching.

But brick by brick, the university has made this kind of intellectual exploration impossible. It has transformed a bastion of free inquiry into a Social Justice factory whose only inputs were race, gender and victim-hood, and whose only outputs were grievance and division.

Students at Portland State are not being taught to think. Rather, they are being trained to mimic the moral certainty of ideologues. Faculty and administrators have abdicated[3] the university's truth-seeking mission and instead drive intolerance of divergent beliefs and opinions. This has created a culture of offence where students are now afraid[4] to speak openly and honestly.

I noticed signs of the illiberalism that has now fully swallowed the academy quite early during my time at Portland State. I witnessed students refusing to engage with different points of view. Questions from faculty at diversity trainings that challenged approved narratives were instantly dismissed. Those who asked for evidence to justify new institutional policies were accused of microaggressions. And professors were accused of bigotry for assigning canonical texts written by philosophers who happened to have been European and male.

At first, I didn't realize how systemic this was and I believed I could question this new culture. So I began asking questions. What is the evidence that trigger warnings and safe spaces contribute to student

---

[3]   FIRE (Foundation for Individual Rights in Education), 29th January 2020, "10 Worst Colleges for Free Speech: 2020", *The FIRE,* https://www.thefire.org/10-worst-colleges-for-free-speech-2020/

[4]   New Discourses channel, 16th March 2020, "The Social Justice Agenda: A Reverse Q&A at Portland State University", *Youtube,* https://www.youtube.com/watch?v=uwNO1PeehWc

learning? Why should racial consciousness be *the* lens through which we view our role as educators? How did we decide that "cultural appropriation" is immoral?

Unlike my colleagues, I asked these questions out loud and in public.

I decided to study the new values that were engulfing Portland State and so many other educational institutions—values that sound wonderful, like diversity, equity and inclusion, but might actually be just the opposite. The more I read the primary source material[5] produced by critical theorists, the more I suspected that their conclusions reflected the postulates of an ideology, not insights based on evidence.

I began networking with student groups[6] who had similar concerns and brought in speakers to explore these subjects from a critical perspective. And it became increasingly clear to me that the incidents of illiberalism I had witnessed over the years were not just isolated events, but part of an institution-wide problem.

The more I spoke out about these issues, the more retaliation I faced.

Early in the 2016–17 academic year, a former student complained about me and the university initiated a Title IX investigation. (Title IX investigations are a part of federal law[7] designed to protect "people from discrimination based on sex in education programs or activities that receive federal financial assistance".) My accuser, a white male, made a slew of baseless accusations against me, which university confidentiality rules unfortunately prohibit me from discussing further. What I can share is that students of mine who were interviewed during the process told me the Title IX investigator asked them if they knew anything about me beating my wife and children. This horrifying accusation soon became a widespread rumour.

With Title IX investigations there is no due process, so I didn't have access to the particular accusations, the ability to confront my accuser, and I had no opportunity to defend myself. Finally, the results of the investigation were revealed in December 2017. Here are the last two sentences of the report: "Global Diversity & Inclusion finds there is insufficient evidence that Boghossian violated PSU's Prohibited

---

5   Delgado, R., Stefancic, J. & Harris, A., 2017, *Critical Race Theory: An Introduction*, 3rd ed., New York: NYU Press.

6   Freethinkers of Portland State University, *Facebook*, https://www.facebook.com/groups/FreethinkersPSU/

7   Office of Civil Rights, August 2021, "Title IX and Sex Discrimination", U.S. Department of Education, https://www2.ed.gov/about/offices/list/ocr/docs/tix_dis.html

Discrimination & Harassment policy. GDI recommends Boghossian receive coaching."

Not only was there no apology for the false accusations, but the investigator also told me that in the future I was not allowed to render my opinion about "protected classes" or teach in such a way that my opinion about protected classes could be known—a bizarre conclusion to absurd charges. Universities can enforce ideological conformity just through the threat of these investigations.

I eventually became convinced that corrupted bodies of scholarship were responsible for justifying radical departures from the traditional role of liberal arts schools and basic civility on campus. There was an urgent need to demonstrate that morally fashionable papers—no matter how absurd—could be published. I believed then that if I exposed the theoretical flaws of this body of literature, I could help the university community avoid building edifices on such shaky ground.

So, in 2017, I co-published an intentionally garbled peer-reviewed paper that took aim at the new orthodoxy. Its title: "The Conceptual Penis as a Social Construct."[8] This example of pseudo-scholarship, which was published in *Cogent Social Sciences*, argued that penises were products of the human mind and responsible for climate change. Immediately thereafter, I revealed the article as a hoax designed to shed light on the flaws of the peer-review and academic publishing systems.

Shortly thereafter, swastikas in the bathroom[9] with my name under them began appearing in two bathrooms near the philosophy department. They also occasionally showed up on my office door, in one instance accompanied by bags of feces. Our university remained silent. When it acted, it was against me, not the perpetrators.

I continued to believe, perhaps naïvely, that if I exposed the flawed thinking on which Portland State's new values were based, I could shake the university from its madness. In 2018 I co-published a series[10] of absurd or morally repugnant peer-reviewed articles[11] in journals that focused on

---

8 Lindsay, J. & Boyle, P., 2017, *Cogent Social Sciences*, **3**: 1330439, https://www.skeptic.com/downloads/conceptual-penis/23311886.2017.1330439.pdf
9 "Peter Boghosian is a secret nazi", swastika in a bathroom, https://peterboghossian.com/wp-content/uploads/2021/08/fot1.jpg
10 Lindsay, J.A., Boghossian, P. & Pluckrose, H., 2nd October 2018, "Academic Grievance Studies and the Corruption of Scholarship", *Areo Magazine*, https://areomagazine.com/2018/10/02/academic-grievance-studies-and-the-corruption-of-scholarship/. See it in a chapter of this book.
11 Nayna, M., 3rd October 2018, "The Grievance Studies Affair—REVEALED", *Youtube*, https://www.youtube.com/watch?v=kVk9a5Jcd1k

issues of race and gender. In one of them we argued[12] that there was an epidemic of dog rape at dog parks and proposed that we leash men the way we leash dogs. Our purpose was to show that certain kinds of "scholarship" are based not on finding truth but on advancing social grievances. This worldview is not scientific, and it is not rigorous.

Administrators and faculty were so angered by the papers that they published an anonymous piece in the student paper[13] and Portland State filed formal charges[14] against me. Their accusation? "Research misconduct" based on the absurd premise that the journal editors who accepted our intentionally deranged articles were "human subjects". I was found guilty of not receiving approval to experiment on human subjects.

Meanwhile, ideological intolerance continued to grow at Portland State. In March 2018, a tenured professor disrupted[15] a public discussion I was holding with author Christina Hoff Sommers and evolutionary biologists Bret Weinstein and Heather Heying. In June 2018, someone triggered the fire alarm[16] during my conversation with popular cultural critic Carl Benjamin. In October 2018, an activist pulled out the speaker wires[17] to interrupt a panel with former Google engineer James Damore. The university did nothing to stop or address this behaviour. No one was punished or disciplined.

For me, the years that followed were marked by continued harassment. I'd find flyers[18] around campus of me with a Pinocchio nose. I was spit on and threatened by passersby while walking to class. I was

---

12   Editors and Publishers of Gender, Place & Culture, 2020, "Statement of Retraction: Human Reactions to Rape Culture and Queer Performativity at Urban Dog Parks in Portland, Oregon", *Gender, Place & Culture*, **27**:2, 307–326, https://www.tandfonline.com/doi/full/10.1080/0966369X.2018.1475346

13   Portland State University, 12th November 2018, "PSU Collective Releases Letter to Students Attacking Peter Boghossian", *Youtube*, https://www.youtube.com/watch?v=kG3QYbDeZso

14   Shibley, R., 8th January 2019, "'Sokal Squared' Hoax Paper Prof Facing Discipline for Not Having Research Reviewed by Institutional Review Board", *The FIRE*, https://www.thefire.org/sokal-squared-hoax-paper-prof-facing-discipline-for-not-having-research-reviewed-by-institutional-review-board/

15   Ngo, A., 5th March 2018, "Gender Studies Critic Shuts Down Heckler at Portland State", *Youtube*, https://www.youtube.com/watch?v=jeAXG3OLzoc

16   Ngo, A., 1st June 2018, "Fire Alarm Pulled at Sargon of Akkad PSU Event", *Youtube*, https://www.youtube.com/watch?v=YPyyvK_4mpg

17   Portland State University, 15th October 2018, "James Damore, Helen Pluckrose and The Second Culture", *Youtube*, https://www.youtube.com/watch?v=87e1aXxruTo

18   "PSU Freethinkers", https://peterboghossian.com/wp-content/uploads/2021/08/fot2.jpg

informed by students that my colleagues were telling them to avoid my classes. And, of course, I was subjected to more investigation.

I wish I could say that what I am describing hasn't taken a personal toll. But it has taken exactly the toll it was intended to: an increasingly intolerable working life and without the protection of tenure.

This isn't about me. This is about the kind of institutions we want[19] and the values we choose. Every idea that has advanced human freedom has always, and without fail, been initially condemned.[20] As individuals, we often seem incapable of remembering this lesson, but that is exactly what our institutions are for: to remind us that the freedom to question is our fundamental right.[21] Educational institutions should remind us that that right is also our duty.

Portland State University has failed in fulfilling this duty. In doing so it has failed not only its students but the public that supports it. While I am grateful for the opportunity to have taught at Portland State for over a decade, it has become clear to me that this institution is no place for people who intend to think freely and explore ideas.

This is not the outcome I wanted. But I feel morally obligated to make this choice. For ten years, I have taught my students the importance of living by your principles. One of mine is to defend our system of liberal education from those who seek to destroy it. Who would I be if I didn't?

Sincerely,

Peter Boghossian

---

[19] The Evergreen State College, 17th January 2019, "PART ONE: Bret Weinstein, Heather Heying & the Evergreen Equity Council", *Youtube*, https://www.youtube.com/watch?v=FH2WeWgcSMk

[20] "Galileo Galilei", *Stanford Encyclopedia of Philosophy*, https://plato.stanford.edu/entries/galileo/

[21] 24th March 2021, "Criticism of Ideas is Not Harassment", *The Chronicle of Higher Education*, https://www.chronicle.com/blogs/letters/criticism-of-ideas-is-not-harassment

Pedro Domingos[1]

Beating Back Cancel Culture

A Case Study from the Field of Artificial Intelligence?[2]

ABSTRACT: Fighting cancel culture isn't impossible. Here, useful principles are given for those seeking to combat cancel culture, and an example is shown in which a social justice bully in *Twitter* was defeated in her attempts to repress culture and expelled from the social net.

TOPICS: censorship, deplatforming and job harassment; general considerations on suppression of academic freedom.
****

It's easy to decry cancel culture, but hard to turn it back. Thankfully, recent developments in my area of academic specialty – artificial intelligence (AI) – show that fighting cancel culture isn't impossible. And as I explain below, the lessons that members of the AI community have learned in this regard can be generalized to other professional subcultures.

To understand the flash point at issue, it's necessary to delve briefly into how AI functions. In many cases, AI algorithms have partly replaced both formal and informal human decision-making systems that pick who gets hired or promoted within organizations. Financial institutions use AI

---

[1]   Professor Emeritus of computer science and engineering at the University of Washington, US. Email: pedrod@cs.washington.edu
[2]   Reprinted from *Quillete*, 27th January 2021, https://quillette.com/2021/01/27/beating-back-cancel-culture-a-case-study-from-the-field-of-artificial-intelligence/

to determine who gets a loan. And some police agencies use AI to antici-pate which neighbourhoods will be afflicted by crime. As such, there has been a great focus on ensuring that algorithms won't replicate their coders' implicit biases against, say, women or visible minorities. Citing[3] evidence that, for instance, "commercial face recognition systems have much higher error rates for dark-skinned women while having minimal errors on light skinned men", computer scientist Timnit Gebru, formerly[4] the co-lead of Google's ethical AI team, has argued that AI systems are contaminated by the biases of the mostly white male programmers that created them. In a paper authored with colleagues at Google and my university, she warned[5] that large language-based AI systems in particu-lar encourage a "hegemonic worldview" that serves to perpetuate hate speech and bigotry.

These issues have also been taken up by the Conference on Neural Information Processing Systems[6] (NeurIPS), the leading conference in the AI community. As of this writing, the NeurIPS home page[7] is dominated by a statement attesting to the organizers' commitment to "principles of ethics, fairness, and inclusivity". This year, NeurIPS has started requiring paper authors to include a section describing the "broader impacts"[8] on society that the underlying science might present, no matter how obscurely technical the underlying content. There is also an ethics board to evaluate whether any paper runs afoul of such concerns. "Regardless of scientific quality or contribution," the organizers have announced,[9] "a submission may be rejected for ethical considerations, including methods,

---

3 Gebru, T., 2019, "Oxford Handbook on AI Ethics Book Chapter on Race and Gender", *arXiv.org*, https://arxiv.org/abs/1908.06165v1
4 Hao, K., 3rd December 2020, "A Leading AI Ethics Researcher Says She's Been Fired from Google", *MIT Technology Review*, https://www.technologyreview.com/2020/12/03/1013065/google-ai-ethics-lead-timnit-gebru-fired/
5 Bender, E.M., Gebru, T., McMillan-Major, A. & Shmitchell, S., 2021, "On the Dangers of Stochastic Parrots: Can Language Models Be Too Big?", *FAccT '21: Proceedings of the 2021 ACM Conference on Fairness, Accountability, and Trans-parency*, p. 610, http://faculty.washington.edu/ebender/papers/Stochastic_Parrots.pdf
6 Thirty-fifth Conference on Neural Information Processing Systems, 2021, https://nips.cc/
7 *Ibid.*
8 Thirty-fifth Conference on Neural Information Processing Systems, 2021, Schedule, https://nips.cc/Conferences/2020/Schedule?showEvent=16144
9 Thirty-fifth Conference on Neural Information Processing Systems, 2021, Schedule, Call for Papers, https://nips.cc/Conferences/2020/CallForPapers

applications, or data that create or reinforce unfair bias" (or, less controversially, "that have a primary purpose of harm or injury").

In early December, I used social media to push back[10] against this fairly obvious use of ideological litmus tests to limit what can and cannot get published. At first, I found plenty of support—as evidenced by the results of an (admittedly unscientific) *Twitter* survey. That was when a small mob of social-justice radicals—already well-known within the field —came after me, led by a California Institute of Technology academic who is also research director at a major tech company.

As so often happens in these confrontations, the discussion was derailed by hyperbolic accusations of racism. Naturally, the mob went after my university, and my own department distanced itself from my critique of the NeurIPS policy. In a matter of just a few days, submission protocols at an academic conference had attained the status of social-justice holy writ, with naysayers—myself foremost among them— denounced as heretics. The mob leader even wrote lengthy *Twitter* threads listing off the names of anyone who'd liked or retweeted my critiques of her position, suggesting they were all bigots.

But as the days passed, and it became clear who the real radicals were, something interesting happened. Many of the usually reticent moderates in our community began to speak up, and denounce the unhinged and ruthless tactics applied against me and my supporters. In the end, I suffered no professional consequences (at least not in any formal way). And the cancel crowd's ringleader even issued a public apology and promised to mend her ways. She is no longer on *Twitter*, and we're rid of the most vicious cancel-culture bully in the AI community. Topics that had been suppressed are now being freely discussed again on our forums. Dozens of computer-science faculty have even signed a letter to the Association for Computing Machinery (ACM),[11] our professional society, calling for an end to "the increasing use of repressive actions aimed at limiting the free and unfettered conduct of scientific research and debate".

It's a tale that illustrates a number of useful principles for those seeking to combat cancel culture. These include:

Find your friends. There's nothing worse than facing a mob alone. Build your network in advance, so that you don't have to cold-call free-speech advocates when a crisis already is upon you. Create relationships

---

[10] Pedro Domingos, 8th December 2020, *Twitter*, https://twitter.com/pmddomingos/status/1336187141366317056?s=20

[11] The Association for Computing Machinery, 8th January 2021, "An Open Letter to the Communications of the ACM", https://docs.google.com/document/d/1ptznKVsJgk7zJCjXKlZ2tl1Ui0KiKQUXfONcilDn2WI/edit

with people in your workplace and field who share your views. Find out whether there are unions or other groups that are responsible for protecting your rights, and find out what they can do to help if a mob ever comes after you. Join and support organizations such as Heterodox Academy,[12] the National Association of Scholars[13] and the Foundation for Individual Rights in Education[14] (FIRE). Connect with like-minded people on social media. Your friends may come to your aid publicly or privately. Both are good. Even just receiving words of encouragement from like-minded individuals can make a big difference when you're under attack.

Pick your battles. All workplaces and professional fields can present their share of dogmatists and unpleasant personalities. You can't take on all of them, and not all battles are worth fighting. Pick the ones with high symbolic value — which is to say, battles that act as proxies for some larger principle — and which you think you have a reasonable chance of winning. In my case, I knew that taking on a notorious bully in the AI community was worth it because her rout would send a message to imitators. I also knew we had an advantage going in, because this individual already had hurt and angered many people. Moreover, her position as research director at a prominent company made her more vulnerable than me.

Know what to expect. The cancel crowd has its own bullet-point playbook. And they'll respond aggressively to any symbolic act that threatens their status, or erodes the impression that they are the ones calling the shots. Remember that behind the social-justice veneer lies the brutal logic of power and ego. To maximize the pain you feel, they'll tag activist groups on social media to inflate their numbers and reach. They'll bombard every organization you're part of with demands to censure, discipline, disown, fire or expel you — often phrasing their appeals in the passive aggressive guise of "concern" and "disappointment". At other times, they will insult, taunt and threaten you in a manner resembling middle-school children having a recess meltdown. In my case, the ringleader called me "a full on misogynist and racist", "shameful bigot", "hypocrite", "clueless", "tone-deaf", "snowflake" and "soulless troll". She assailed my "privilege and patriarchy", "lack of basic empathy and ethics" and "zero self-awareness". She also questioned whether I'm really a human, and called on NeurIPS to ban me, and for my department to expunge me. Her goal, in short, was to ruin my life. The cancellers will

---

[12] Heterodox Academy, https://heterodoxacademy.org/
[13] National Academy of Scholars, https://www.nas.org/
[14] Foundation for Individual Rights in Education, https://www.thefire.org/

dig up anything they can from your past. And if they can't find anything, they'll make it up. This will all seem terrifying, but much less so if you realize that you're just the latest victim in what is basically a mechanical and dehumanizing process. Insofar as you don't actually get fired from your job or suffer some other equivalent setback, these are all just words, and they don't define who you are.

Don't back down. Don't apologize. Don't make clarifications, and don't try to appease the mob. All of these will only be taken as concessions, and embolden the mob to demand more. The real Achilles' Heel of the cancel crowd is its short attention span. Once they bully someone into submission, they move on to the next victim. It's a system designed for quick wins. If you don't back down, they'll raise the pitch as far as they can—but eventually they'll be at a loss for what to do next, and all but the most fanatical will lose interest. The few that remain, now bereft of their backup, are just what you need to teach all of them a lesson, as we did in my case.

Don't let them make it about you. You have the right to defend yourself when attacked, and it's only natural to do so. Fight sanctions against you through the appropriate channels. But focusing your efforts on your own actions, even if they are the subject of spurious accusations, is generally a mistake. That's because it changes the subject from the real underlying issues[15] to your own supposed failings—and that's what the cancel crowd wants, because it effectively forces you to fight for a draw instead of a win. The appropriate response to low attacks is to point out how low *they* are. For example, if someone threatens you with Title IX sex-discrimination proceedings[16] on the basis of alleged "sexism"—as they did in my case—don't bother dignifying this kind of ludicrous claim with a substantive rebuttal. Rather, just thank them for illustrating the misuse of Title IX to crush free speech, as I did.[17]

Hold the moral high ground. Never descend to the level of insults, taunts and *ad hominem* attacks, no matter how strong the temptation. Let the cancellers do it to their heart's content, and the onlookers will judge accordingly. In my confrontation with the AI cancel crowd, I was particularly helped by the fact that several of the ringleaders are (or call

---

[15] Pedro Domingos, 12th December 2020, *Twitter*, https://twitter.com/ pmddomingos/status/1337594183033389058?s=20

[16] Office for Civil Rights, August 2021, "Title IX and Sex Discrimination", *U.S. Department of Education*, https://www2.ed.gov/about/offices/list/ocr/docs/ tix_dis.html

[17] Pedro Domingos, 12th December 2020, *Twitter*, https://twitter.com/ pmddomingos/status/1337595958599667713?s=20

themselves) professional AI ethicists. Some of them are even well-known within their field. When they serially engaged in childish and unethical behaviour in full view of their colleagues, they did my job for me.

Mock them mercilessly. Fear is what keeps the silent majority from speaking up, and laughter is the best antidote. The cancellers take themselves extremely seriously, imagining themselves to be social-justice angels whose holy ends justify every imaginable means. Their sanctimonious spirit is a gift to you, if you call it out instead of playing along with its conceit.

Don't let their narrative outrun yours. Once a false narrative is entrenched, it's hard to overturn, no matter how many facts you have on your side. So while, as noted above, I generally would discourage you from focusing too much on defending your own actions, there should be some resource you can point to so that everyone can know the truth. Once you have established that resource—a blog post, a published article, a podcast, even a set of tweets or *Facebook* posts—point people to it where necessary, including your own professional contacts and potential allies. Keep it short, crisp and compelling so that it gets widely circulated and isn't thwarted by short attention spans. And keep the tone confident (and possibly even funny), so that it's clear who the real inhuman fanatics are.

Goad them into overreaching. The cancellers' overconfidence is your greatest asset, as I learned when the ringleader of the mob that came after me resorted to posting the above-referenced list of people whom she wanted cancelled, many of them junior researchers whose only crime was to have followed me or liked one of my tweets. This crossed a line for a lot of observers, and of course the people on the list itself were aghast. Word spread of the shocking behaviour. Even people on her side started turning against her.

Turn their weapons against them. You may find this to be the most controversial principle, but it's also arguably the most crucial—as the cancellers won't stop until they fear that they'll endure the same consequences that they seek to impose on others. In my case, I watched as investors and customers leaned on the ringleader's company to rein her in. Even companies that posture heavily in the area of social justice don't actually want to be stained by the disgraceful behaviour of mob leaders. Indeed, I have no doubt that it was an ultimatum from her employer that finally led the ringleader to stop her *Twitter* outbursts and apologize publicly to her victims, for all to see. Some will say that once we resort to this step we become as bad as the cancellers. But that's a false equivalence. The cancel crowd tries to ban people because of their views. We try to stop bullying—behaviour that is reprehensible regardless of ideology.

Use the courts. The courts can be your friend when confrontations with the cancel crowd can't be resolved through less formal and expensive means—for two reasons. One is that they invoke principles of due process, and look askance at show trials and kangaroo courts. They also tend to be less politically skewed than universities, tech firms and human resources departments. Even just the threat of a lawsuit can be enough to stop the cancellers. It worked for me when some of them crossed the line from insult to defamation. FIRE[18] and other pro-free-speech organizations employ lawyers whose job is to fight on your behalf. Oh, and universities hate lawsuits. Whether you end up suing or not, moreover, *always* keep records on the assumption that you will need documents to prove your case. It's easier to gather them at each step rather than after the fact.

Bring administrators around. Some administrators are themselves members of the cancel crowd, and will always be part of the problem until such time that they conclude that this attitude is no longer helpful to their own careers. But most are just decent people trying to do their job and find a path to safe harbour. And in this regard, it's actually useful to them when they can see pressure coming from both sides, not just one. Despite being bombarded with demands, my department ultimately took no action against me (besides dissociating itself from my positions)—in part, I think, because I helped them see the situation clearly, including what was really at stake and how much the department had to lose by doing the wrong thing.

Don't antagonize. Educate. Even many neutral onlookers who find cancel-culture tactics repellent dismiss the phenomenon as afflicting just a few privileged souls—acceptable collateral damage, as they see it, in the battle against patriarchy, white privilege and so forth. (They're just "false positives", as one MIT professor put it when he attempted[19] to dissuade people from signing our letter to ACM.) It's easy to get angry at these naïve enablers of the mob, but it's better to make them *aware*. Point them to resources such as the National Association of Scholars' database of

---

18   Foundation for Individual Rights in Education, https://www.thefire.org/
19   Karger, D., 3rd January 2021, "A Rebuttal to Some CS Academics' 'Free Speech' Open Letter to the ACM", *David Karger's blog*, https://david-karger.medium.com/a-rebuttal-to-some-cs-academics-free-speech-open-letter-to-the-acm-729ce1cb6caf

cancellations,[20] the *Canceled People* website[21] or *Quillette's Panics and Persecutions*.[22] Give them examples of cancellations of journalists,[23] tech workers[24] and even high-school students.[25] Patiently explain what they're missing (as I did in my response[26] to the above-referenced MIT professor).

Get the majority on your side. In the end, most cancellers can't be dissuaded in the short run: they've invested too much in their roles as inquisitors to give them up easily. The goal isn't to win them over — you won't — but rather to persuade the much larger number of people in the middle. Just because these people aren't vocal doesn't mean they aren't out there watching, reading, thinking.

Perhaps most importantly, *remember that most cancellation attempts end in failure*. It's hard to know that, however, because we seldom hear about the mobbings that fizzle out. Instead, the mob relies on its high-status wins to keep everyone in line. They enjoy the illusion that their movement is unstoppable, when in fact it becomes a subject of mockery as soon as a critical mass of people raise their voices against it.

And so even if you're never targeted by the mob, play your part in opposing its attacks. As Solzhenitsyn famously put it, one man who tells the truth can bring down a tyranny. Together, we can bring down cancel culture.

---

[20] Acevedo, D., 14th December 2021, "Tracking Cancel Culture in Higher Education", *National Association of Scholars*, https://www.nas.org/blogs/article/tracking-cancel-culture-in-higher-education

[21] *Canceled People Database*, https://www.canceledpeople.com/

[22] Quillette, 2021, *Panics and Persecutions – 20 Quillette Tales of Excommunication in the Digital Age*, London: Eyewear Publishing.

[23] Weiss, B., Resignation letter, *Bari Weiss blog*, https://www.bariweiss.com/resignation-letter

[24] "Google's Ideological Echo Chamber", *Wikipedia*, https://en.wikipedia.org/wiki/Google%27s_Ideological_Echo_Chamber

[25] Currier, J., 5th January 2021, "White Villa Duchesne Student and Parents Accuse School of Discrimination", *St. Louis Post-Dispatch*, https://www.stltoday.com/news/local/crime-and-courts/white-villa-duchesne-student-and-parents-accuse-school-of-discrimination/article_ff6417ce-d5dc-5083-9a38-426ec91c0302.html

[26] Domingo, P., 3rd January 2021, "Rebuttal of David Karger's Defense of Cancel Culture", *Pedro Domingos' blog*, https://pedromdd.medium.com/rebuttal-of-david-kargers-defense-of-cancel-culture-1780484d03ce

Part V.

General Considerations on Suppression of Academic Freedom

Civitas Research Team[1]

Academic Freedom in Our Universities

The Best and the Worst[2]

ABSTRACT: This report analyses over three years of campus censorship (January 2017–August 2020), examining the multiple policies and actions of all the 137 registered UK universities. Building on previous research, this study employs a unique approach, methodology and data to measure restrictions on free speech. In all cases, our policy analysis of each university is summarized by assessing 22 variables and providing a censorship score. This new study has found, *inter alia*, that 48 of the universities (35%) — including the three highest ranked UK universities — are performing badly on free speech. A further 70 of the universities (51%) are not performing as well as they should.

TOPICS: general considerations on suppression of academic freedom; censorship, deplatforming and job harassment; diversity, inclusion and equity programmes
****

Objective

This report has carried out an analysis of over three years of campus censorship (2017–2020), examining the policies and actions of all 137

---

[1] Institute for the Study of Civil Society, London, UK. Website: https://www. civitas.org.uk/; Email: jim.mcconalogue@civitas.org.uk
[2] The full text of the report is available at: https://www.civitas.org.uk/content/ files/Academic-Freedom-in-Our-Universities.pdf, partially reprinted here.

registered UK universities[3] – including their students' unions – to provide a detailed understanding of the state of free speech across UK academia. *Civitas* is grateful to the Nigel Vinson Charitable Trust for its support for this research.

This study employs a new and unique approach, methodology and data to measure restrictions on free speech. We would like to acknowledge previous studies on the separate *Free Speech University Rankings* by online magazine *Spiked* over four years (2015-2018), along with all its team, who deserve clear credit for the UK's first annual nationwide analysis of campus censorship.

Assessment

In all cases, our policy analysis of each university is summarized by assessing 22 variables, including: controversies surrounding free speech censorship on or near campus; external pressure group involvement and university society groups in curbing free speech; the restrictive nature of the internal Policy on Free Speech on free speech itself; extreme curbs on free speech listed in harassment policies; through to the number of offensive "speech acts" listed in student and stall Codes of Conduct. The number of restrictions imposed by specific university actions and policies are collated and aggregated into an overall **censorship score** for each university. For better understanding, each score is then provided with a category:

- Those universities which are graded as between 1 and 150 fall into the **MOST FRIENDLY** category;
- Those scoring between 151 and 300 fall into a **MODERATELY RESTRICTIVE** category and;
- Those scoring 301 or more come under the **MOST RESTRICTIVE** category.

Those three categories that we gave to free speech on campuses: MOST FRIENDLY, MODERATELY RESTRICTIVE or MOST RESTRICTIVE. We assess the policies and reported free speech restrictions imposed jointly by university and student unions in their policies and register an individual censorship score for each university.

---

[3]   Members of the representative organization Universities UK as of June 2020. Data cover the period between January 2017 through to August 2020. All data were collated between March and August 2020.

It is intended that the findings summarized here—presented as a data table[4]—can help universities to compare experiences on their approaches to free speech and help academics, students and the public to observe the scale of censorship and differences in the treatment of free speech across UK academia. It analyses both the practical curbs on free speech within universities whilst also presenting a distinct focus on policies which can be used to explain and justify restrictions. The high level of restrictions strongly suggest that UK universities should adopt a US-style "Chicago statement" on free speech or a version of the Academics for Academic Freedom (AFAF) statement, or, if not, directly reaffirm the existing free speech commitments in section 43 (No. 2) of the 1986 Education Act (see Appendix). All UK universities should now sign up to a written statement to protect free speech. The magnitude of restrictions in policies merits further Government-level and parliamentary Select Committee investigation. Little research work has genuinely reflected on the state of the "auto-censor" culture imposed by highly vocal, sometimes aggressive activist groups or student networks in modern campus life.

Key Findings

- **MOST FRIENDLY:** 19 of the universities (14%) have allowed some restrictions to free speech in its actions and regular policies but **not** at the level which might warrant external intervention.
- **MODERATELY RESTRICTIVE:** 70 of the universities (51%) are not performing as well as they should and the Office for Students (OfS) should tell the university how it could improve.
- **MOST RESTRICTIVE:** 48 of the universities (35%)—including the three highest ranked UK universities—are performing badly on free speech and the government should take some action to resolve the issues by a change of policy and legislation.

Below, we summarize the findings by reporting the defining features of the MOST RESTRICTIVE, MODERATELY RESTRICTIVE and MOST FRIENDLY categories and what it means for censoring free speech in the 137 UK universities.

---

[4] Academic Freedom database, *Civitas*, http://civitas.org.uk/content/files/ACADEMIC-FREEDOM.xlsx

	MOST RESTRICTIVE	MODERATELY RESTRICTIVE	MOST FRIENDLY
Censorship score	301 or higher	151–300	1–150
No. of universities	48 (35%)	70 (51%)	19 (14%)
Example universities	University of St Andrews, University of Cambridge, University of Oxford, University of London, University of Liverpool, University of Sheffield, University College London, University of Exeter, Imperial College London, Nottingham Trent University, Oxford Brookes University	University of Manchester, University of Sussex, Durham University, Queen's University Belfast, King's College London, University of Edinburgh, University of Birmingham, Cardiff University, Newcastle University, University of Essex, LSE, SOAS, University of Bristol, University of Kent	University of Hull, Aberystwyth University, University of York, Lancaster University, London Business School, Manchester Metropolitan University, University of Buckingham, University of Northampton
Free speech curbed by a perceived transphobic episode	65%	47%	36%
No. universities in which curbs to free speech are due to external pressure groups	33%	21%	5%
No. universities curbed free speech due to a "cancel culture" of open letters/petitions	69%	48%	47%
No. universities in which curbs to free speech are due to social media activism	58%	40%	16%
Universities with cases of disinvitation or no platforming	16%	20%	0%
Universities with publicly available (yet restrictive) Free Speech Policy	73%	74%	58%
Average number of restrictions imposed on free speech in Free Speech Policy	12	10	5
Average number of restrictions imposed on speech by policy on bullying and harassment	182	90	15

	MOST RESTRICTIVE	MODERATELY RESTRICTIVE	MOST FRIENDLY
Censorship score	301 or higher	151–300	1–150
No. of universities	48 (35%)	70 (51%)	19 (14%)
Universities with IT Regulations or social media policy with over 50 levels of restriction	60%	30%	21%
Average number of restrictions imposed by "Equal Opportunities policy"	27	22	18
Universities listing 30+ restrictions in their student and stall Codes of Conduct	81%	64%	26%
Universities with a Transgender policy defining gender offensive speech terms/pronouns	65%	63%	11%
Harassment policies defining gender offensive speech	52%	26%	5%
Universities without an External Speaker policy imposing restrictions	71%	51%	84%

Broad Findings across
UK University Landscape

When looking at all universities across the UK, we find overall:

- 93 of all 137 (68%) university institutions experienced a controversy relating to censorship of free speech.
- Of the "Russell Group" of world-class universities, a concerning 42% were recorded overall as receiving the MOST RESTRICTIVE censorship score; over half (54%) came in with a MODERATELY RESTRICTIVE censorship score, while just one registered with a MOST FRIENDLY score.
- Over half (53%) of all 137 universities experienced alleged "transphobic" episodes that led to demands for censoring speech. To draw a comparison, just 7% of all universities experienced reported "Islamophobic" issues that led to active demands for censoring of speech or written material.

- Just under a quarter (23%) of all universities experienced episodes that led to demands for censoring speech due to the intervention of external pressure groups. Similarly, just under a quarter (24%) of the universities experienced episodes of free speech restrictions due to the intervention of their own university societies.
- Over half (55%) of all universities experienced a "cancel culture" of open letters or petitions which pushed for the restriction of views of stall, students or visiting speakers on campus.
- 50 of the 137 universities (37%) experienced incidents that led to demands for censorship of speech or written material due to social media activism.
- 22 institutions have been involved in direct instances of disinvitation and "no platforming" of external speakers. On the counterterror Prevent strategy specifically, only one reported case was found of event cancellation, or disinvitation of an external speaker — or even of radical students or student societies on campus prevented from speaking — due directly to those counter-terror legislation duties.
- 98 of the 137 universities (72%) have taken steps to introduce a documented policy on free speech/expression that has by itself imposed a restrictive set of conditions on free speech. Overall, 45 universities had policies which placed 10 or more levels of restrictions on free speech in their own free speech document. This included the perceived offence or insult based on age or gender identity and, for example, sets out the right to debar speakers/ organizations where it believes that their presence on campus is "not conducive to good order" or might "offend the principles of scholarly inquiry".
- 89% of universities have a policy on bullying and harassment in which speech can be curbed, for example, by claims to personal offence, unwanted conduct, or conduct which is reported as "insulting", even in cases where it would "undermine" an individual or create an "offensive environment". Harassment policies in universities can stifle students in their discourse, including through the perceived "intrusive questioning" of a person's life, insulting jokes, patronizing language, or unwanted conduct or perceived offensive environments. Overall, 68 universities (50%)

had harassment policies placing over 100 levels of practical restrictions on free speech.

- 93% of universities host IT Regulations or social media policy in which written text is limited. A common example is a restriction on sending content which is deemed offensive in reference to some-one's gender reassignment, sexual orientation, political beliefs, national origin or maternity. Overall, 115 universities (84%) had IT policies placing over 20 levels of practical restrictions on free speech.
- 81% of universities have an "Equal Opportunities Policy" which is restrictive of speech deemed offensive.
- Approximately 87% of all the 137 UK universities do not have a current "safe space" policy — well-publicized spaces which restricted free speech on campuses — which suggests that the policies devised by the previous government to remove those restrictions can have a beneficial effect when responding to free speech issues.
- 93% of universities list in their student and stall Code of Conduct a series of unacceptable speech acts. Overall, 83 of 137 universities (64%) had Codes of Conduct placing over 30 levels of practical restrictions on free speech.
- 58% of universities have a policy for Transgender Persons defining the terms for referencing transgender persons — while it was found that some 31% had bullying and harassment policies defining gender offensive speech.
- In 22 universities, there was at least one reported allegation of hate crime in relation to speech acts.
- Over 50 institutions now host a University External Speaker Policy — in most cases, designed to prevent disinvitation or no plat-forming of invited speakers — which have themselves become a cause for curbing free speech. For example, of some concern in those universities, undermining community relations, unacceptable risk to well-being or challenge to equality criteria apparently consti-tutes an acceptable restriction. Others found reasons for curbing free speech where it might "spread intolerance" or discriminate on grounds of sex or gender reassignment. Certain restrictions could be placed on speakers who are political, religious extremists or

where it was claimed to be against fascism based on what it perceived as extremism, or prejudice.

José Luis González Quirós[1] and
David Díaz Pardo de Vera[2]

The Pleasure of Orthodoxy

ABSTRACT: Human beings find it difficult to distinguish reality from fantasy. We find it hard to understand that facts which resist formalization are very difficult to communicate, even in the academic world where authority and schools of thought play a fundamental role. We are amazed that others do not share "obvious truths". Faced with this impediment, it has been common to create groups of devotees and to orchestrate intense campaigns that are nothing more than expressions of force. There is always a risk that these groups will try to gain power and impose their views, indulging in what might be called the pleasure of orthodoxy: to speak in the name of truth.

TOPICS: general considerations on suppression of academic freedom; feminism and gender mainstreaming.
****

The invention of the *academic world*, of a secular *collegium invisibile* whose members are those who are knowledgeable about something, unaccountable to external bodies, was an extraordinary achievement of civilization. It made freedom of thought, the most fundamental form of freedom we may posit, the first rule of an intellectual community based on the exchange of texts between thinkers, first in the shape of letters, later through books, journals, conferences and multifarious other channels and activities.

---

[1] Professor Emeritus of Philosophy, Universidad "Rey Juan Carlos I", Madrid, Spain. Email: jlgonzalezquiros@gmail.com
[2] Doctor of Telecommunications Engineering, Universidad Politécnica de Madrid, Spain. Email: dpardo@gaps.ssr.upm.es

The second foundational principle of these arenas of thought was respect for the truth. Practices were developed to ensure these principles were followed, which involved the idea of *tolerance*, that is, enshrining the right to dissent from any manner of imposition of truths, however inescapable these might be taken to be.

Reconciling both principles is problematic, not only in practice. The coexistence of what is held to be true, at any moment in time, with what is deemed to be erroneous has always been arduous and controversial. Indeed, the idea of tolerance was born out of efforts to overcome wars of religion with the adoption of peaceful dispositions in matters in which it did not seem possible to reach unanimous agreement on an unquestionable truth.

Such is the space in which scientific inquiry takes place, a complex interplay between what is held to be true and a new object of concern that is not (yet) knowable with certainty. When Rudolf Carnap proposed adopting a pluralism of *forms of language* that could convey different meanings, which requires an interpretative *distancing* from propositions whose meanings elude rigid frameworks, he was establishing a principle of tolerance within epistemology. This is to go beyond mere benevolence.

It is comparatively easy to uphold freedom of thought in the academic sphere because this freedom lies in the very essence of its purpose of inquiry. It would be inconceivable that the knowledge it seeks were to be supposed known at the outset and any fanciful deviation quenched, lest it lead to baneful error. So far, at least, whenever it has been presumed that the limits of knowledge have been reached, that no further advance is imaginable and seeking it could only lead astray—a supposition that was made of physics near the end of the nineteenth century—new exploits, setbacks and discoveries have soon dispelled the notion.

The source of misunderstandings on this point, the need to uphold well-established truths against the dangerous temptations of error, is at the very root of our intuitions about truth. Philosophers have debated endlessly on the idea of truth, and, put very simply, they have agreed that truth is a kind of concordance, be it between understanding and its objects, between understanding and its subjects (people) or between people and that which presents itself to them as being patently the case. The common element in these views on truth is a primary mode of conformity that allows recognition of a firm base upon which scientists can work, politicians can legislate, and a common language can be used for people to understand each other.

Now, agreements do not preclude freedom of thought, nor can they forbid it, because scientists work from an accepted truth that is sometimes adulterated, politicians must modify laws that were once adequate but are so no more, and ordinary people change their manner of speech unceasingly, if only to say the same things. In none of these three scopes, science, politics and conversation, do intransigence and dogmatism — which Aquinas regarded as manifestations of a rigid and hard pride[3] — have a place. Conformity is a greater danger to the advancement of knowledge than nonconformity, although the latter poses its own problems. Feynman recommended not believing anything that is taught in physics lectures until one can ascertain it for oneself. This audacity in handling the legacy passed down in the sciences is a fundamental requirement for their continual renewal.

The moral and intellectual ideals of science, hand in hand with those of liberal democracy, presuppose knowing how to combine respect for the truth with cultivating experience and reason as the paths to search for it. This indispensable condition presupposes, in turn, an ethic of tolerance such that, when disputes arise that are hard to settle, or confusion sets in that is hard to dispel, there is respect for the judgment of arbitrating institutions that remain true to their fundamental role of ensuring the field remains open to rational disagreement. As Richard Rorty put it, "if you take care of freedom, truth takes care of itself."[4]

Where they have taken root, science and liberal democracy, both, have led to great improvements in welfare. They have been able to do so primarily by virtue of their judicious harmonization of a respect for received legacy with the boldness to invent new ways of thinking. Nevertheless, today the truth of these statements is being put into question, quite injudiciously, in favour of supposedly inescapable alternatives.

Hannah Arendt observed repeatedly that politics and truth have always had a turbulent relationship. The essence of politics is in debate, and debates often have difficulty with facts that no one should reasonably doubt. In the academic world the opposite is usually the case. The essence of intellectual discovery is not debating, not confrontation, but a Popperian *endless search*, which in a way is a revival of Aristotle's formulation of the essence of a foundational philosophy. Scientific facts can be discussed, and their implications for our understanding of the world may be debated, seeking to advance said understanding, which may necessitate refining or indeed replacing theories with new ones. The observed or proven facts themselves, however, cannot be debated before the general

---

[3] "Ille autem qui in suo sensu perseverat, rigidus et durus per similitudinem vocatur", *Summa Theol. III, sup. 1. 1. resp.*

[4] Rorty, R. & Mendieta, E., 2006, *Take Care of Freedom and Truth Will Take Care of Itself: Interviews with Richard Rorty*, Stanford, CA: Stanford University Press.

public as if they were contingent beliefs. As Neil deGrasse Tyson has put it,[5] debates are often "won" in the public eye by whoever is most charismatic or has the better debating skills, and not necessarily the person presenting "objective truths" (as we commonly understand the term, leaving aside philosophical deliberations about the nature of objectivity). The realm of debate is either contemplative or political, it is well suited for discerning and contrasting perspectives and experiences or for illuminating what should be done in the face of the facts that are the case in the world, to paraphrase Wittgenstein. Of course, freedom of thought entitles one to believe whatever one wishes, even flying in the face of hard fact. However, we are in grave danger, as deGrasse Tyson goes on to observe, when those who wield political power impose upon society beliefs and rules of conduct grounded in them.

When someone believes they have reached the end of their search, when they turn a supposedly scientific truth into a religious dogma worth dying for, the door is opened to two parallel and terrible processes. The first we might call *the pleasure of orthodoxy*: the intimate satisfaction one feels when in possession of a weighty truth, leaving behind a path fraught with error, doubt, vacillation and setbacks; the second is a belligerent attitude against anyone who dares question a truth one holds to be definitive, one that demands we defend and impose it.

Any truth, however insignificant, is a form of power. Therein lies the danger of knowing it, or believing one knows it. The pre-eminent expression of power, political power, often fails to show respect for the truth when it is held by others, precisely because the freedom to hold the latter can always threaten the preservation of the former. Correspondingly, the symbiosis of force with something that is held to be true, or that is presented as such, provides authoritarianism with an indispensable instrument for its own affirmation, one that enables it to curtail dissent, freedom of thought and, of course, the capacity to develop any science.

Up to now, freedom of thought has always managed to bury its would-be undertakers, but the outcome of this ongoing battle is beginning to look uncertain. Today, riding on unprecedented heights of impudence and media power, we are witnessing two trends that share the same essence: the rising ambition to dictate certain beliefs, and the acceptance as *alternative facts* of such falsehoods, however patently preposterous, as may be deemed useful or necessary to advocate. Both inclinations assume

---

[5]   "3 Scientists School Flat Earthers on the Evidence", *Big Think*, https://bigthink.com/videos/flat-earth-myth-bust.

that an unquestionable truth has been revealed, and with it the right to foist it upon others. The value of truth is thus subordinated to the will of those who purport to defend it and strive to prescribe it with expedience.

Ironically, it may be argued that these freedom-stifling dispositions have been nurtured since the mid-twentieth century (although roots in history always go deeper) by the increasing denaturalization and radicalization of novel academic endeavours to understand society, most salient of which might be those that fall under the conceptual umbrella of *critical theory*. The irony is two-fold: first, it lies in the fact that a belief-dictating, freedom-limiting drive should arise from, and find justification in, the academic realm, which can only thrive in freedom. Secondly, it is in its abuse of academic reflection on inherited dogma and the power structures it supports, only to impose new dogmas.

The ability to impose a *new orthodoxy* that is felt with the joy of a paradise attained is the same that allows lying unknowingly, if we are permitted the oxymoron. Just as lies become transparent to the dogmatic, all manner of outrage is regarded as dust along the path, an utterly unimportant contingency, to the revolutionary bent on dictating a new form of liberation of those oppressed by a dogma that must be banished.

Let us succinctly concretize these reflections with the example of a peculiar variety of radical feminism in Spain which is succeeding in undermining presumption of innocence in cases of sexual abuse. An elementary principle, one grounded in reason, is thus sacrificed at the altar of a revealed, primordial truth that demands redress, something along the lines that there exists an ancestral prejudice, the *patriarchy*, that pervades all pores of society. Hence, not only must it be extirpated at all costs from the legal system, but it must also be uprooted from the cultural niches in which it supposedly subsists and reproduces. One such arena of special importance is academia, which finds itself under pressure, not least through the imposition of legislation—the surest way to curtail freedoms—to accept the new doctrine without the possibility of honest discussion, and to banish all alternatives that were heretofore considered perfectly legitimate.

Just as the law can be applied arbitrarily and conditionally, contorting its seemingly abstract and impersonal rules to suit higher interests, such as the oft brandished *raison d'état*, so the crusade to excise prejudice has been extended to much of academia, which is now falling under a reign of intellectual terror. Ideological indoctrination of various flavours—radical feminism and nationalism being two of the most prominent—is taking root in textbooks, research programmes and through the creation of vacuous courses of study. Some feminists have gone so far as to denounce *modus tollens* as sexist, although such nonsense has fortunately not (yet) caught on. It is a veritable onslaught intent on subjecting science and independent thought to a new form of power.

The contamination of the academic sphere with new supposed truths that strive to subdue it can take place mainly via three routes. First, through logical error, that is, arriving at mistaken conclusions; secondly, through ethical error, by meaning to dictate interpretations of reality that seemingly lay a bridge over the chasm separating reality from a demanding moral conscience; and thirdly, by allowing scientific inquiry to be led astray by an aesthetic ideal, as denounced by Sabine Hossenfelder in her field of physics.[6] If it can happen in the hardest of sciences, it is no wonder how far afield certain escapades in the social sciences have been able to go.

It is costly to follow one's conscience against the prevailing current. Being able to recognize the truth, to reject ignorance, error and lies are qualities everyone believes they possess to an equal or greater degree than anyone else. And yet it is easy to fall prey to groupthink. When agreement borders on unanimity it tends to become strongly expansive. The motivation driving argument turns from holding an honest discussion meant to convince, and indeed also to learn and dispel error from one's own position, into a will to impose what is held to be true, with the self-indulgent excuse of opposing the advance of error and ignorance and preventing the harm these would cause.

We sometimes seem to think that, just like people, beliefs and ideals themselves possess rights that must be enshrined in the law. We ought to be fearful of this happening, particularly by imposition, even if those beliefs appear true also to us. There is a clear moral distinction between respecting the truth and trying to impose it. Turning the truth into an asset for the public authorities to control as they please is to abuse it both morally and intellectually. The views of the majority can be an excellent guide for decision-making, fallible as it may be, but it can be very harmful to take them as a criterion of truth, wisdom or morality.

---

6   Hossenfelder, S., 2018, *Lost in Math: How Beauty Leads Physics Astray*, London: Hachette UK.

Jorge Gibert Galassi[1]

Murphy's Law Meets Neoliberalism in Chilean Academia

ABSTRACT: This work deals with academic freedom in Chile, whose higher education, because it is highly commercialized, functions as a business where students are clients, and teachers and authorities are service providers. In this scenario, the notions of fairness and inclusion engender mediocrity because the customer comes first. Thus, academic freedom is restricted to handbooks on handling overcrowding and the diminishing skills of the students. Finally, the teacher is a mere human resource in permanent danger of being fired for opinions and behaviours that department heads or clients do not like.

TOPICS: general considerations on suppression of academic freedom; diversity, inclusion and equity programmes.
****

The purpose of this chapter is to provide a holistic picture of Chilean academia, and how the structural features of the higher education (HE) system constitute a threat to academic freedom.

Murphy's Law is a very popular adage or epigram which says that "anything that can go wrong, will go wrong" and is very similar to the Unintended Consequences Law. What we will try to do here is to interpret changes in Chilean academia in terms of unintended consequences, meaning that actions of individuals and organizations always have collateral effects that are unanticipated or unintended. Social science has

---

[1] Professor of Sociology, Facultad de Ciencias Económicas y Administrativas, Universidad de Valparaíso, Chile. Email: Jorge.gibert@uv.cl

paid attention to this phenomenon for many decades, but public opinion and political systems have not. The classic reference to the concept of unintended consequences is the 1976 article by the American sociologist Robert K. Merton,[2] which, in a nutshell, states that the sources of unanticipated consequences are ignorance, error, the "imperious immediacy of interest", basic values and the self-fulfilling prophecy.

This chapter deals with academic freedom in Chile, whose HE system, due to being highly commercialized, functions like a business where students are clients, and professors and university administrators are service providers. In this scenario, the notions of fairness and inclusion engender mediocrity because the customer comes first no matter what the other considerations are, including quality and the achievement of academic goals. Thus, academic freedom is restricted to handbooks to deal with an excess number of students and the limited skills of the majority of them. Finally, the professor is a mere human resource in permanent danger of being fired for opinions and behaviours that department chairs or clients do not like. If the work of any individual at institutions of HE should be assessed purely based on their academic merits and achievements, why should we tolerate mediocrity?

The literature regarding why HE globally is in such an enormous transformation process is broader than we can take into account here. Of course, what Halffman and Radder (2015) have said could be summarized in this idea: "Management has proclaimed academics the enemy within: academics cannot be trusted, and so have to be tested and monitored, under the permanent threat of reorganisation, termination and dismissal." Academic capitalism is the fancy word to describe the managerial university of the present day (Slaughter and Rhodes, 2009). Instead, my next pages are devoted to one local case. The causes of the failure of Chilean universities are more profound than those related to academic capitalism. Indeed, they are related to the historical roots of universities in Latin America, in addition to closer unanticipated consequences of neoliberal rules. These are as follows:

1. Ignorance about the real meaning of what a university is. The institution of the university in Latin America is shaped by the Spanish Counterreformation, which did not serve the goal of searching for truth but rather the training of administrative servants of the Spanish Empire. In the Chilean case, the first "real universities" emerged in the early twentieth century, and their research or scientific function was only

---

2   Merton, R.K., 1976, *Sociological Ambivalence and Other Essays*, New York: Free Press.

formally established in the Universidad de Chile's normative code in 1931.[3] So, there is a long tradition of the university as a continuation of high school, with teaching conceived as primarily focused on professional training skills. I think that university is a bad example of an institution transplanted from abroad. Therefore, in recent times (Bernasconi, 2010) the main features of a small group of Chilean universities are closer to the international standards, mainly because of the emergence of an academic research culture arising from novel scientific communities (Gibert, 2011). That is good, but not good enough to overcome tradition.

2. Erroneous lack of a proper notion of what a university is. Since the mid-70s, by dictatorial decree, the whole educational system has been running on the idea of educational services as a market. Thus, education is a profitable business. People who are administrators or owners of the universities rule without appropriate background, meaning they lack the proper academic credentials or experience: the epitome of academic capitalism.

3. The "imperious immediacy of interest" has transformed universities into mercantile organizations that are always thinking about profit and efficiency in the short-term instead of long-term efficacy. The result of this, academically speaking, is a culture of an "easy way of doing things" or the routine of doing things without quality standards: the prevalence of a checklist approach only searching for profit.

4. The situation gets worse because of the effect of basic values of per-missive sympathy in evaluating student performance, and employment self-protection of the faculty members. This last feature is caused by a culture of fear as an outcome of an atmosphere of intolerance coming from many political subcultures like feminism, equalitarianism, racial or indigenous movements. It is well known that there is an excess of identity politics in global academia. In many ways, these basic values function as blackmail to the learning context which gets denigrated or simplified.

5. The self-fulfilling prophecy is obvious in terms of the fact that higher HE enrolment rates are not improving the system's quality.

The Chilean case can be qualified as the North Korea of neoliberalism. The magnitude of macroeconomic structural adjustment was very extensive and the expansion of the marketization process greatly affected the education sector as well. During the 90s, the participatory rate of

---

3 "Historia del Estatuto de la Universidad de Chile", Universidad de Chile, https://www.uchile.cl/portal/presentacion/senado-universitario/proceso-de-modificaciones-al-estatuto-vigente/estatuto/110422/historia-del-estatuto-vigente

students in HE increased due to the serious stagnation during the dictatorship. The HE system reached a 20% enrolment rate in the early 90s, in contrast to 5% in the early 70s. In 2007, the growth of that rate in HE was 50% which qualified, according to experts, as a universal access status.[4] Beginning in 1990, the growth of the participation rate of students in HE institutions put an end to the Chilean elite university and a system made up of four universities that had a concentration of human capital with scientific prestige.

Data from 2019 indicate that only seven universities offer a PhD in 50% of their full faculties, and that is far below international standards of academic excellence.[5] That means that HE expansion was done without quality improvement. A short description shows that, in 56 institutions, probably 52 are very heterogeneous, with some having excellent programmes, but, as a whole, the system is very deficient. It seems that only 16% of the faculty in the university system can be considered to be active researchers.[6] Therefore, many institutions function as a mere business, a transaction between a supplier of degrees and a consumer of them. This is easy supply for quick consumption.

In a lot of cases, it appears to be that a university degree is a scam and a path to unemployment. Academic freedom becomes educational freedom, the capacity to provide educational services as a business without regulations and, of course, without any kind of academic quality. The goal was, initially, a good one: the State cannot forbid individuals from developing educational initiatives. However, the university ideal gets challenging for the common organizational and practical issues of Chilean universities. The most obvious is related to property issues. The university owners set the goals and means to reach those goals. Some Catholic universities forbid biomedical research with human beings and censor teachers or instructional contents even if those are religious, but faculties who teach them belong to another faction inside the Catholic Church and are, in turn, in opposition to the administrative board.[7] In the

---

[4] "Evolución reciente de la cobertura de la educación superior en Chile", http://accioneducar.cl/wp-content/uploads/2016/08/Evoluci%C3%B3n-reciente-de-la-cobertura-de-la-educaci%C3%B3n-superior-en-Chile.pdf

[5] Fuente: www.mifuturo.cl, Mineduc, 2019.

[6] DATACIENCIA. Dimensiones de la Producción Científica Nacional, https://dataciencia.anid.cl/authors

[7] 24th March 2015, "Críticas a Ezzati por despido de profesor de la Facultad de Teología UC", *cooperativa.cl*, https://www.cooperativa.cl/noticias/pais/educacion/universidades/criticas-a-ezzati-por-despido-de-profesor-de-la-facultad-de-teologia-uc/2015-03-24/205252.html

larger private universities with a strong managerial style, the contents of teaching are strictly supervised by department chairs. The employment contract and the permanency within institutions depend on how teaching is linked to handbooks or fixed syllabi. Professorships do not have the right to keep their ideas because they might upset the university experience of student-clients. The administrators cannot hire faculties with freedom, and in many cases have to obey nepotistic recommendations from the owners. The result of this is the expansion of what I call Wiki-Professorship, mere repeaters of trivial content that students can learn on their own. This is the real threat to academic freedom and the core idea of a university.

Table 1 shows that, despite the increasing number of PhD and full-time academics due to accreditation phenomena, the percentage of PhDs is lower among full-time academics. This fact suggests a non-competitive academic market.

	2011	2020	Variation %
Total academics	61,600	70,000	14%
Total full-time academics	8,200	33,300	306%
PhD academics	7,400	13,700	85%
Full-time PhD academics	5,100	10,800	111%
% PhD of total of academics	12%	19%	58%
% PhD of the total full-time academics	62%	32%	–48%

Table 1. Academics within university system 2011–2020

It seems that academia was transformed by a new professorship group. In Chile, from 1975 to 1990, faculty deferred to the dictatorship, while from 1990 to 2010 it deferred to managerial university (or academic capitalism). Does today's faculty defer to the copy-paste or millennial generation?

Maybe there is a strong match between the millennial generation and Wiki-Professorship in the socioeconomic and educational structures of Chilean society. In 2005, seven out of every ten students were first-generation university enrolees, in a context of deficient secondary education which did not socialize students to civic and political adult life, nor prepare them in basic twenty-first-century skills. According to the OECD, Chile's PISA score is lower than the average of OECD countries (Programme for International Student Assessment, 2019). Therefore, the only available mechanism is to lower the educational level to acquire the necessary competencies at the university level. The cost of that operation is academic facility, the easy way to get a degree. A student's lower cultural capital is irrelevant to academic failure. In fact, it is better for success. The majority of students come from lower socioeconomic classes, and campus activists and others might refer to all their academic deficits as a matter of pride. Therefore, speaking with slang or without the use of proper vocabulary is a sign of the necessity of special treatment from the administrators' point of view. They even see justification for handing in academic assignments late because of cultural routines in vulnerable families. If faculties try to improve those characteristics to amplify their cultural background, it is considered as an offence or "micro-aggression" and students might use various forums to publicize them. The victimhood culture has been installed in the Chilean university system (Campbell & Manning, 2014).

Moreover, due to administrative concerns and the establishment of the institutional framework for the quality assurance of HE, a lowering of academic standards continues to be constantly promoted because—for our argument—the main components of accreditation are the passing rate and the timely degree: that is, it is assumed that all students are the same. This could be fairly true in Belgium or Finland, but not in Chile. Therefore, institutions should not have student failure problems or unnecessarily prolong the degree completion time. All of this means that faculties cannot exercise academic freedom in terms of minimum requirements. There is pressure to pass students without merit. In addition, as the university is a business for the masses and a for-profit enterprise, a way to better manage it is through the homogenization of the content via manuals, which ends up killing the little academic freedom that faculty members exercise in their work.

The critics of meritocracy like Michael Sandel (2020) made a pertinent point that even fair meritocracy led to the wrong impression that one succeeded on one's own and that success is morally justified. The problem with this is the societal divide implied between winners and losers. But we can create fake justice. So, to give a chance to lower classes in the Chilean case, the HE system is meant to provide a university degree by means of a false meritocracy. This means that everybody can pass courses throughout the years. Meritocracy can be run by mediocrity. Of course, rewards depend on the feudal and symbolic halo of the institutions in a rather unequal and oligarchic society such as Chile. If meritocracy does not imply an effort to get a real education, then the problem remains unsolved. Young people don't deserve real education in general, but in elite universities where ordinary people can get in. So, the neoliberal promise is broken because students don't receive an education useful enough to acquire new competencies or improve their natural ones.

The massification and commodification of HE, together with the diversity, inclusion and equity (DIE) movements, generate a paradoxical effect, affecting academic freedom by it being impossible to defend a minimum standard of excellence. In addition, freedom in the development of research and especially freedom of action and communication in the field both external and internal to the university – freedom of political action and freedom of criticism respectively – have been greatly weakened in recent decades, such that it has become necessary to vindicate it through academic organization initiatives.[8]

After 17 years of a dictatorial regime and 30 years of a neoliberal regime, getting democracy to work appears complicated. Following Kitcher's statements (2001), we are under the threat of a vulgar democracy. The convulsive times we are living in directly affect these university trends, both managerial and academic. The key issue, I think, is the confusion between democracy and mediocracy, the rule of mediocrity.

Political discontent has driven a huge change in the neoliberal regime in Chilean society. The first hit was in 2011 and the last was 2019, a youth-led fight that initiated an interesting social movement to transform the basis of a very unequal society and a weak and restrictive democracy. That is a good thing. But in some sense, youthful will and desires for a better society have produced a second consequence, an unintended one, characterized by a discretional will to manage any kind of social spaces. One of them is the university space. It seems that young people think that, given that unfair matters happen (high fees, unequal quality, poor benefits, useless certificates, etc.), they must impose their rights by force. The worst trend in that sense is the complicity of faculty. The deal is this: the academics feign to teach, and students feign to learn. The outcome of that deal is an atmosphere of university idleness where faculty and students are permanently on holiday. In short, the university degree is a gift obtained only by the fact of paying fees and attendance. The academic environment is a transactional marketplace, where faculty have to teach as simply as possible without bothering students, who are trying to change the world and make a difference by posting on Snapchat, Tik-Tok, and Instagram. Of course, there is no problem with posting. The problem is this: are you good enough to save the world? Or in other words, do you have time for this?

Is there an intolerant political ideology in favour of mediocrity in the Chilean university system? It could be the case.

My first experience of academic discrimination was more than 20 years ago. Since that date I've been witness to the acceleration of the university

---

8   19th January 2018, "Docentes de educación superior constituyen la Asociación Chilena de Profesores Universitarios para proteger la libertad académica", *elmostrador.cl*,   https://www.elmostrador.cl/noticias/opinion/2018/01/19/docentes-de-educacion-superior-constituyen-la-asociacion-chilena-de-profesores-universitarios-para-proteger-la-libertad-academica/

government of mediocrity in the whole HE system. A modest summary includes:

- Being appointed department chair as punishment because increasing resistance from students against academic quality made the job too hard.
- Getting fired due to high academic production that was offensive to many faculty colleagues, as well as the fact that prolific research activity was seen as showing a lack of engagement with teaching duties.
- Prohibition of attending conferences because that "wasn't part of the academic duties".
- Being censored for opinions against academic regulations and normative codes that promote student laziness.
- Being transferred from one department to another because the first-year students "evaluated" the professor's work as inadequate and not related to the syllabus... made by himself.
- Being harassed and marginalized at work because opinions were not the same as those of the majority.
- Beginning the semester without course assignment due to personal opinions from administrative staff, with the complicity of the rest of faculty.
- Being censored by the department's chairs due to students' complaints of supposed micro-aggressions related to being opposed to academic habits of laziness or the use of slang in academic papers.
- Being censored by administrators or department's chairs for opinions contrary to student strikes.[9]

In conclusion, it seems that expansion of HE in Chile, without a secondary education of excellence, results in a system without quality which now converges with recent waves of intolerance and unintended consequences of DIE politics, which, in turn, emphasizes academic laziness and "buying–selling degrees mechanisms". The neoliberal structural feature of the system has an outcome that is too close to mediocrity, and is justified

---

9   The number of student strikes in 2011 was more than 1,000 and, from 2018 to 2019, have risen from 250 to more than 400 behind the 2019 Chilean social revolt. Since 2011 the regular academic term has been reduced by 25% due to student strikes, https://coes.cl/publicaciones/informe-anual-del-observatorio -de-conflictos.

by the argument of inclusion, mainly for students with academic deficits, as well as for Wiki-Professorship.

References

Bernasconi, A., 2010, "The Apotheosis of the Researcher and the Institutionalization of the Academic Profession in Chile", *Estudios sobre Educación*, **19**: 139–163 (in Spanish).

Campbell, B. and Manning, J., 2014, "Microaggression and Moral Cultures", *Comparative Sociology*, **13**(6): 692–726, doi: https://doi.org/10.1163/15691330-12341332

Gibert, J., 2011, "The Social Construction of Scientific Profession: Notes on Intellectual and Social Identities of Scientific Communities in Chile", *Revista Estudios Sociales*, **119**: 169–206 (in Spanish).

Halffman, W. and Radder, H., 2015, "The Academic Manifesto: From an Occupied to a Public University", *Minerva*, **53**: 165–187, doi: 10.1007/s11024-015-9270-9

Kitcher, Ph., 2001, *Science, Truth, and Democracy*, New York: Oxford University Press.

Sandel, M.J., 2020, *The Tyranny of Merit: What's Become of the Common Good?*, New York: Farrar, Straus and Giroux.

Slaughter, Sh. and Rhoades, G., 2009, *Academic Capitalism and the New Economy: Markets, State, and Higher Education*, Baltimore, MD Johns Hopkins University Press.

Erik J. Olsson[1]

Feminine Culture in Academia

The Threat to Academic Freedom Coming from Soft Values

ABSTRACT: As many of us know, and quite a few have learned the hard way, academic rights are far from always being respected in scholarly life. Scholars working in sensitive areas find their talks cancelled or their lectures investigated on vague charges of harassment or discrimination, or their research criticism is silenced out of concern for the "psycho-social work environment". My concern in the first part of this chapter will be some rather basic questions. What is academic freedom, and why do we need it? What specific rights do or should we have as researchers and teachers? My next question will be: how come having these rights apparently fails to protect us from violations? As I will try to explain, one major threat to academic freedom comes from a perhaps unlikely source, namely, an excessive emphasis on soft values, such as equality, diversity and the like at the expense of more fundamental academic principles. Finally, I ask what can be done to protect academic freedom in practice. In this connection, I describe the activities of an academic watchdog, *Academic Rights Watch*, and the extent to which these activities have been successful. In a postscript, I describe a surprising event — the censorship of a presentation of this article — that lends further support to its main thesis.

[1] Professor of Theoretical Philosophy, Department of Philosophy, Lund University, Sweden. Co-founder and Chairman of Academic Rights Watch. Email: erik_j.olsson@fil.lu.se

TOPICS: general considerations on suppression of academic freedom; censorship, deplatforming and job harassment; feminism and gender mainstreaming.
****

1. What is Academic Freedom and Why Do We Need it?

My first question, about the nature of academic freedom, can be answered succinctly as follows: academic freedom is the freedom that researchers have to pursue their own research questions in whatever direction it takes them and communicate the results to whoever they want, provided they adhere to strict scientific and ethical standards. It follows that academic freedom is not something that is handed out gratuitously to anyone asking for it, but only to those that adhere to high scholarly standards.

Why, then, do we need academic freedom? As we will see, some insightful answers can be found in an international agreement of, I am tempted to add, unusual value and insight, namely the UNESCO Recommendation Concerning the Status of Higher Education Teaching Personnel (1997). The principles endorsed in the recommendation are not mandatory regulations but have the status of non-binding "soft laws". Even so, they were adopted by UNESCO by simple majority and arguably capture the norms that have traditionally governed western universities over the centuries as codified in the principles of the Humboldt University. Moreover, they require member states and their higher education institutions to take "all feasible steps" to apply the recommendations (Article 74). It is worth noting that the recommendations apply to all "higher-education teaching personnel", defined broadly as "all those persons in institutions or programmes of higher education who are engaged to teach and/or to undertake scholarship and/or to undertake research and/or to provide educational services to students or to the community at large". Thus, the UNESCO recommendations also cover many PhD students' and retired, but still active, scholars' academic rights.

Now the answer provided in the UNESCO recommendations is that we need academic freedom for universities to be able to fulfil their societal role. This role serves to "preserve, disseminate and express freely opinions on traditional knowledge and culture". It also enables academics to "pursue new knowledge and its application without constriction by prescribed doctrines" and, not least, to "maintain a critical distance to society" and "take a longer-term view". Surely, we cannot do any of this without considerable freedom to pursue our own research questions.

Teachers and researchers can enjoy academic freedom only if a number of more specific principles are respected. An important such principle is stated in Article 25: "Access to the higher education academic profession should be based solely on appropriate academic qualifications, competence and experience and be equal for all members of society without any discrimination." Scholars' civil rights are covered in Article 26: "Higher-education teaching personnel... should enjoy freedom of thought, conscience, religion, expression, assembly and association as well as the right to liberty and security of the person and liberty of movement."

Another important principle is that of freedom of teaching (*Lehrfreiheit*) which is the topic of Article 28: "Higher-education teaching personnel have the right to teach without any interference... and... not be forced to instruct against their own best knowledge and conscience... Higher education teaching personnel should play a significant role in determining the curriculum." Article 29 concerns the fundamental principle of freedom of inquiry: "Higher-education teaching personnel have a right to carry out research work without any interference... They should also have the right to publish and communicate the conclusions of the research of which they are authors or co-authors..."

Academic freedom concerns not only the freedom of individual scholars, but also the freedom of the institution of which they are a part, as stated in Article 17 on institutional autonomy: "The proper enjoyment of academic freedom and compliance with the duties and responsibilities listed below require the autonomy of institutions of higher education..." Indeed, if the university itself is not free from outside influence, it is difficult to see how its academic staff can in practice enjoy academic freedom.

Two further important principles are those of self-governance and collegiality, as codified in Articles 31 and 32, respectively: "Higher-education teaching personnel should have the right and opportunity... to take part in the governing bodies and to criticize the functioning of higher education institutions, including their own... and... the right to elect a majority of representatives to academic bodies within the higher education institution."

Finally, academic freedom requires in practice security of employment and protection from arbitrary dismissal, as laid out in Articles 46 and 48, respectively: "Security of employment in the profession, including tenure or its functional equivalent, where applicable, should be safeguarded as it is essential to the interests of higher education as well as those of higher-education teaching personnel." "No member of the academic community should be subject to discipline, including dismissal, except for just and sufficient cause demonstrable before an independent third-party hearing of peers, and/or before an impartial body such as arbitrators or the courts."

2. Academic Freedom in Practice:
Two Main Threats

Some rights are legally protected, some not. In Sweden, for instance, civil rights and freedom of speech are guaranteed to all citizens in the constitution (*"Regeringsformen"*). However, several other rights are not legally protected at all, such as freedom of teaching, or only insufficiently protected, such as freedom from arbitrary dismissal (for the legal protection of academic freedom in Europe, see Karran et al., 2017).

Moreover, some rights that are legally protected are protected only in principle. In Sweden, again, violating a scholar's right to free speech is normally not a crime and there are no personal consequences for the perpetrator. Moreover, while a decision to dismiss a scholar can be appealed in court, the financial risk thereby incurred is often humbling.

In short: there is plenty of room for violations of academic freedom in practice. And as we all know, it does not take much nowadays to have one's lecture cancelled or subject to internal investigations for discrimination, harassment and the like. In essence, it suffices to assert something that is perceived to be difficult to reconcile with ideas that happen to be fashionable in society at the present point in time. Regrettably, the notion that universities need to "maintain a critical distance to society" to fulfil their societal role is, to put it mildly, not widely appreciated.

One cause of violations of academic freedom is the fact that the ideal of an independent self-governed university guaranteeing academic freedom to its scholars can be quite far removed from reality. In fact, various external bodies and organizations want to have their say regarding what academics should study and teach. Thus, some violations can be traced to an insufficient *de facto* protection of institutional autonomy. To some extent, it is reasonable that the state should have some control over what research is being conducted and what subjects are taught in publicly run universities. After all, taxpayers are paying the bill. Yet, there is a limit to which even the state can legitimately influence academic activity without introducing what the American pragmatist philosopher C.S. Pierce famously called "roadblocks of inquiry" (Peirce, 1955). Of course, the state is not the only external body that may want to interfere in scholarly activity. This goes for the church, private companies and other organizations as well.

However, my focus in this article is on two other causes of violations. One of them is New Public Management (NPM) and, more generally, the influence of neoliberalism on university governance. Essentially, the idea is to run public universities as if they were private enterprises. The reasons for so doing may vary, but one frequently mentioned motive is that universities will thereby become more efficient. The tacit assumption here is that private enterprises are more efficient than public organizations and, moreover, that this has to do with the way they are governed as opposed to, say, the fact that they compete on an open market.

In practice, NPM is often implemented by setting simplistic, measurable goals regarding education and research outcomes whose achievement is monitored by an ever-growing administration (Sörensen and Olsson, 2017). More to the point, NPM clashes with two pillars of academic freedom, namely, the possibility for scholars to enjoy civil rights, including free speech, and collegial governance. In practice, NPM limits scholars' freedom to publicly criticize their own university and how it is run due to concerns for the university "brand". Outspoken scholars are dismissed, bought out or subjected to internal investigations or other administrative sanctions. Since such actions may clash with constitutional requirements, I have argued with Jens Sörensen that NPM introduces uncertainty and double standards regarding basic civil rights and that the system of legal Ombudsmen can make matters worse ("shadow management", Sörensen and Olsson, 2020).

But there is a further threat that is perhaps even more surprising. In many western countries, the traditional focus on academic values like meritocracy and free speech is gradually being shifted to human relations and "soft values", i.e. equality, diversity and the like. In the terminology of leading sociologist Geert Hofstede, this amounts to a transition from a masculine to a feminine culture (e.g. Hofstede et al., 2010, chapter 5). I will argue that, if taken to the extreme, a feminine culture constitutes a direct threat to several fundamental academic principles. A strongly masculine culture obviously threatens academic freedom, too, for example in China and Turkey where there are limits to how much academics can criticize power, but excessive masculinity is less of a threat in the West and not the topic of this article.

Following Hofstede et al. (2010, chapter 5), the key insight is that feminine and masculine cultures differ systematically in attitudes to education and work. Here are some of the most salient differences. In a feminine culture the average student is a norm and weak students are praised, whereas in a masculine culture the best student is the norm and excellent students are praised. In a feminine culture, those who try to excel are met with jealousy. A masculine culture, by contrast, encourages competition in class. In a feminine culture, friendliness in a teacher is appreciated, whereas brilliance is appreciated in a masculine culture. In a feminine culture, conflicts are resolved by compromise and negotiation, in a masculine culture by letting the strongest win. Rewards in a feminine culture are based on equality, whereas they are based on meritocracy in a masculine culture. In a feminine culture, people work in order to live. In a masculine culture, people live in order to work.

Now, it is but a small step from these observations by Hofstede and his colleagues to the conclusion that a feminine culture will clash with two of the aforementioned academic principles, namely meritocratic hiring and freedom of expression, but that a feminine culture should promote collegial governance.

Consider UNESCO on meritocratic hiring again: "Access to the higher education academic profession should be based solely on appropriate academic qualifications, competence and experience and be equal for all members of society without any discrimination." A feminine culture will be in full agreement with the second part, about equality. However, it will have difficulties with the first part: that hiring should be based on quali-fications, competence and experience. A feminine culture values instead friendliness, good relations and cooperation in potential candidates for an academic position, and there is therefore a tendency to hire above all people who are nice and friendly (and a corresponding tendency to ostracize and in extreme cases dismiss people who are not nice and friendly).

A feminine culture will also have problems with freedom of expression. Severe research criticism is perceived as aggressive, unfriendly and uncooperative and there is a tendency to not invite, or cancel already invited, speakers perceived to exhibit these masculine traits. On the other hand, we should expect a feminine culture to promote collegial governance viewed as a venue for negotiation and compromise regarding the more important decisions that have to be taken for an academic unit.

Combining New Public Management with a feminine culture results in a particularly toxic mix, as witnessed by a top-down, governmental decision to introduce gender mainstreaming at Swedish universities 2017–2019. The effect on academic freedom is described as follows in a recent paper by myself and Sörensen (2020, p. 1):

> [W]e conclude that gender mainstreaming was introduced as a form of identity politics though government action and de facto supervision; that the latter was problematic from the perspective of institutional autonomy; that the choice of gender studies as a preferred scientific framework for university policy had a chilling effect on inquiry and free speech in other areas of research; and, finally, that gender mainstreaming led to violations of some scholars' individual rights.

The violations concerned freedom of expression and of teaching. (Some examples are given in section 3.)

Two final remarks: we can expect people in a feminine culture to react with jealousy at the academic achievements of others and a corresponding tendency to verbally derogate the successful other (cf. Buss, 2016, p. 372, on *Schadenfreude* as a strategy for coping with a subordinate position in a hierarchy). Moreover, we can foresee a general shift of focus away from a search for knowledge and truth to factors that promote quality of life for academic personnel. These factors involve securing a safe employment with a decent salary to provide for one's family, a pleasant work environment with good human relations and also working 9 to 5 rather than long hours. Thus, we should expect brilliant people wanting to work hard to achieve ambitious academic goals to be relatively unappreciated and struggle in a feminine culture and, in extreme cases, become the targets of administrative sanctions and investigations. There will be a general energy drain in universities whereby energy traditionally devoted to academic work is transferred to activities aimed at increasing the quality of life. The likely effect is a reduction in terms of both quantity and quality of academic work.

3. Academic Rights Watch —
Monitoring Academic Freedom in Sweden

Obviously, it is a good thing to have good academic laws and regulation. Regrettably, however, violations of academic freedom occur nonetheless, and in countries with a large higher education sector perhaps even on a daily basis. So, what can we do to protect academic freedom, not only in theory but also in practice?

One way to go is to make sure that academic violations are properly monitored and documented. In 2012, I co-founded an organization called Academic Rights Watch (ARW) with my colleague Magnus Zetterholm. Starting out as a loose network, it was transformed into a legal entity, a foundation, in 2015. The main purpose from the start has been to document violations of academic rights at Swedish universities on our website academicrightswatch.se (some cases appear in English translation on academicrightswatch.com), using the 1997 UNESCO recommendations and Swedish and European law as our gold standards.

Members of ARW have also, in different constellations, published opinion pieces in newspapers and other official outlets and written legal complaints to authorities and Ombudsmen, most notably the Parliamentary Ombudsman (JO) and the Chancellor of Justice (JK). Our guiding principle is "sunlight is the best disinfectant": what academic offenders fear the most is to have their actions publicly documented and discussed.

Thus, apart from informing the public and stakeholders about the meaning and practice of academic freedom, we rely on producing a significant "shaming effect" in those who have violated scholars' rights, deterring others from doing the same in the future.

Fortunately, Swedish law, well known for its commitment to openness, allows for easy access to public documents, such as internal university decisions, and for publishing names of high-ranked managers and leaders. Looking back, ARW has published around 300 postings documenting violations of 50 individual scholars' academic rights, a third of whom are female. Members have published 50 opinions pieces in the media.

Many cases documented by ARW illustrate the threat to academic freedom coming from an excessively feminine culture. This is hardly surprising since Sweden is considered by sociologists the most feminine country in the developed world (Masculinity Index, MAS; see Hofstede et al., 2010, chapter 5). In a recent case, a lecturer was effectively forced to reconsider course literature on early twentieth-century fascism due to pressure to have more female authors. Because there were simply too few female fascist writers at the time, the course eventually had to be cancelled. In another case, a professor was investigated for expressing his scholarly view on biological sex differences while teaching at Medical School after a student made complaints (conclusion: "risk for discrimination" and need for new, even more far-reaching gender policies than the radical ones already in place). An active case at the time of writing involves a high-profile professorial couple in astronomy found to have violated Swedish work environment law following complaints of "excessive" scientific criticism and other supposedly unfriendly behaviour (such as not contributing to coffee making at the department, an accusation which was, for the record, firmly denied by the accused).

Yet, the documentation also includes cases that highlight other academic shortcomings, some of which are traceable to NPM and concern for the university brand. Thus, a university confirmed the dismissal of a lecturer even though an independent court had found the university's original grounds for dismissing her on the pretext of scientific fraud wanting. In another case a professor critical of a hiring process was prohibited from expressing her views to anyone else but her superiors. In the latter case, the university was criticized by the Parliamentary Ombudsman (JO) following a complaint by ARW (Dnr 2058-2016).

So, what effect has ARW's activities had? Have they contributed to a greater respect for the values that underlie academic activity if such activity is to be seriously pursued? These are questions that do not have a simple answer. It seems clear, though, that because of ARW it has become more risky for university managers and others to infringe on academic rights. After all, before ARW there was essentially no risk at all. After ARW, there is the risk that the whole affair will be documented online or reported to Ombudsmen and other authorities. It seems likely that this increased personal risk has had a deterring effect, even though that effect is difficult to assess.

What can also be said, with some confidence, is that ARW started a conversation that has been continued and largely taken over by other participants in the public sphere. The number of occurrences of "Academic Rights Watch" in Swedish media reached its peak in 2018 (source: National Library of Sweden). Interestingly, before ARW was founded there was practically no mention of (the Swedish equivalent of) "academic freedom" in Swedish media, and occurrences in the period 2013–2015 are largely in connection with ARW. However, even after 2018 as the media interest in ARW cooled somewhat, mentions of "academic freedom" continued to increase mainly due to editorials and opinion pieces on the topic. The conversation culminated in a new law (in the Higher Education Act) being adopted unanimously by the Swedish parliament in which universities are required, as a general principle, to safeguard and promote academic freedom in their activities. While this is certainly a welcome legal development, it remains to be seen what practical significance it will have.

Postscript

Interestingly, a presentation of the contents of this article was censored at a research seminar, for exactly the reasons that would confirm my main thesis. The article was presented under the title "Academic freedom — what it means, how we protect it" at the Institute of Astrophysics at the Canary Islands (Instituto de Astrofísica de Canarias, IAC) in Tenerife, Spain, 18th November 2021. A video of the talk was published on the IAC's *Youtube* channel shortly thereafter. However, only two hours after being published, the video was taken off *Youtube* by the Seminar Committee (Comisión de Seminarios) for violating the institute's equalty policies, supporting my thesis about the repressive potential of an excessive focus on soft values. The Committee explained its action in the following terms:

> Many of you who have expressed your disagreement and concerns with the contents of the seminar given yesterday November 18th by Professor Erik Olsson. To begin with, the members of the Seminar Commission [CS] would like to stress their unconditional support of the equality policies carried out to promote inclusion and diversity in Academia.

We would also like to clarify some elements of the context of the seminar. This seminar was proposed by a senior researcher from the IAC. In general, the role of filtering or vetting seminars is not among the tasks of the CS, since it is also its duty to ensure that the Institute is a forum for debate in a free and open scientific environment. We understand that it is the responsibility of the researchers of the IAC who suggest speakers, to decide whether a seminar is appropriate, and who, therefore, share responsibility for their content. In any case, neither the profile of the speaker, nor the title, nor the abstract of the talk made the CS expect that the content could go against the principles of equality and be in conflict with our code of conduct.

All your reactions have been collected, and they have been transmitted to the Comité de Dirección, which is aware of the discomfort generated by this seminar, and which will take the measures it deems appropriate.

At the request of IAC's direction, in a preventive manner, and until the Comité de Dirección can evaluate the content of the seminar, its recording has been removed from the Institute's digital platforms and is no longer accessible online.

The final decision to censor the talk was announced by the IAC Director Prof. Rafael Rebolo López on 24th November 2021. The Director cited the following declaration agreed by the IAC Committee of Directors:

Concerning the seminar given recently at the IAC by Prof Erik J. Olsson (Univ. of Lund), the Management of the IAC deeply regrets that during this seminar statements were made that are utterly contrary to our firm commitment to gender equality and the principles of our Code of Ethics.

This professor was not on a working visit at our institution. On an ad hoc basis, his presentation was proposed by an IAC researcher to the Seminar Committee, who reviewed the provided title and abstract of the presentation. From the provided information, this Commission could not have possibly deduced the totally inappropriate contents that were actually presented in several slides and expressed verbally by the aforementioned speaker.

The IAC's Management expresses its firm disapproval of what happened and maintains the measure of cancelling the distribution of and access to the presentation through its own media, thus confirming the action taken as a preventive measure by the Director shortly after the seminar when he became aware of what had happened.

All staff are reminded of their responsibility to comply with our Code of Ethics and the principles and aims of the IAC when carrying out our activities. This commitment applies to external staff invited for activities at our Institute.

The Director did not explicitly state which parts of the presentation he considers to be contrary to gender equality and IAC's Code of Ethics, and why. Nor did he comment on the truthfulness or empirical support for the statements made in the lecture. The censorship of this paper has been fully documented on *Academic Rights Watch*'s international homepage (https://academicrightswatch.com/?p=2973).

References

Buss, D.M., 2016, *Evolutionary Psychology: The New Science of the Mind*, Fifth Edition, London and New York: Routledge.

Hofstede, G., Hofstede, G.J. & Minkov, M., 2010, *Cultures and Organizations: Intercultural Cooperation and Its Importance for Survival*, New York: McGraw Hill.

Karran, T., Beiter, K. & Appiagyei-Atua, K., 2017, "Measuring Academic Freedom in Europe: A criterion referenced approach", *Policy Reviews in Higher Education*, 12: 209–239.

Olsson, E.J. & Sörensen, J.S., 2020, "What Price Equality? The Academic Cost of Government Supervised Gender Mainstreaming at Swedish Universities", *Societies*, 10. MDPI AG.

Peirce, C.S., 1955, *Philosophical Writings of Peirce*, Justus Buchler (ed.), New York: Dover Publications.

Sörensen, J.S. & Olsson, E.J., 2017, "Academic Freedom and Its Enemies: Lessons from Sweden", in Halvorsen, T., Ibsen, H., Evans, H.-C. & Penderis, S. (Red.) *Knowledge for Justice: Critical Perspectives from Southern African-Nordic Research Partnerships*, pp. 57–70, African Minds.

Sörensen, J. & Olsson, E.J., 2020, "Shadow Management: Neoliberalism and the Erosion of Democratic Legitimacy through Ombudsmen with Cases Studies from Swedish Higher Education", *Societies*, MDPI AG.

UNESCO, 1997, *UNESCO Recommendation Concerning the Status of Higher Education Teaching Personnel*.